REREADING SHEPARD

Also by Leonard Wilcox

V. F. CALVERTON AND RADICALISM
IN THE NORTH AMERICAN GRAIN

Rereading Shepard

Contemporary Critical Essays on the Plays of Sam Shepard

Edited by

Leonard Wilcox

Senior Lecturer in English
University of Canterbury, Christchurch, New Zealand

St. Martin's Press

First published in Great Britain 1993 by
THE MACMILLAN PRESS LTD
Houndmills, Basingstoke, Hampshire RG21 2XS
and London
Companies and representatives
throughout the world

A catalogue record for this book is available
from the British Library.

ISBN 0–333–53849–8

Reprinted and bound 1994
in Great Britain by
Antony Rowe Ltd, Chippenham, Wiltshire

First published in the United States of America 1993 by
Scholarly and Reference Division,
ST. MARTIN'S PRESS, INC.,
175 Fifth Avenue,
New York, N.Y. 10010

ISBN 0–312–07479–4

Library of Congress Cataloging-in-Publication Data
Rereading Shepard : contemporary critical essays on the plays of Sam
Shepard / edited by Leonard Wilcox.
p. cm.
Includes index.
ISBN 0–312–07479–4
1. Shepard, Sam, 1943– —Criticism and interpretation.
I. Wilcox, Leonard, 1943– .
PS3569.H394Z85 1993
812'.54—dc20
92–9850
CIP

To Candace and Geordan

Contents

Acknowledgements

The editor and publishers are grateful to Bantam Books, a division of Bantam Doubleday Dell Publishing Group Inc., for permission to quote from *Seven Plays* by Sam Shepard © 1981 by Sam Shepard.

I wish to thank Jane Gregg for reading and commenting on a number of these essays, as well as Carole Acheson for her assistance with the manuscript. I am particularly indebted to Rosemary Russo Grigor who gave her time generously in preparing the manuscript.

Notes on the Contributors

Susan Bennett is Assistant Professor in the Department of English at the University of Calgary with research and teaching interests in contemporary drama and theory. Her book *Theatre Audiences: A Theory of Production and Reception* was published by Routledge.

Dennis Carroll is Professor of Drama and Theatre at the University of Hawaii at Manaoa. He has published on American, Australian and Hawaiian drama. His book *David Mamet* was published by Macmillan in 1987.

Jane Ann Crum is an Assistant Professor at The Catholic University of America. She has worked as a dramaturg at the Yale Repertory Theatre, Center Stage, Arizona Theatre Company, and Playmakers Repertory Company. A graduate from the Dramaturgy and Dramatic Criticism Department of the Yale School of Drama, Ms Crum has taught at the Yale College of Theatre Studies Program, The University of North Carolina at Chapel Hill, and Odessa College. Her essays have been published in *Theater*, *Notable Women in the American Theater*, *Sam Shepard: A Casebook*, *Before My Eyes: Essays in Honor of Stanley Kauffmann*, and *George Bernard Shaw: The Neglected Plays*.

David DeRose is Assistant Professor in Theatre Studies at Yale University. His interests include post-Vietnam drama in the United States, and he is writing a book on Sam Shepard for Twayne Publishers.

Sherrill Grace is Professor of English at the University of British Columbia. She has written widely on modern and contemporary American and Canadian literature with books on Malcolm Lowry, Margaret Atwood, and Expressionism. She is author of an annotated edition of *The Collected Letters of Malcolm Lowry*.

Ann C. Hall is Assistant Professor in English at Marquette University in Milwaukee, Wisconsin. She recently completed a Ph.D. dissertation on 'Women in the plays of Eugene O'Neill, Harold Pinter, and Sam Shepard,' and has published on the topics of sexual politics in Pinter and women in the plays of O'Neill.

Felicia Hardison Londré is Curators' Professor of Theatre at the

University of Missouri, Kansas City, and Dramaturg for Missouri Repertory Theatre. She has published numerous articles on French, Spanish, and Russian Theatre. Her books include *Federico Garcia Lorca*, *Tom Stoppard*, and *Tennessee Williams* (all from Ungar), *Tennessee Williams: Life, Works, Criticism* (York Press Monographs), and *Shakespeare Around the Globe* (Greenwood Press), for which she was associate editor. Her *History of World Theatre: the Eighteenth Century to the Present* was published in 1991. She is a produced playwright and a translator of plays; her translation of the Argentine play *Trio* by Kado Kostzer was produced at the Missouri Repertory Theatre. She serves on the editorial boards of five theatre journals. In October 1989 she presented a paper on current methodology in theatre history as part of a joint USA-USSR Commission on Theatre Research in Moscow.

Charles R. Lyons is Margery Bailey Professor of English and Dramatic Literature at Stanford University, where he chairs the Department of Drama. He is author of *Bertold Brecht: The Despair and the Polemic*, *Shakespeare and the Ambiguity of Love's Triumph*, *Henrik Ibsen: the Divided Consciousness*, and *Samuel Beckett*, as well as numerous articles on drama. Professor Lyons, who held both Guggenheim and N.E.H. fellowships, is on the editorial boards of *Comparative Drama*, *Literature in Performance*, and *Theatre Journal*.

Gerry McCarthy is Director of the Department of Drama and Theatre Arts at the University of Birmingham, Birmingham, England. His book, *Edward Albee*, was published by St. Martin's Press in 1987.

Sheila Rabillard is an Assistant Professor in the Department of English at the University of Western Ontario. She has published on Shepard, T. S. Eliot, Albee, Rabe, and Beckett.

Gerald Weales is Professor of English, University of Pennsylvania, and drama critic for the *Reporter* and *Commonweal*. He is author of *Religion in Modern English Drama*, *American Drama since World War II*, *A Play and Its Parts*, *Tennessee Williams*, *American Drama in the 1960s*, *Clifford Odets*, and *Canned Goods as Caviar: American Film Comedy in the 1930s*.

Leonard Wilcox is Senior Lecturer in the American Studies Department at the University of Canterbury in Christchurch, New Zealand. He has published essays in American literature and American political culture, and his essays on Sam Shepard have appeared in *Modern Drama* and *Sam Shepard: A Casebook*.

Ann Wilson, Assistant Professor in the Department of Drama, University of Guelph, is interested in contemporary theatre and theory, particularly feminist theory. She has published on a range of issues dealing with Canadian theatre and on contemporary American and British playwrights, including Sam Shepard, Joan Schenkar and Christopher Hampton. An Associate Editor of *Canadian Theatre Review,* she has edited a collection of essays on Howard Brenton.

Introduction

In his prodigious career, Sam Shepard has written over forty plays. He is winner of an Obie Award for 'substantial achievement' in the theatre; he received a Pulitzer Prize for *Buried Child* in 1979, and the New York Drama Critics Circle Award for *A Lie of the Mind*. His work spans more than two decades, from his early one act plays, emerging from the experimental theatre of New York in the sixties, to the more fully developed family plays of the seventies and eighties. Regardless of the period in which they were written, his plays share certain recognisable characteristics: they are startlingly imaginative, bizarrely disjunctive, linguistically creative, and imagistically provocative.

As Shepard has gained recognition, critical commentary on his drama has proliferated. Yet Shepard criticism is in its early stages, and the terms of the debate over his work are now just beginning to emerge. One of the key issues around which this debate is developing is Shepard's relationship to modernism and postmodernism. Is Shepard's primary legacy the avant-garde of European Modernism? Do his family plays primarily reflect the modernist influences of Ibsen and O'Neil? Is Shepard fundamentally an expressionist who quests after 'essence' and some inner, transcendental truth? Do his texts exhibit a nostalgic impulse, a desire to return to origins, to a more 'authentic' period in the American past? Or is he a postmodernist for whom essence is illusory, for whom origins are irretrievable, for whom an inner hermeneutical core of truth has been eclipsed by textuality? Are his plays ultimately products of a postmodern world of media saturation and the 'canned goods' of popular culture?

This volume addresses this central question of modernism and postmodernism in relation to Shepard's plays. A collection of original essays, it seeks to bring a diverse range of viewpoints to the subject, viewpoints which are informed by contemporary theory and critical methodology. It seeks to extend the discussion of modernism and postmodernism to the emerging debate about the family plays: to what extent do these plays represent a return to a modernist tradition? To what extent do they exhibit the characteristics of postmodern texts? Finally it focuses on the feminist debate over the family plays:

1

are they representations which reflect and reinforce a patriarchal world, or do they provide space for oppositional readings, and for resistance to the hegemony of patriarchal 'master narratives'? Any volume of Shepard criticism ought to include the venerable Gerald Weales who has forgotten more about Shepard than most of us shall ever know. His essay provides a good starting point, not only because he surveys the early plays, but because he provides a more traditional approach to Shepard. Interestingly, Weales sees two major influences on Shepard's work that are not usually considered: the conventional theatre of Thornton Wilder, Mary Chase, and Christopher Fry (where Shepard may have picked up ideas on monologue), and the comic genius of Laurel and Hardy, and Groucho Marx (where he may have gleaned ideas about role-playing). Yet in spite of this remarkable admixture in the early plays, and in spite of their inventiveness, Weales sees them much like Shepard himself now views them, as efforts, often not entirely successful, in learning how to write. Weales regards the early plays as dated 'artifacts' of the East Village culture of the 1960s, and argues that their relevance is primarily to that milieu and historical context.

With Dennis Carroll's semiotic reading of several early plays, we move into contemporary critical analysis. Anyone who has seen a Shepard play performed is struck, no doubt, by the remarkable, often stunning, convergence of stage setting and iconicity on the one hand and language on the other. Carroll's analysis of the 'polyphony of emission' of sign systems in *The Rock Garden* and *4-H Club* reveals the processes involved in this distinctive aspect of Shepard's plays. Carroll contends that the early plays are a rich and dense network of sign systems which provide the director or anyone interested in 'potential performance' with an abundance of possibilities to draw upon. Carroll's semiotic analysis also reveals that the early plays contain many elements that are developed in the later plays, thus suggesting a continuity in Shepard's *oeuvre*.

I introduce the issue of postmodernism and the problem of origins in my essay on the desert and the city in *Operation Sidewinder*. The play fascinates me, because like many of Shepard's works the desert appears to be associated with origins, with the authentic and the natural, as opposed to the city, the realm of the image and the simulacrum. Yet the play, which takes place in the desert, suggests that the matter isn't that straightforward; in fact the desert comes to represent a 'postmodern' landscape where origins are foreclosed and where the authentic is disclaimed. For the quest for origins (personal as well as cultural and historical) that occurs in the play is depicted in allegorical terms (one might argue that this play is the most allegorical of Shepard's works); and as an allegory the play pursues origins, presence and the 'primal scene' while simultaneously acknowledging the impossibility of apprehending or representing them directly.

Gerry McCarthy's essay has relevance for the issue of origins and 'presence,' for he is interested in the issue of metatheatre in Shepard's works, and focuses on *Geography of a Horse Dreamer* as a metaphor of performance and theatre. Shepard's play, McCarthy argues, foregrounds the processes of the acting performance and is concerned with the theatrical imagination itself. Its subject is precisely the central issue of all dramatic performance: the experience of time and the use of memory. The play suggests that memory experience in acting cannot be forced and subjected to the instrumental tyranny of intentionality (which results in self-consciousness and paralysis), but is linked to the rhythms of sensory experience. This has its analogies in the dramatic action of the play: with those characters who see the dreamer as a source of material profit on the one hand, and with mental modes which place actor and audience in the context of sensation and the imaginative modalities of myth, memory and image on the other.

Sheila Rabillard examines Shepard's challenge to myths of origins and the authority of authorship in *Angel City* and *True West*. As she reads them, these plays represent postmodern destabilisations of the author role in two ways: first, in a disruption of the author's mysterious (absent) authority, and second, in a discursive construction of the authorial function, which depicts that function as a conduit rather than a source or wellspring. Moreover, in both plays, modernist myths of origin are further undermined insofar as the characters are representations of actors acting and performing: we find no ground in the essential element of the dramatic medium, but rather a sign of the actor's performance gesturing toward an always-absent point of origin.

Ann Wilson approaches the issue of origins via autobiographical material. She begins with the notion of the celebrity interview and its assumed unmediated content, its supposition that the interview is a transparent transmitter of the celebrity's self-revelations. Shepard has on more than one occasion been interviewed, and such interviews have purported to reveal his true self. Yet Shepard himself throws in doubt the notion that the interview excavates the intact and fully present self in 'True Dylan', a short piece based on an interview, and a play which implies that the self is a fiction, a tissue of textuality. Wilson extends this notion to *Buried Child*, arguing that Shelley occupies a position analogous to the interviewer – observing the family, scrutinizing family photographs, looking for the essence of the family's collective selfhood. Yet what emerges is less truth than Shelley's desire to record and to know. In that sense, Shelley is not only a paradigmatic interviewer searching for the elusive meaning of her subject, but the paradigmatic reader, whose activities lead not to the unearthing of a hermeneutical core of meaning in the text but rather reflect a desire to find meaning and order in narrative form.

Charles R. Lyons' essay brings us into the terrain of the family plays. Professor Lyons has worked extensively in the field of European modernism and he situates three of Shepard's family plays within the 'conventions of modern realism'. Lyons forcefully argues that Shepard's family trilogy 'extends and amplifies' certain problems in the realist project that modernist works had already foregrounded. Shepard's early work was characterized by the 'play' and associative logic of 1960s avant-garde; in the late seventies Shepard took up the conventions of dramatic realism and reconfigured their structure to accommodate the more open, fluid conventions of his writings. Shepard's later works consistently exhibit the conventions of dramatic realism since Ibsen: the use of a retrospective structure, the *kindermord*, the dispossession of the characters from the space represented, the 'problematic' father, the relationship of fathers and sons. Yet Shepard conflates in a variety of ways the 'transformational' technique, legacy of the 1960s, with a much older legacy, the family dynamic of modern realism, and the result is what Lyons calls 'pseudo-realism,' a variation which both exploits and ironically displaces the conventional structure of realistic drama. For Lyons, Shepard's postmodernism consists in his 'self-conscious assimilation' of modernist conventions and archetypal patterns and his foregrounding of their artifice. Lyons' illuminating discussion suggests that Shepard's plays owe more to tradition than we might have thought. Moreover, in terms of the 'origins' of Shepard's drama, Lyons concludes that Shepard's plays seem 'more public than private, more aesthetic than psychological, more theatrical than autobiographical'.

David DeRose's essay introduces central aspects of the current debate on the family dramas and their relationship to the earlier plays. In this debate DeRose disagrees with Weales. Where Weales sees the early plays as artifacts, traces of a developing dramatic technique, DeRose locates Shepard's 'postmodernism of resistance' (to use Hal Foster's term) precisely in his early experimental theatre with its 1960s preoccupation with heightened consciousness. This altered awareness, a 'superpresence' associated with 'schizoid' states, provided the innovative, destabilizing impetus of his early works and was related to a legacy of his modernist forebears, the European avant-garde. This schizoid modality both reflected the discontinuous postmodern condition and challenged old verities of a 'persistent reality' and of a stable selfhood. Those moments of bizarre 'superpresence' persisted in the earlier family plays, but DeRose sees an unfortunate decline of this impulse as Shepard moves into his more recent work. The balance between a resistant postmodern form and postmodern 'content' is lost in the later plays which refer in ever more non-dramatic terms to the postmodern condition while their form becomes increasingly conventional. Consequently their postmodernism has become 'retrograde' while the experimental impetus of the early plays has been written off and labelled, in Shepard's own assessment (providing a clear-cut case for the 'death of the author'), an adolescent learning experience, 'a kind of cavorting'.

DeRose's essay points to the critical disagreement surrounding Shepard's later family plays. Interestingly, the feminists in this collection see many of these later plays as retaining a 'resistant' dimension of postmodernism insofar as they challenge patriarchal values. Ann C. Hall examines *Fool for Love* and finds relevant the Lacanian drama of the subject's development from the mirror stage to its inscription in the symbolic, a symbolic order which, however, is haunted by the myths of the imaginary: the notion of a unified self, the belief that sexual difference is based on the biological 'fact' of phallic possession. Both male and female characters in the play struggle with fantasies emerging from the 'imaginary', yet it is the men who view woman as lack, as castrated, as (fetishised) 'other', in order to maintain the fiction of their self-sufficiency and wholeness. Ultimately May evades this representation of women not only by denying the hegemonic male narrative of the family drama (thus aligning herself with a 'community' of women), but by becoming 'an anxiety producing question to a system which claims complete control over women'.

Susan Bennett disagrees with Hall. Analysing female spectatorship in Shepard's plays, Bennett concludes that *Fool for Love* is not

a 'resistant' text because it provides only limited points of entry for
the female spectator. Moreover, while May becomes aware of the
control of the male gaze during the course of the play, this awareness
ultimately does not empower her. Shepard asserts the play is from
May's point of view; yet her view is mediated by The Old Man and
the hegemonic male gaze which reduces her reality to an image,
and denies the audience its own (perhaps different) reading of her
condition. Yet contrary to DeRose (who views *A Lie of the Mind* as
an example *par excellence* of Shepard's 'retrograde' postmodernism)
Bennett sees *A Lie of the Mind* containing, unlike *Fool for Love*, a
resistant impetus, an 'enabling double focus'. The play's focus on
the 'split between the woman as she is and as she is viewed' sets
up an oscillation between masculine and feminine identification
which offers a more active role for the female audience. Audience
attention is focused towards Beth's conflict with male authority, and
toward her act of rebuilding her life. Her actions finally construct an
opportunity for resistance. While May remains passive, destined to
repeat her mother's history, Beth, struggling against male violence,
power, and hegemony, represents 'a new kind of voice in Shepard's
work'.

Sherrill Grace's article has relevance for the issue of 'origins' as
well as for the debate on the feminist dimensions of Shepard's
later plays. Grace, who has written extensively on expressionism,
believes that Shepard's plays emerge from the expressionistic tradition. Indeed, Shepard's works embody one of the central tenets
of expressionism: faced with an alienating reality the individual
turns inward in a nostalgic longing for some inner, essential,
'transcendent' truth. Examining *Buried Child, Fool for Love*, and *A Lie
of the Mind*, Grace finds examples of an expressionist poetics: details
of staging, lighting and sound effects that push Shepard's characters
and audience into the mysterious and dangerous 'territory within'.
Yet Grace's intriguing reading locates a contradiction or 'central
paradox' in Shepard's art: it calls our attention to the fact that our
world is constructed in language, yet because of its expressionist
bent it runs headlong into the 'expressive fallacy,' the notion that
there is some essence prior to language. Grace finds evidence of
this expressive fallacy in *A Lie of the Mind*, which condemns the
patriarchal system and its violence yet depicts Beth in terms of
the male dream of 'inner territory', of pure origin and essence.
Grace's reading raises important questions about Shepard's last
play. How does it allow for change if its vision ultimately succumbs

to a withdrawal inwards and back to a lost past, to the lure of origins in the 'territory within'?

Jane Ann Crum's lyric reading of *A Lie of the Mind* concludes the debate on Shepard's family drama. For Crum, the play underscores differing feminine reaction to male oppression: the first a ritualised burning of the father's house, the second a gradual transformation of the sexual and economic exchanges between the sexes. In terms of the latter, Crum draws theoretical impetus from Cixous' 'Realm of the Gift' as a means by which the feminine can subvert the patriarchal order. The Realm of the Gift, a system of feminine economy based on an open-ended notion of exchange, is the basis of Meg and Beth's revolution in *A Lie of the Mind*. Two possible responses to the patriarchy are thus offered in the play: flight from the 'fatherland' (Lorraine and Sally's choice) or an effort to redeem the men made invalids by the patriarchal system through the new feminine economy of the gift. Neither solution is without cost, yet clearly the latter, in Crum's interpretation, holds out the greater promise of substantial change. In any case, Crum argues that in his last play Shepard has at last embraced 'the feminine'.

Felicia Hardison Londré's essay serves as a kind of coda to the discussion of the family plays. She examines scenic metaphors in *Fool for Love* and *A Lie of the Mind*, and isolates the motel as an 'antechamber' which not only suggests the dislocation and transience in Shepard's world but an 'outer edge of consciousness'. Shepard's motel rooms are occupied by characters whose perceptions – resembling the Strindbergian artist dreamer – shape (and distort) the reality offered to the audience. However Shepard's postmodern sensibility enables him to shift the identity of the dreamer from one character to another. In *Fool for Love* this leads to an interesting ambiguity: May and Eddie, situated in the 'antechamber' of the motel may be dreaming The Old Man, or conversely The Old Man may be dreaming his progeny. Other props may signify this dream state, such as the blanket/flag in *A Lie of the Mind* with its connotations of the security and hegemony of American dreams. Yet the motel is a primary 'fantasy arena', a place that signifies both self invention and entrapment; it is a site of language and signification that takes place against surrounding darkness and emptiness.

The essays in this collection, then, seek to outline and clarify the terms of the current debates in Shepard criticism, fill gaps in the existing critical commentary, and invite further rereadings of Shepard's texts.

1

Artifacts: The Early Plays Reconsidered

Gerald Weales

> My work is not written in granite . . . it goes out into the air and dissolves forever.
>
> Sam Shepard to Daniel Nagrin, 12 December 1978

'The Hopis say the top of the head has a door and if you keep that door open all kinda' wonders come to ya', says Billy, the old prospector in *Operation Sidewinder* (1970).[1] In the Prologue to *The Mad Dog Blues* (1971), in which Kosmo and Yahoodi introduce themselves (even more than Slim and Shadow in *Back Bog Beast Bait* or the brothers in *True West*, they seem to be a split portrait of Sam Shepard), Kosmo says, 'intuitive decisions based on a leaking-roof brain. Lots of dashing images'.[2] When Hoss in *The Tooth of Crime* (1972) says, 'Everything just happened. Just fell like cards. I never made a choice',[3] is he talking about his endangered celebrity or the creative process? 'He has a revelation. Or rather, a revelation presents itself. Stabs at him', says Louis in the long monologue in *Suicide in B♭* (1976) in which he presents his theory of how and why Niles disappeared.[4] As late as 1982, Shepard, still surprised at the process of making *Tongues* and *Savage/Love*, could write to Joseph Chaikin, 'It never occurred to me before that you could begin with an actual subject and work around it like we did'. Much earlier (1973), he had written to Chaikin from London, 'I don't understand how I work really'.[5]

It was during the 1970s, as these quotations indicate, that Shepard began to be nagged by questions about how the imagination works, how his plays were born if not how they were made. When Shepard began with the one-acts that made his name as an off-off-Broadway playwright (1964–1966), he lacked the technique perhaps, but he

8

had something – a 'leaking-roof brain', if not genius that gave him the images he needed. He told the editors of *Theatre Quarterly* in 1974, 'the so-called originality of the early work just comes from ignorance. I just didn't know'.[6] When Lupe starts to soft-shoe sitting down in *Action* (1975), as Jeep and Shooter have earlier, Jeep says, 'There's something to be said for not being able to do something well'.[7] Lupe has a speech that almost certainly reflects what Shepard felt as his work carried him beyond the safe communal confines of Theatre Genesis, LaMama, Caffe Cino and the Judson Poets' Theatre:

> It was like somebody was watching me. Judging me. Sort of making an evaluation. Chalking up points. I mean especially the references to all those stars. You know. I mean I know I'm not as good as Judy Garland. But so what? I wasn't trying to be as good as Judy Garland. It started off like it was just for fun you know. And then it turned into murder. It was like being murdered. You know what I mean?[8]

Shepard tried to build a fence to keep the critics away from the American Place Theatre when *La Turista*, his first long play, was done there in 1967, but Elizabeth Hardwick broke through and, mixing deprecating platitudes about the audience with high praise for the young playwright, made it clear to the readers of the *New York Review of Books* that superior folks had to keep a sharp eye out for this boy; he was a comer.[9]

She had learned what his off-off-Broadway audience already knew – that there was something special about Sam Shepard's plays. From then on somebody was watching, judging, making an evaluation, chalking up points. So the 1970s plays began to consider the artist in various disguises, and the author, who told the *Theatre Quarterly* that he never doctored his early plays for production ('I never changed the words'), admitted that he had come to understand the need for revision: 'I hate to rewrite, but I can see the importance of it'.[10] By the 1980s, as he moved to the more carefully structured family plays, the writing 'turned into murder'. According to Don Shewey, he rewrote *True West* thirteen times, *Fool for Love* sixteen times.[11]

That was certainly not the way he wrote back when 'it was just for fun'. Yet it may not have been quite as spontaneous as reconstructions of the period suggest. In her essay on acting Shepard,

Joyce Aaron, his first New York lover as well as a performer in
Up to Thursday, *Red Cross* and *La Turista*, says, 'I saw how and
where he didn't rewrite, and how and where he did'.[12] For the
most part, he wrote rapidly ('Yeah, I used to write very fast, I mean
I wrote *Chicago* in one day')[13] and frequently. In the introduction to
the expanded version of *The Unseen Hand and Other Plays* (1986),
Shepard says, 'I wrote all the time. Everywhere. When I wasn't
writing, I was thinking about it or continuing to "write" in my head.
I'd have six or seven ideas for plays rolling at once'.[14] The word *ideas*
may be misleading in this context – a 1990s word for a 1960s activity
– for, as Shepard told *Theatre Quarterly*, 'I would have like a picture,
and just start from there. A picture of a guy in a bathtub or of two
guys on stage with a sign blinking – you know, things like that'.[15]
The point of *The Unseen Hand* introductory quotation, however, is
not method, but bulk, busyness. Shepard told Mel Gussow in 1969
that he wrote 100 plays during his off-off-Broadway days,[16] and
Joyce Aaron told Don Shewey that 'she has a whole suitcase full
of manuscripts Shepard gave her that no one else has ever seen'.[17]

The image of the boy playwright, the innocent from the West
– fostered by Shepard and most of the people who write about
him – is not as pure as it seems. When one looks at the early
plays – at their lack of plot, character development, extractable
theme – one can almost believe that he washed up on the banks
of the East River, newborn, but in fact he bused into town with
theatrical equipment in his luggage. Increasingly, critics have begun
to place Shepard within a larger dramatic context – Lynda Hart in
Sam Shepard's Metaphorical Stages (1987), for instance – but the roots
they are after tend to lie within the European and American avant
garde. Shepard's early introduction to *Waiting for Godot* and the
wonder of words has been well-documented, as has his attraction
to Chaikin's Open Theatre. I am more interested in his brushes with
conventional theatre. During his three semesters in junior college, he
acted (*Harvey*, *The Skin of Our Teeth*) and wrote a Tennessee Williams
imitation. He then escaped both the college and his California home
by signing on with the Bishop's Company Repertory Players and
touring for eight months playing one-night stands; *Winnie the Pooh*
and *A Sleep of Prisoners* are the two items from the repertory that
Shewey mentions. I find it difficult to believe that Shepard's early
plays took the shape they did – or the shapelessness they did –
because he was unaware of conventional stage possibilities. He
may not have arrived in New York knowing how to act, and how

to write, with the kind of technique Pop was talking about in *The Holy Ghostly*, but having written one bad Williams play, he almost certainly chose to stick with his own impulses, a reaction against a kind of theatre that did not much interest him.

Not that the influences need all have been negative. Of the two plays he performed in college, one is about a man who chats with an invisible seven foot white rabbit and the other has a memorable four-page monologue, delivered amid moving scenery. Even *A Sleep of Prisoners* allows its soldiers to role-play in their dreams. Mary Chase, Thornton Wilder and Christopher Fry had their own rows to hoe – to write a Broadway comedy, an expressionist play, a religious drama – but their devices (monologues, role-playing) do not seem that foreign to what Shepard was doing. His pieces eschewed linearity and avoided recognisable subject matter; they were to *be*, not be 'about' ('I mean it to be a theatrical event, that's all', he said of *La Turista*),[18] but conventional theatre fed into his work as did movies, music, his past and his present.

The juvenilia of most writers lie buried in basements and attics and the back pages of forgotten journals until a well-meaning editor drags them out and holds them up for all the world to see. In Shepard's case his youthful effusions took to the stage and, very quickly, the page – *Five Plays* was published by Bobbs-Merrill in 1967. For a time, in the 1960s, it was almost impossible to walk across an American campus without falling over a production of one of the early one act plays, and in 1972–73, after both Shepard and *The Tooth of Crime* hit England, his early plays blossomed all over London.

Things are quieter now. In the introduction to *Unseen Hand*, Shepard says, 'the plays themselves seem to drift back to me as flimsy ghosts, in the same way a conversation with someone in the distant past is half-remembered'.[19] The ghostliness set in early; in the *Theatre Quarterly* interview, he sometimes misremembers details, as when he says that *The Rock Garden* 'happened in two scenes',[20] forgetting the opening pantomimic scene of one character (the teenage girl) and the spilled milk. With the 1986 collection, he has the texts at hand if he wishes to flesh out the ghostly flimsiness – as do we. There are several reasons why one might want to look back at these early plays: to search for biographical elements hidden in the interstices of theatrical fancy; to see how the deceptively primitive plays anticipate the more accessible later ones; to consider the early one act plays as still viable theatre pieces.

The two characteristics of the early Shepard plays that were most celebrated when the works were new were his startling images (the blood on Jim's forehead at the end of *Red Cross*) and the monologues (the train ride that Stu evokes in *Chicago*). These remain Shepard characteristics. Consider the naked Wesley carrying the lamb in *Curse of the Starving Class*, Tilden's covering Dodge with corn shucks in *Buried Child*, Lee's chomping down on the buttered toast to seal the tenuous bargain in *True West*; or Wesley's recollection of the night before in *Curse*, Vince's family speech in *Buried Child*, Eddie's account of the walk with his father to May's house in *Fool for Love*. In these later examples, the images and the monologues – feeding as they do, theme as well as theatricality – are more obviously integral to the plays as a whole than was the case in the early plays, but still, it is still an instance of the boy playwright growing into the man, the lineage clearly visible, as in those faces on Vince's windshield.

It would be possible to follow or imagine a clear trail from *Cowboys* to *A Lie of the Mind*, but I propose something less systematic – to contemplate the method of the early plays. Of the ten plays produced between 1964 and 1966, seven are extant – eight if one counts *Cowboys #2* (1967) as a legitimate remaking of *Cowboys* – and all of them, except for *Up to Thursday*, were printed within a few years of first production and are included in the 1986 *The Unseen Hand and Other Plays*.

Don Shewey explains how, after Wynn Handman had accepted *La Turista* for production at the American Place, Shepard carried off the final two acts of *Cowboys* 1964 for revision (it was originally a three-act play), and returned 'with a single act drastically different from both the first act and the two he'd discarded'.[21] If this was rewriting, early Shepard style, then *Cowboys #2* need not be a *Cowboys* clone. Still, there is outside evidence to suggest that the two plays ride the same range. Jerry Tallmer's New York *Post* review of the original play gives a detailed account of the action on stage – if only to dismiss it – which might pass for a description of *Cowboys #2*.[22]

There are echoes of *Cowboys #2* all through the Shepard canon – the playful, quarrelling pair of buddies; the chronicle of decline and rot; the mutability of character. In the last instance, Stu and Chet switch to the voices of old men, become Clem and Mel, and, among other things, perform pieces from Western movies. They finally become trapped in, and victims of, their fantasy as the two other men come onstage and begin – tentatively and without expression –

to assume the roles of Stu and Chet. In time, Shepard would develop
a theory of character more complex than the one implicit in *Cowboys*.
In his 'Note to the Actors' in *Angel City* (1976), he dismisses the idea
of a single, developing character and suggests that the performer
'should consider instead a fractured whole with bits and pieces
of character flying off the central theme' and to take the 'abrupt
changes' as 'full-blown manifestations of a passing thought or
fantasy'.[23] One can read Stu-Clem and Chet-Mel – or the other
Stu's old-woman voice in *Chicago* or the ever-changing Mexican
boy in *La Turista* – in terms of the *Angel City* formulation, but that
is too heavy a burden for *Cowboys* to carry. Whether the shifting
roles are exterior – assumed for whatever reason by a character or a
performer – or interior – a character's 'bits and pieces' – at this point
in Shepard's career it is all a game. Critics have assumed that the
shifting roles grew out of the acting exercises, the transformations,
of the Open Theatre, but although Shepard met Joseph Chaikin in
1964, the year in which *Cowboys* and *The Rock Garden* marked his
debut as a playwright, and although he did attend some of the
Open Theatre workshops, it seems more likely that he found there
a confirmation of what he was already doing.

If Shepard needed a source outside himself, he could have found
it in the movies. I do not think that Groucho Marx ever turned up
as one of the influences Shepard used to trot out for gullible theatre
reporters, but the programme for the 1965 Cherry Lane production
of *Up to Thursday* promises a new play called *Quackenbush*, which
never materialised[24] and that is a name identified with Groucho
even though it was changed to Hackenbush before *A Day at the
Races* was released. A look at the balcony scene in *Monkey Business*,
in which Groucho courts Thelma Todd by imitating a tomcat and
then moving on to one parody role after another, will show how
much Shepard's kind of role-playing is part of popular culture.
Don Shewey suggests that 'Shepard's style of writing was largely
determined by his style of living'.[25] Shepard told *Theatre Quarterly*
that 'Charles Mingus, a friend from California and his first New
York roommate and me used to run around the streets playing
cowboys in New York',[26] and Shewey reports that *Cowboys* was
so obviously 'a typical conversation between the two roommates'
that Mingus's father, the jazzman, was angry at his son for letting
'Shepard steal his words'.[27] The biographer also says that some
of the playwright's friends, whom he does not identify, 'found
it disturbing the way Shepard could switch personalities from

one minute to the next',[28] but there seems nothing unusual or dangerous about it unless, like Stu and Chet, one gets trapped in one of the roles. In *Cowboys*, working out of himself, Shepard recorded a fantasy game so ubiquitous that it could become the basis of a theory of dramatic character which was also a theory of personality.

The other half of Shepard's debut double-bill, *The Rock Garden* (1966), he says, 'is about leaving my mom and dad'.[29] I would not take the autobiographical note too seriously, even though the boy does run out at the end of the scene with the woman, and his 'monologue about orgasm' in the third scene might be taken as an attempt to differentiate between himself and the man. The speech has nothing to do with adult sexuality. It is a masturbatory fantasy that 'ends in him coming all over the place', or so the author tells us. It is not an obvious masturbation scene, like Hänschen's speech to 'Venus' in Wedekind's *Spring Awakening*, but it could be played that way, particularly if the staging followed the text, placing the boy on a chair facing upstage, his back to the man and presumably to the audience. In his introduction to *Angel City & Other Plays*, Jack Gelber sees the man and woman as 'endlessly mouthing boring American claptrap' which so irritates the boy that he uses his monologue to kill the 'puritanical old man'.[30] This response to the play has a nice Gelber ring to it, but the thing that is most interesting about the boy's monologue is how tedious it is. It is constructed just like the man's speeches on lawn care and painting and the building of rock gardens – full of relentless detail and punctuated throughout with the repetition of 'You know?'. It is true that the man falls off the couch at the end, but there is no reason why his reaction should be different from that of the boy who several times '*nods out from boredom and falls off his chair*' (40). Gelber's reading imposes a cause-effect plot on the play, and I distrust any analysis of these early works that gets too specific. Michael Smith indicated that danger in his 'Notes on *Icarus's Mother*' in *Five Plays*: 'As a director I approached the play all wrong. I started rehearsals by talking about its content and overall meaning'.[31] That is the temptation for anyone – director, scholar, critic – who deals with the early plays.

In the light of Shepard's later work, the scene with the woman has become more fascinating than the orgasmic speech, which finally found its natural home as a hillbilly sketch in *Oh! Calcutta!* The woman lies in bed, chattering about her father and her husband to the largely silent boy, and every time she compares the boy to Pop (his legs, his toes) or to Bill (his torso), the boy, who began the scene in his underwear, exits and comes back with the pants, the shoes, the shirt that hides the family resemblance. This repeated business seems to me a more effective way to leave 'mom and pop', if that is what the author wants, but he would learn like Vince in *Buried Child*, that you cannot escape the family. In *Curse of the Starving Class*, there is a funny reprise of the resemblance routine. After Wesley urinates on the charts his sister has prepared for her demonstration, his mother says, 'Why aren't you sensitive like your Grandfather was? I always thought you were just like him . . . You're circumcised just like him. It's almost identical in fact'.[32] This leads not to Wesley's covering himself (he has already 'put his joint back in his pants'), but to a brief, cross-purposes discussion of how Ella came to see her father's penis. Later in *Curse*, after Wesley has stripped and walked naked about the place, he puts on his father's discarded clothes, suggesting still another identification – one that is also an echo of *The Rock Garden*. After the boy dresses, even donning an overcoat, the father comes in, similarly dressed, and strips to his underwear. This seems to indicate some ambiguity about 'leaving mom and pop'. The dressing/undressing game that the boy and the man play emphasises familial connections – as do the shared speech patterns indicated in the paragraph above – which suggest some ambiguity about leaving mom and pop.

Up To Thursday (1964), the first Shepard play to be produced commercially (by Theater 1965 in its New Playwrights Series), has been dismissed by its author as 'a bad exercise in absurdity' and 'a terrible play, really'.[33] In his review of *Icarus's Mother*, Edward Albee – one of the producers of *Thursday* – praised 'the resonance, the overtone' of the earlier play which he seems to think was 'about a boy about to be drafted'.[34] If we ignore the brief first scene, in which a crane removes a rock that the Young Man is sitting on, the play presents the character in bed, covered by an American flag, waiting for clean underwear, while two couples chat, quarrel, laugh and occasionally join him in bed; at the end, the cranemen from the first scene lead him off. Is that being drafted? Presumably, that is what Albee's intuition told him. In the *Icarus* review, he said, 'It is the nature of Shepard's art, so far, that while his plays are, of course, ABOUT something, we must SENSE his intention – his subject, if you like – and react through intuition'. Whatever *Thursday* was about, Shepard chose never to have it printed. A look at the manuscript indicates that despite the author's rejection of his work, the play is not particularly inferior to the other early works.[35]

If Shewey is right that *Chicago* (1965) grew out of Joyce Aaron's having accepted a job in Chicago, that would explain the title, (if titles needed explaining in Shepard). The autobiographical element would also give comfort to critics and playgoers who want a plot (the offstage phonecall about Joy's job) to explain the bathtub as a security base for Stu. I prefer another order of realism. The policeman and the Gettysburg Address notwithstanding, the play opens with Stu's playing in the bathtub while Joy, offstage, calls him to breakfast. Her impatience leads to what still seems to me a very funny line, one that has the demented logic common to American farce: 'Do you dig cold biscuits? The butter's cold, too. The jam's cold. I hope you're glad'.[36] The bathtub is going to be transformed, as is Stu, and the play will move on to unrelated visual and verbal images, ending with release when Stu gets out of the tub and leads the breathing exercises. Release from what? For whom? Joy finally gets that wagon full of suitcases offstage.

4-H Club (1965) draws on Shepard's membership of the 4-H Club as a high school boy in California. Jeep in *Action* says, 'I was being taken away by something bigger . . . Bigger than family. Bigger than school. Bigger than the 4-H Club'.[37] An ironic build-up, as though the 4-H Club were the pinnacle of discarded past associations, but references to 4-H sprinkle Shepard's work. Sally in *A Lie of the Mind* remembers 4-H pictures on the wall of her father's shack in the long scene about his death. Emma in *Curse of the Starving Class* is preparing her demonstration on how to cut up a frying chicken for a 4-H event at the fair until Wesley destroys her plans – ostensibly for her own good: 'She'll look back and remember the day her brother pissed all over her charts and see that day as a turning point in her life'.[38] Shepard's new 'direction', his movement away from 4-H, was hardly as explosive as Emma's, but it did lead him to the East Village and a play about three men in a cabin with the unlikely title *4-H Club*. Perhaps mouse-stomping is a 4-H event not widely publicized. Perhaps, too, heart-head-hands-health can work wonders, for John's last long speech begins with the dangers of mice, rats and baboons and ends by conjuring a benign place where 'You just float and stare at the sky' (100). Although the line is repeated four times, the final image is of Joe's pounding the coffee pot noisily against the hot plate. My playing games with Shepard's evocation of the 4-H Club gives a texture to the play which is a critical imposition. The reality of the work is what is onstage. There is the mouse-stomping, which seems to go on for too long a time, and Joe's monologue about the gardener and the dying town, which never achieves the verbal power of comparable speeches in *Red Cross*. More interesting in the light of later work, are the dramatic tensions, never explicit, in which first Joe, then John becomes an outsider in relation to the other two, and tries to force his way into the excluding centre by threatening to leave or attempting to disrupt the game or the story.

With *Icarus's Mother* (1965), Shepard shows a certain facility for the side-step. In the *Theatre Quarterly*, the interviewers kept trying to lead him, to get him to be specific about 'the almost political sense of an outside threat' and about the meaning of that circling airplane. The best they got out of him was that the play grew out of a Fourth of July celebration in Milwaukee and 'this emotional thing' was in response to the fireworks, creating 'a certain kind of chaos, a kind of terror, you don't know what the fuck's going on'.[39] A close reading of Frank's speech about the plane crash, 'a recognized world tragedy of the greatest proportion'[40] may give fuel to Michael Smith's suggestion that the play is about 'the so-called paranoia of the nuclear present',[41] but Frank's is only one of several long monologues. Certainly, this play invites close thematic analysis more obviously than the other plays, except *Red Cross*, but those smoke signals that Bill and Howard keep trying to send when the others are offstage suggest very garbled messages: smoke screens, perhaps.

'They told me for this movie my model should be Gary Cooper', Shepard says of his role in *The Right Stuff* (1983). 'I could never connect with Gary Cooper. When I think of a rugged individualist, I right away think of Stan Laurel. Out of all the silent comics, he sort of sticks out in my mind as the truest and also the funniest'.[42] Shepard is not only parodying movie publicity in this quotation, he is making a genuine point about Laurel. Shepard is also harking back to an early enthusiasm. Charles Mingus, recalling the East Village days, told Ellen Oumano, 'Our heroes were Laurel and Hardy . . . There's a grace and stupidity and naturalness, and the possibility of being a genius like they were, based on really studying them'.[43] As Shepard describes the paintbrush fight in *Fourteen Hundred Thousand* (1966), it is not exactly a Laurel and Hardy routine – not enough deliberation – and he saddles Tom and Donna with words that his heroes did not need. There is much more physical business in this play than in the other early plays, even *4-H Club* and *Red Cross* – business that depends on precision playing which most actors cannot achieve. The building of bookshelves and their collapse, the book carrying and the paint fight, these call for a tension between the physical and the verbal which the play cannot easily capture onstage. There are happy lines in the play based on an oblique use of words – 'I happen not to be a professional carpenter or an expert nailing person' (107) – and despite, or perhaps because of, Shepard's sense of the linear city as 'a strong visual conception', the deadliest extended passage in his work. Stan Laurel would have been a godsend to the show.

I saw an off-Broadway production of *Red Cross* (1968), directed by Jacques Levy, who had staged the original version at Judson Poets' Theatre. He began by throwing a bright light into the eyes of the audience, about as wrong-headed a directorial decision as one can imagine for this play. Although Shepard was capable of attacks on the audience in his early plays (the audience becomes the Indians in *Cowboys #2*), and audience abuse by light and sound was rather popular at the time, *Red Cross* cries out for distance that keeps the viewer out there looking in. The all-white set, costumes and props are to be absorbed, the initial surprise settling into acceptance so that the final splash of blood on Jim's forehead can come as a shock. There were other disruptive elements in the performance I saw, but they cannot be laid at Levy's door. Two elderly women, sitting in the first row of the tiny Provincetown Playhouse, listened for awhile and then tripped up the aisle and asked the usher, very audibly, what it all meant; when he declined an explanation, they returned to their seats. After a few minutes, back the women came, this time wondering if the theatre manager was around. He was not or he chose not to be. Back to their seats again and, after a beat or two, once more up the aisle, asking now if the author were available. Finally, they settled down, waited out *Red Cross* and took what comfort they could from John Guare's *Muzeeka*, the second half of the bill.

I confess to having enjoyed the women who might have been written into a Shepard play without doing any structural damage. The remarkable thing about *Red Cross* is that it retained its theatrical integrity against those odds. It is clearly the most accomplished of the early works. The set pieces – Carol's monologue, the swimming lesson, the Maid's speech about becoming a fish – have force in their own right, and do not need to be held together by the whisper of plot or the visual/verbal echoes (blood on the snow, blood on the forehead) or an imported theory of any kind. There is a temptation to make complex readings of *Red Cross*, of text and subtext, but I think more is to be learned about the play by concentrating on the separate elements. Once, in a class of mine, a young woman, a skier, climbed up on my desk and skied her way through Carol's monologue, insisting that it was designed to fit a downhill run. I suspect that if one could find a way to speak and hold one's breath at the same time, a session in a swimming pool could show how much the Maid's speech is designed as a slow settling to the bottom.

In October 1984, *Red Cross* was performed by the Quaigh Theatre in New York as a part of its Lunch Series. There were no other listings for the early Shepard plays in the *Best Plays* catalogues for the 1980s. There were presumably some amateur productions, and college productions, but Samuel French, which handles the early plays, has not vouchsafed any figures on their appeal. It is as though these works, which once stirred such excitement, had dwindled to biographical matter, critical matter, as though the stage had forsaken them. I feel, in this essay, like an archaeologist, digging among the ruins of a once-thriving civilization trying to understand its customs and its people and bemused to find so many traces that still mark the present. There have been finds – single lines, long speeches, images, confrontations – attractive enough to make me want to put them on display in the Museum of East Village Art of the 1960s – an institution that has not yet been established. It would be valuable to see first-rate productions of all eight of these plays, but only *Red Cross* has the look of living theatre about it, and even it is an artifact. As Shepard said in 1985, 'Today, I don't see how these plays make any real sense unless they're put into perspective with that time'.[44]

Notes

1. Sam Shepard, *The Unseen Hand and Other Plays* (New York: Bantam, 1986), p. 241.
2. Ibid., p. 257.
3. Sam Shepard, *Seven Plays* (New York: Bantam, 1984), p. 218.
4. Sam Shepard, *Buried Child and Suicide in Bb* (New York: Urizen Books, 1979), p. 122.
5. Joseph Chaikin and Sam Shepard, *Letters and Texts: 1972–1984*, ed.

Barry Daniels (New York: New American Library, 1989), pp. 117, 10.
6. Sam Shepard, 'Metaphors, Mad Dogs and Old Time Cowboys', Interview with the Editors and Kenneth Chubb, *Theatre Quarterly*, 4 (1974), 3–16.
7. Sam Shepard, *Angel City and Other Plays* (New York: Urizen Books, 1976), pp. 129–30.
8. Ibid.
9. Elizabeth Hardwick,'Word of Mouth', *New York Review of Books*, 6 April 1967, pp. 6, 8. The review was taken over by the playwright or his first publisher and, with a few added paragraphs, used as the introduction to *La Turista* (Indianapolis: Bobbs-Merrill, 1968), pp. ix–xv, and again in Sam Shepard, *Four Two-Act Plays* (New York: Urizen Books, 1980), pp. 11-16.
10. Kenneth Chubb and the Editors of *Theatre Quarterly*, 'Metaphors, Mad Dogs and Old Time Cowboys: Interview with Sam Shepard', *Theatre Quarterly* 4 (1974), 7, 8.
11. Don Shewey, *Sam Shepard* (New York: Dell, 1985), pp. 139–47.
12. Joyce Aaron, 'Clues in a Memory', in *American Dreams*, ed. Bonnie Marranca (New York: Performing Arts Journal Publications, 1981), p. 173.
13. Chubb, p. 6.
14. Sam Shepard, *The Unseen Hand and Other Plays* (New York: Bantam, 1986), p. ix.
15. Chubb, p. 6.
16. Mel Gussow, 'Sam Shepard: Writer on the Way Up', *New York Times*, 12 November 1969, p. 42.
17. Shewey, p. 42.
18. Lewis Funke, 'Singing the Rialto Blues', *New York Times*, 5 March, 1967, Section 2, p. 5.
19. *The Unseen Hand*, p. ix.
20. Chubb, p. 8.
21. Shewey, p. 56.
22. Ibid., p. 39.
23. *Angel City*, p. 3.
24. Unless it turned into *4-H Club*. The programme promised that the Playwrights Unit of Theatre 1965 would offer *Quackenbush* in March; it did offer *4-H Club* in September.
25. Shewey, p. 52.
26. Chubb, p. 5.
27. Shewey, p. 53.
28. Ibid., p. 38.
29. Chubb, p. 8.
30. *Angel City*, p. 3.
31. Sam Shepard, *Five Plays* (Indianapolis: Bobs-Merrill, 1967), p. 27.
32. *Seven Plays*, pp. 143–44.
33. Chubb, p. 8.
34. Edward Albee, 'Theatre: *Icarus's Mother*', *Village Voice*, 25 November 1965, 19.

35. In the Performing Arts Research Centre, New York Public Library at Lincoln Centre.
36. *Five Plays*, p. 49.
37. Sam Shepard, *Fool for Love and Other Plays* (New York: Bantam, 1984), p. 189.
38. *Seven Plays*, p. 143.
39. Chubb, p. 9.
40. *Five Plays*, p. 34.
41. Ibid., p. 34.
42. Shewey, p. 175.
43. Ellen Oumano, *Sam Shepard* (New York: St. Martin's, 1986), pp. 24–25.
44. *The Unseen Hand*, p. 37.

2

Potential Performance Texts for *The Rock Garden* and *4-H Club*

Dennis Carroll

I wish to examine here some features of potential 'performance texts' of two of Shepard's early, comparatively neglected short plays. The investigation will fall mid-way between a literary structural analysis and a director's 'production book'. Features of possible 'performance texts' suggested here are conservative in that they depend heavily on the evidence of the text and on the staging implied and specified through words – both of dialogue and of stage directions. Actual performance texts might depart far more from, even confront, such specifications – as Richard Schechner's realisation of Shepard's *The Tooth of Crime* did; and Patrice Pavis recognises the viability, indeed the virtue, of such a radical approach on the part of a director.[1]

'Performance text' might be defined as the 'polyphony of emission' of parallel sign-systems operating in the rhythm-time continuum of performance, comprising a system of codes.[2] Pavis suggests that one concomitant towards the establishment of a performance text is deciding on a system and level of formalisation of the elements of performance, and its limits.[3] The phrase 'polyphony of emission' should not imply a Wagnerian *Gesamtkunstwerk* approach, which Pavis, Honzl and others reject on the grounds that throughout the audience 'reception' of a theatrical performance various sign-systems are perceived as foregrounded singly or in stranded combinations.[4] In the theatre, of course, the chief 'conductor' of this foregrounding process is the director.

In specifying and isolating sign-systems in a semiotic-based analysis, several difficulties immediately present themselves. One has to do with the permissable extent of 'interpretation' when a critic or potential director moves beyond defining the articulating systems to what is being articulated, from 'signifiers' to 'signifieds'. Some leading semioticians such as Umberto Eco, as well as film and theatre theorists such as Pavis and Dudley Andrew, have in recent years pleaded for a catholic and flexible use of semiotic analysis in an age where a plurality of critical methods can cast valuable light on a text.[5] It might be argued, indeed, that such a flexible (rather than narrowly 'rigorous') approach is the most valuable kind for any potential director of a play. Of course, any director of Shepard will be aware of content 'motifs' and 'themes' uncovered either by his or her reading of Shepard's other work, or by a more conventional type of dramatic criticism of it.

Another problem also treated in Pavis' important study is the dialectical tension, in the theatrical realisation of a playtext, between textuality and iconicity – the counterpoint or parallelism between image-referents in the text of the play's dialogue and those which actually appear as part of the scenography. The tension in such counterpoint, of course, is particularly germane to Shepard's work. Here we can agree with Pavis that when potential or actual performance is analysed, neither textuality nor iconicity is privileged; that they form a continuum/parallel (perhaps like a musical score), which may often operate dialectically.[6] At certain times, iconicity (articulated through scenic and performative sign-systems) may be foregrounded; at other times, textuality (articulated through the performative and textual). Pavis reminds us that there can be latitude in the notion of definition of the theatrical 'sign' – that there is no dichotomy and no hierarchy between '*mise en scène*' and 'text' as the locus for signifiers; and he follows Honzl in stressing that any 'signified' can be suggested by signs in several different sign-systems, in the process called by some critics 'transcodification'.[7]

A third difficulty implicitly problematic in any model for performance texts is that one might overlook temporal and rhythmic qualities that operate in any time-continuum of actual performance. Time and time again, Pavis draws our attention to this shortcoming of earlier semiological theatrical analysis.[8] To some extent, though, the model suggested here allows for this; there are carefully indicated synchronic and diachronic cues which make it possible to apprehend the sum total of all sign systems at any point in time on stage during the performance; and the diachronic axis indicates

TABLE I *Sign-System Categories*

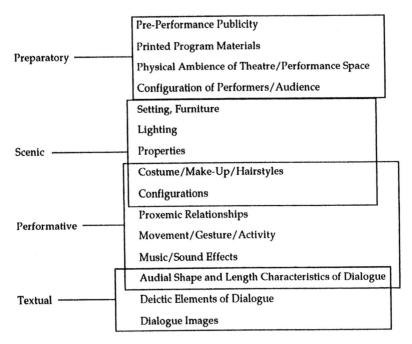

Preparatory	Pre-Performance Publicity
	Printed Program Materials
	Physical Ambience of Theatre/Performance Space
	Configuration of Performers/Audience
Scenic	Setting, Furniture
	Lighting
	Properties
	Costume/Make-Up/Hairstyles
	Configurations
Performative	Proxemic Relationships
	Movement/Gesture/Activity
	Music/Sound Effects
	Audial Shape and Length Characteristics of Dialogue
Textual	Deictic Elements of Dialogue
	Dialogue Images

the progression of each sign-system *through* time. What is not adequately indicated, perhaps, is significant patterns of intersecting, interweaving, and 'bunching' of sign-systems, especially at the climactic points of performance.

This table of sign-systems (Table I) is a variant of others such as those proposed by Tadeus Kowzan and Martin Esslin.[9] 'Framing and preparatory indicators', adapted from Esslin's model, include such things as the space of performance, the architectural disposition of audience and performers, and generic description, prepublicity, and programme brochure. 'Configurations' specify what and how many characters are on stage a time, taking into account exits and entrances, but not specifically spatial picturisation on stage.[10] The latter is noted in a separate sign-system, with proxemic relationships, which analyses figures' distance from each other as well as body-focus. Following earlier theorists such as Serpieri and Benveniste, Elam makes a valuable distinction between 'deictic language' – which refers to the 'here and now' of the dramatic interfigural interaction and which is comparatively dense with

'shifters' (personal, possessive or demonstrative adjectives or pronouns) – and 'anaphoric language' that is narrative or descriptive
or choric in function and refers to some other time and place.[11] The
'audial shape' and dialogue-unit length category pinpoints rhythmic qualities of the text, particularly in terms of rhythmic verbal
motifs which recur. 'Gesture' and 'activity' can be conveniently
grouped together in the same category, but need to be discretely
analyzed within it as well; certainly in *The Rock Garden*, as we shall
see, the lack of gesture as opposed to activity is significant.

Dividing the text along a diachronic axis is both a more difficult
and, for the potential director at least, inevitably a more subjective undertaking. A number of possibilities present themselves:
mechanically by text-page, which is artistically not very revealing;
by the directorial motivational-unit method, which is geared to conventional realist drama; and by employment of Smiley's dialogue-
beat system, which seems to me to have the most useful potential
of all. Smiley defines a dialogue beat as a 'thought unit' on the
part of the playwright and his characters are defined by topic or
motive, structured by stimulus, rise, climax and ending.[12] Several
such 'beats' might be conjoined in a longer textual unit, defined by
a directorial sense of rhythm-tempo bracketing, by any additional
formal divisions in the text, and by significant 'bunching' of sign
systems. Table I makes it clear that the major categories of sign
systems overlap.

A. THE ROCK GARDEN (1964)

In practice, to indicate progressions precisely (i.e., especially in
respect to the diachronic axis) a large chart would have to be
used, so that parallelism and simultaneity can be exactly established, especially in those sign-systems dealing with degrees of
deixis and to exactly calibrate imagistic recurrence in time. In what
follows, signficant patterns in the development of sign systems are
summarized, and two full sign-system tables (Tables II and III) are
offered for *The Rock Garden* Scene 3.

In Scene 1, only the scenic and performative categories are in
operation; there is no dialogue. A bare stage surrounds a solid
kitchen set; the lighting is plain, and the man, girl and boy are
seated there. The props consist of a magazine, used by the man, and
glasses of milk, drunk by the two teenagers. Costumes, presumably

TABLE II The Rock Garden: Scenic and Performative Sign Systems for Scene 3

Music and Sound Effects	Movement, Gesture Activity	Proxemic Relationships	Configuration	Costumes, Make-Up, Hair-style	Props	Lighting	Setting, Furniture	Unit Definition
None	(1. 12.) Boy falls off his chair from boredom, sits again	Man facing D.R, Boy U.L.	Man, Boy	Both in underwear	None	[Even.] Early Afternoon	Bare Stage; Couch D.L. Angled D.L.; Chair U.R. Angled	#1 pp. 222–23 Ends: MAN/It Only takes a couple of coats No. of lines = 27
"	"	"	"	"	"	"	"	#2 pp. 223–24 Begins: BOY/ Two coats? Ends: BOY/White would be Good. No. of lines = 23
"	(1. 6.) Boy falls off chair, sits again (1. 16.) Falls, sits	"	"	"	"	"	"	#3 pp. 224–25 Begins: MAN/Sure. Maybe a kind of off-white. Ends: MAN/We could do it in our spare time. No. of lines = 37

TABLE II *continued*

Music and Sound Effects	Movement, Gesture, Activity	Proxemic Relationships	Configuration	Costumes, Make-Up, Hair-style	Props	Lighting	Setting, Furniture	Unit Definition
"	"	"	"	"	"	"	"	#4 p. 225 Begins: BOY / Together? Ends: MAN/Sure. No. of lines = 13
"	"	"	"	"	"	"	"	#5 pp. 225 – 26 Begins: MAN/It wouldn't be hard work at all. Ends: MAN/ . . . sprinkler heads and all that You know? No. of lines = 32
"	"	"	"	"	"	"	"	#6 p. 226 Begins: BOY/When I come it's like a river. No. of lines = 28

TABLE III The Rock Garden: *Textual Sign-Systems for Scene 3*

Dialogue images	Deictic elements	Audial shape and length characteristics
UNIT 1: lawn: lines 1, 6, 7, 8, 9, 10, 11, 12 sprinkler-heads: lines 2, 3, 14, 17 lawn-mowing: lines 4, 5 fence-painting: Lines 19, 20, 21 saturation: Lines 22, 24	I: lines 2, 3, 4, 5, 7 (twice) 8 (twice), 10, 13, 21, 11 QUESTION FORM: lines 6, 9, 10, 12, 14, 21, 23, 25, 26 This: lines 7, 12 you: Lines 9, 10, 12, 19, 21, 23 that: lines 6, 12, 13, 14 (twice), 15, 16 17 we: lines 18, 19	LONG PAUSE: lines 1, 3, 6, 12, 18, 21 23, 27 I guess: lines 3, 4, 5, 6, 8, 13, 21 I mean: lines 7, 8, 9 You know: lines 9, 10, 12, 13, 20, 22, 25 NOTES: Monologue, rejoinder, 1. 1. Short sentences
UNIT 2: white: lines 16, 17, 19, 20, 23	QUESTION FORM: lines 1, 3, 5, 7, 11, 12, 13, 14, 17, 19, 20	two: lines 1, 2, 3, 4, 7, a couple: lines 2, 6 Stychomythia: 1 – 7 words
UNIT 3: white: lines 1, 2, 4 rocks, rock-garden: lines 7, 11, 13, 17, 20 21, 24, 27, 28, 29, 30, 33. trips, Arizona: lines 11, 18, 31, 32 carrying rocks: lines 12, 15, 16 fountains: lines 34, 35	QUESTION FORM: lines 1, 2 (twice), 3, 4, 5, 6, 7, 10, 13, 14, 18, 19, 21, 23, 27, 29, 32, 35 I, me: lines 2, 5, 7, 11, 13, 16 (twice), 17, 18, 22, 25, 28 (twice), 31, 34, 35 that: lines 7, 10, 12, 19, 29 my, our: lines 9, 23, 32, 34, 36 we: lines 11, 17, 18, 20, 22, 23, 30, 31, 32, 33, 35, 36 (twice) you: lines 1, 2, 3, 4 (twice), 6, 7, 8 (twice), 10, 12, 15 24, 29, 31, 35	different: lines 2, 3 (twice), 4, 6 you know: lines 1, 2, 3, 4, 6, 10, 14 15, 16, 24, 25, 26 LONG PAUSE: lines 20, 22 NOTES: Monologue, rejoinders lines 21, 23 short sentences
UNIT 4: sandwiches: lines 2 working: lines 4, 8, 11, 12	QUESTION FORM: lines 1, 4, 7, 10, 12 we: lines 2, 4, 6, 9, 11	sure: lines 2, 5, 13 Stychomythia: 1 – 17 words

TABLE III *Continued*

Dialogue images	Deictic elements	Audial shape and length characteristics
UNIT 5:		
work: lines 2, 4, 11, 12	we, us: lines 2, 7, 8, 9,	LONG PAUSE: lines 1,
orchard: lines 3, 5, 8, 9	10, 16, 19, 20 (twice),	3
	23, 24, 25	you know?: lines 4, 8,
rocks, rock-garden: lines	QUESTION FORM: lines	11, 13, 14, 16, 18,
4, 8, 27, 29	4, 8, 11, 14, 16, 18	27, 30, 32
Arizona: lines 9, 24	20, 22, 27, 30, 32	NOTES: Monologue, 2
spraying trees: lines 10,	I: lines 6, 7, 16	rejoinders lines 19, 22
22, 23	that, those: lines 12, 17	Sentences lengthen, then
irrigation: lines 11, 29	19, 26	shorten near end. Fewer
laying pipes: lines 13,	you: lines 3, 6, 8, 11,	pauses.
14, 15, 16, 17, 18, 19	13, 14, 16, 18, 27,	
fountain: line 26	28, 30	
fence: line 29		
sprinkler-heads: line 31		
UNIT 6:		
'Come': lines 1, 2, 10	I, me: lines 1, 2 (three	you know?: lines 2, 5
vagina: lines 2, 5, 16	times), 3, 5, 9, 11,	6, 7, 8, 9, 10, 12,
penetration: lines 5, 9,	12, 13 (twice), 14, 16	14, 16, 21, 23, 25,
25, 26, 27, 28	18, 22, 23, 25 (twice)	26, 28
undressing: lines 12, 13,	28	I mean: lines 4, 6,
14	QUESTION FORM: lines	10, 12, 14, 17, 19,
'head': lines 14, 15, 16	2, 6, 7, 8, 9, 10, 12,	23
intercourse: lines 17, 18,	15, 16, 20, 22, 24,	
19	27	NOTES: Monologue (this
finger, thumb insertion:	She, her: lines 6, 7, 8,	time by the boy), no
lines 20, 21, 22, 23,	9 (twice), 10, 13, 15	rejoinders. Sentence
24, 25	(twice), 19	patterns similar to
	you: lines 2, 4, 5, 6,	Man's but more
	7 (twice), 8, 9, 10,	pronounced.
	11 (twice), 13, 15, 17,	
	18, 20 (twice), 21, 22,	
	24, 25, 27	
	NOTE: The 'you' here is	
	not always deictic, some-	
	times generalized	
	impersonal pronoun.	

everyday clothes, are not specified. The proxemic relationships are formal, as the three are seated around the table. The repeated activities are of two kinds – the boy and girl glance at each other in turn and sip milk, and the end of the scene is marked by the girl spilling her milk. 'Sound effects' consist of slurping as the milk is being drunk. Lights go up rapidly, and black out fast. Since there is no spoken text, the last four systems in any sign-system diagram would be blank.

In Scene 2, the scenic and performative categories significantly interweave, and particularly significant is the way that the costume and prop sign systems interweave with those involving configurations and proxemic relationships. A bed is upstage, in front of a bay window through which outlines of trees can be seen. There is a rocking chair D.L., otherwise the stage is bare. Shepard does not indicate whether the bay window is in a single flat or whether this forms part of a box set. The light is specified as blue. Configurations are restricted to no more than two figures at any time in the acting (i.e., 'bedroom') area, and proxemic relationships are characterised by distance and isolation. The woman is lying in bed, under five blankets, and the boy of the previous scene, rocking in the chair, is in his underwear. They do not face each other. Six times the boy rises, exits, returns with something, and sits. The first two times, he complies with the woman's request for a glass of water, which he gives her before sitting. The third time, he brings her a blanket, then two more glasses, then another blanket, and each time but the first he comes back also with an additional item of clothing for himself – pants, shoes, shirt, overcoat.

At the end of the scene, several important sign-systems 'bunch' climactically with the entrance of the man from the previous scene; the rate and texture of the movements as described in the stage directions appear both sporadic and abrupt, punctuated with unsettling, threatening sound effects:

> (*Footsteps are heard offstage. The footsteps get louder. A* MAN *walks by the window from stage right to stage left dressed in a hat and overcoat. The* BOY *stands suddenly. The* MAN *can be heard scraping his feet offstage. The* BOY *runs offstage right. The* MAN *enters stage left. He walks across the stage and exits right. After a while the* MAN *comes back on dressed in underwear. He crosses to the rocking chair and sits. For a long while the* MAN *just sits rocking. The* WOMAN *stares at the ceiling*).[13]

After a brief exchange between the man and woman, the lights dim out slowly after a 'long silence'. When the boy is on stage in this scene, the woman has nine-tenths of the dialogue, but the woman's sentences are simple, marked by a large number of phrase-sentences. The rhythm is broken, sporadic and disjointed. Many of the anecdotes during the woman's fevered rambling are of reminiscence, but they are also often deictic insofar as they are active and dialogic – aimed at making the boy aware that she is comparing the unseen 'pop' – the grandfather – both to her husband and to her son, and implying perhaps that the younger men don't measure up. Thus, the reminiscence seems selective and aimed *at* the listening character, as an implied challenge. And the brief questions of the boy are more than merely mechanical rejoinders to keep the woman talking. They operate deictically, for they increasingly suggest ironic provocation to draw direct response:

> WOMAN: . . . Pop had the same kind of legs.
> BOY: What do you mean?
> WOMAN: Well I mean they were bony and – and kind of skinny.
> BOY: They were?
> WOMAN: Yes. And he had knobby knees.
> BOY: He did?
> WOMAN: And fuzzy brown hair all over them.
>
> (220)

This nascent pattern of ironic challenge in apparently innocuous rejoinders intensifies in the following Scene 3 with the Man. At the end, the dialogue abruptly changes character in the brief, guardedly innocuous exchange between husband and wife, after the boy has abruptly left – apparently to avoid the father.

As far as the dialogue-image sign system is concerned, the scene begins with food images – 'angels on horseback', burned over an open fire, made and enjoyed by 'pop', the woman's father. Images of an attic, forest, rain and beach follow. 'Pop' is then equated with images of poisoned food – mushrooms and a stew, then vomit and starvation – and a proliferation of befouling cats which he kept confined to the attic. Then pop's legs, and his physique, are compared with the boy's. Finally the woman compares her sickness to cold, draft, and rain. Her next monologue relates the father's poor physique to images of draft-closing putty, useless work, and an orchard, and finally reverts back to her own state – to rain, cold, and blankets. The final images, shared between the man and the woman, are of draft and leaky windows – suggesting the exposure, the lack of comfort and stability, in this particular family domestic 'interior'.

Tables II and III represent a detailed analysis of Scene 3 of the play. Table II represents the performative and scenic groups of sign systems described in Table I. The scene has been divided into six units indicated in the right hand column and geared to the text of the play as it appears in the Urizen Books edition. Since this scene is static and there is a relative emphasis on the language spoken, the textual sign-systems are separately and more exhaustively analysed in Table III. Here each beat is divided more rigorously by line; significant images, rhythmic phrases, and deictic integers are noted on the line on which they occur and repetitions are indicated in a vertical column of asterisks, placed on the relevant lines, running down from the first letter of the image or word. Deictic integers include questions from one figure to another, demonstrative pronouns, personal pronouns, and possessives. I have included significant (i.e., significantly often repeated) images or words only, just occasionally mentioning an image not to be repeated but significant from a broader reading of Shepard's work (e.g., the image of a sandwich with mayonnaise which appears only once, Beat #4, line 2). The tables also include brief, general notes on characteristics and patterning at the end of each beat, and in fact the synchronic and diachronic axes are preserved in these tables. What follows is essentially a summary of the evidence diagrammed in them.

Once again the scenic sign systems reveal the predisposition towards static tableaux in this play. This is not to imply a pejorative criticism, for, as in *4-H Club*, the stage picture, its aridity and austerity, provides its own mordant and counterpointing comment on the tinsel-visions set up by the monologues; and here in *The Rock Garden* the separation of the figures, their facing away from each other, makes further ironic the largely false diegetic 'communication' implied by the 'questions' of the man's monologues. As far as the set is concerned, we are back to the apparently 'wall-less' construction of Scene 1, with the separation of furniture pieces of Scene 2. Proxemic relationships are set by the spatial separation of the sofa and chairs and the different body focus of the two figures. Lighting is clear coloured. The major activity is the falling of the boy off the chair, specified as from boredom, capped at the end by the man's falling off the sofa – apparently from shock- reaction to the potency of the boy's speech – before the blackout. Given the context of stasis, these movements have the emphatic force of thunderclaps.

In the textual categories, the sign-systems of audial shape/unit length and deixis are closely linked. The alternation between virtual monologues and short, sharp one-line exchanges (called 'stychomythia' in ancient Greek tragedy) is obvious, and have been a major influence in my beat division. Equally obvious are the implications of the oft repeated rhetorical question tag 'You know?'. When an actual answer to this tag is expected, the man usually supplies it himself, preceded by the tag 'I mean'. Other questions of a non-rhetorical kind are not followed by a pause for a response, but are also self-answered; and non-questions or statements sometimes elicit a long pause of non-response, or, sometimes, an unexpected and usually unnecessary question for clarification which then leads into a stychomythic burst of dialogue. These latter banal exchanges, usually 'questions' by the son about what is already obvious, can hardly be other than challenges. The monologues are punctuated by long silences which seem to increase the man's unease and nervousness, as his attempts to strike up a rapport with the boy meet with a mechanical or equivocal response – or no response at all. These silences elicit an even more short-breathed structure in the sentence-pattern, including an increase in the number of 'You know?'s. In the final monologue of the son, this pattern intensifies, probably as a parodic challenge. Another interesting feature is a syntactic pattern in the monologues – the comparatively short-term repetition of a key image or word which, eliciting no response, is then dropped. An illustration (my emphasis):

> Sure. Maybe a kind of off-white. You know? What about a kind of off-white? You know what I mean? A kind of *different white*. *You know? Just a little different.* Not too much *different* from the way it is now. What do you think? A *different* kind of white. You know? So it won't be too much the same. It could be almost the same but still be a little *different*. You know? (223)

This seems to indicate the persistence of the man's attempts to connect, and his self-conscious dickering with key-words to do so – after he has recognised that they are futile.

Implicit in this 'audial shape' category is a deictic attitude of the speaker to listener and vice versa. When the number of questions is examined, the implied orientation for a needed response is stronger. What is even more significant is the pattern of 'shifter' personal pronouns used. In Beat #1, 'I', gradually changes to 'we', and this pronoun, with its implications of a bonding between father and son (which remains a wish-fulfilment on the father's part) reaches its highest level of density in Beat #3. No other figures are referred to by the father. In Beat #6, the 'I' aggressively returns; 'we' is not mentioned at all, and the sex-object 'she/her' recurs often – the only other figure referred to in this scene.

Patterns in the dialogue-image system are clear and easily suggest a 'theme'. Major images are of sprinklers, mowers, lawns, sprinkler heads, and the colour white. Then the rock garden image is introduced. The white and green colour images are interspersed with people – action images of father and son working – at painting fences, and getting more and more rocks. Sterility is suggested by images of repetitive and useless work and of Arizona, desert, and Oriental decorative statuary. There is finally another vision of a sort of false fecundity, when the man talks of irrigating the desert and garden and describes his vision of a sprinkler-ridden and neatly-mown *Home and Garden* suburban paradise. Then comes a transition to the son's explicitly sexual imagery, beginning with the reference to a river of 'come', and then to various permutations of sexual activity. The speech climaxes in the following passage:

> BOY: Actually girls really like fingers almost as well as a penis. You know? If you move your fingers fast enough they'd rather have it that way almost. I learned to use my thumb, you know? You can get your thumb in much further, actually. I mean the thumb can go almost eight inches whereas a finger goes only five or six. You know? I don't know. I really like to come almost out and then go all the way into the womb. You know, very slowly. Just come down to the end and all the way back in and hold it. You know what I mean? (226)

The boy's speech breaks through the aridity and shatters the stasis of rock-garden suburbia which is presided over by the figure of the father. Evidence from the scenic and performative sign-systems confirms these 'thematic' implications. The setting illustrates the typical combination of 'dangerous' open space surrounding the fragile-domestic interior, so characteristic of the later Shepard. The ritual of domestic, 'trivial' activity is suddenly subverted by violence: the teenage girl's apparently deliberate upsetting of her milk glass; the boy's 'shocking', climactic story which 'floors' its target (the father falls off the couch), instead of the 'nodding off' in boredom – the son falling off his chair while contemplating the father's arid domain of suburban tasks like lawn mowing and constructing a rock garden. And in addition there is the stasis of tableau; the absence of living, meaningful gesture; the blue or pallid light.

But when the model analysis is examined, it is the 'textual' sign-systems – those of audial shape/length, the deictic, and the image-referent – which reveal the greatest density, more so in this play than in many of Shepard's others. The audial shape/rhythmic patterns and deictic sign-systems indicate a pattern in which monologue – disjointed, loaded with cliché-ridden or hermetic fantasy or personal memory (as well as a false or superficial deictic orientation to the son-listener) is subverted by an increasingly provocative pattern of defiance from the boy, capped by the final monologue. And this pattern of the man's selfish sterility and its implied rejection by the boy is paralleled by the image sign-system. The images of nature – forest, rain, beach, sheep – and images of healthy food give way to poisoned food, cat-shit, and putrefaction. Images of ineffectual labour emerge – puttying windows in which cracks reappear, useless painting, and irrigation which results in sterility. Then in contrast we get the sexuality of the boy's final monologue, with all the rage and the thrill of nascent experience, foreshadowed in the latent sexual images of the sprinkle-heads and sprinklers, running water in rain and irrigation, and – just before the boy's monologue – spraying.

The evidence of the sign-systems confirms Shepard's statement about the play – that it is a play about 'leaving my mom and dad'[14] – and about lethal but also life-asserting energy, which symbolically 'kills' the father and enables the boy to move to adulthood. Of course, the father-son rivalry is an important theme in the mature Shepard plays. In *Curse of the Starving Class*, for instance, it is doubtful whether Wesley can transcend his father's mistakes and criminal dabbling – and father and son are destructively conjoined in the final memorable image in the play, that of the airborne eagle and tom cat crashing to earth, tearing at each other, like 'one whole thing'.[15] More positively, in *Buried Child*, Vince's aggressive insistence on claiming his heritage may just counteract powerfully enough the 'negative' image of the shrouded infant-corpse which dominates the final tableau.

B.   *4-H CLUB* (1964)

4-H Club is a longer play than *The Rock Garden*, and is less anchored
in stasis and tableau. It will be dealt with here in a more summarised
form, with the salient features and implications of the various
sign-systems noted.

One unusual feature of this play compared to *The Rock Garden* is
that reference is made to the framing and preparatory category of
sign-systems. Twice, characters refer to the presence of the audience
in the theatre, foregrounding the formal construct of the play-frame
and the non-representational stylistic strategies of the play as a
whole.

The action is not broken into scenes, and the scenic sign-systems
remain fairly constant, except for a significant lighting change near
the end. A 'kitchen' cluttered with cans and garbage demarcated
with three dirty stage flats, the upstage one containing swinging
doors, is placed at the up left area of a bare stage – again, we
have the image of an 'interior', surrounded by amorphous and
abstract space. In the 'kitchen', there is a garbage can up right
and a coffee pot on a hot plate down left. Other props are a broom
onstage, and apples that will be introduced and proliferated later.
The three figures are dressed in 'torn, grimy' clothes which do not
change. The 'kitchen area' at lights up is littered with paper, cans
and trash. The lighting remains even until Bob and Joe go into the
kitchen to 'kill the mice' – and at that point the kitchen lights go out,
obscuring the bodies, but not the voices, of the two, and isolating
John, who remains visible and spatially apart, outside it.[16]

Configuratively and proxemically, the image of two-on-one is
reinforced from the beginning, but its permutations change. The
first tableau sets all three men slightly apart from each other, in
the kitchen area. It soon becomes clear, though, that John and Bob
are first bonded, leaving Joe as the 'odd man out' – privileged,
as the textual sign-systems reveal, with monologue – a privilege
which remains through two-thirds of the play. Later, the balance
shifts. John is the isolated member of the three, and at the final
tableau he is apart, down right, while Joe and Bob have teamed
up, and, absorbed in their own rivalries over strategies to hunt out
the mice, ignore or even subvert his final vision of peace and escape
in a tropical country. John is the character who most often restlessly
exits from the stage and returns; the final 'bonding' of Bob and Joe
occurs when he is offstage.

The movement sign-system reveals evidence that essentially supports the shifting of the fulcrum among the three, and the alliance. Much of the movement and activity centres on the floor (of the raised proscenium stage) since there are no chairs on stage – and in this play, the movement and activity tracks are closely linked. There are two lengthy sections of circular movement, the first between Joe (advancing to eat the apple) and John, a stalking movement; the second, between Bob and Joe, is the cooperative bonding during an aggression-fantasy while John is offstage. More palpably linked with activity is the violence done to food – especially the coffee cups, broken in unison by the three men, and the violent kicking of trash over the floor of the kitchen, and stomping on the floor – at first done by John and Bob, with Joe the tidier who ineffectually attempts to sweep after them, and later by Bob and Joe, with John protesting at this further trashing. At the end, fantasies of violence build to actual physical wrestling between Bob and Joe. The other activity that is important is the eating of the apples. That too undergoes a change, and it helps to underscore the bonding alliances. It is John – the eventual odd man out – who initiates the apple-eating; but Bob finds one of his own and shares it with Joe. Later, the apple-eating activity is John's exclusively, with a reserve of apples stashed under his shirt as he eats down right.

The audial shape and deictic sign-systems intertwine to highlight the creation of compulsive team fantasies of proliferation, violence, and dispersal. Stychomythic dialogue techniques, in turn game-like, desperate, and hysterical, build such fantasies. More extended monologue indicates patterns of 'odd man out' among the trio, at first identifying Joe as the outsider, later John. Significant also is the development of more extreme registers of dynamics. The savage yelling of Bob and Joe, challenging the mice to come out of their hiding place, yields to a more fantastical, game-like delivery as they try to trick them out by being quiet. Whispering in the dark 'interior' builds to a voiced terror in reaction to John's story about the savage mandrills, but finally evolves into a ritual, non-verbal protest, as the coffee pot is bashed on the hot plate by Joe in a steady rhythm.

A genuine (as opposed to token or ironic) deixis is much more in evidence here than in *The Rock Garden*; it follows the patterning of the bonding, and reinforces it as fantasies are created and reinforced; but the 'solo' monologues genuinely affect reactions of the bonded pair who listen and absorb them. The food and props also reinforce the deixis in the dialogue – apples are desired

by a hungry Joe and Bob from John, who appears to control the
store; John wants hot coffee, and seems willing to barter apples,
but Bob reminds him that the cups have been broken and that he
was a collaborator in this. This pattern is reinforced by the 'shifters'
present and the gestic (social-attitudinal) dialogue implications.

But again, it is the dialogue-image sign-system which is of major
importance. The images of dirt, stasis and separation of elements in
the *mise en scène* are again counterpointed by a significant diachronic
stream of images which is foregrounded through much of the play.
These are summarised below; they begin with food images, progress
to images of proliferation and dispersal in which water is a major
'cleansing' element, and climax in two imagistic narratives: Joe's of
a 'suburban' paradise which proliferates and decays, then John's of a
'tropical' paradise which finally comes to rest in an apogee of idyllic
peace.

In the beginning, in what appears to be a parody of a 4-H cooking
manual, hot coffee is laid out in images; after the coffee and cups
are violated, Joe, alone on stage for his first monologue, introduces
images of neatness and cleaning with a jet of water – a jet which then
becomes destructive and draws a crowd of people as the firemen
called to the scene disperse. This is the first of a significant series of
images of proliferation turning to dispersal which are introduced
through dialogue in the image-sound system of the play. Apples, at
first positively characterised in the dialogue, are turned gradually
into a rather foul multi-purpose stew, and they proliferate. They
then are characterised as weapons (on John's exit with his apple),
and the men's collective fantasy of the proliferation of apples as
offensive weaponry – 'all these apples sailing through the air and
crashing their skulls!' (213) – brings the National Guard, a mob and
armoured cars.

Now the images change as Joe – in a series of monologues –
launches into an anecdotal fantasy-recollection of proliferation and
dispersal, centring on remembered competitiveness: a high school
peer built a lawn-and-drive-mowing service into a kind of general
human services movement which attracted hordes of old ladies, neat
houses all in green and white, mown lawns, and reliance on the boy
who, at the height of his mesmeric success, 'escapes' – drives off in
a Rolls-Royce – and his beneficiaries, with nothing left to live for,
die one by one. Joe recalls wending blindfold through the decayed
town by night with his friends, and the anecdote of one of them who
entered a decaying house. This monologue is comparatively gentle

in tone and surreal in ambience; the intruder walked into a typically cosy mid-American interior, with books, lamps, and pictures of 'swallows and dogs'. But it ends with a disturbing image. He went down a hallway and ' . . . walked into a huge bathroom that was painted blue and there was this old lady lying on her stomach with a spoon in her hand' (218). This suggests the death at the heart of the suburban *Home and Garden* American dream just as potently as the Man's image of artificially green lawns, sprinklers and rock gardens in the earlier play.

Now begin two successive fantasy images – patterns building in violence. Bob and Joe create a composite picture of mice that will be routed out of their hiding places, slaughtered, and turned into food. Then comes the final set of images in John's monologue, delivered at the proscenium in his separate space: he evokes a jungle landscape with wolverines and mandrills. The image of humans doing violence to rats and mice is inverted as the mandrills – savage baboons – are pictured slaughtering and dismembering humans. Images of wolverines, who close their eyes in the dark so that they cannot be seen, prompt Bob and Joe's final activity to drive the mice out. The final images of John's monologue, however, are of him eating a leisurely breakfast by a picture window viewing a tourist-scene and of floating face-upward in a clear and blue ocean where you can see 'all the way down to the bottom'. In the final 'bunching' of the sign-systems at the curtain tableau, the verbal images of hypnotic peace and beauty – 'You just sit there and eat and look out over the ocean . . . I'm going to do some swimming too. Floating on my back. You just float and stare at the sky' (233) – are juxtaposed with the stark reality of the scenic ones, in which the grimy stage's presence is reinforced by the sound effects of the two men in the kitchen fighting over strategies to rout out the mice, and Joe beating rhythmically and savagely against the coffee pot. The sum effect of this disparity is to hold the verbal and scenic sign-systems in a dialectic, in which two fantasies, one of peaceful escape and the other of savage victimization, compete. But John, in isolation to the side, seems overpowered by the fantasy of the bonded pair, who build their fantasy on the actual scenic sordidness – the 'reality' – embodied in the set.

The title of *4-H Club* is of course a parody, and the settings and action *in toto* represent a repudiation of the kind of civic pieties the 4-H Club stands for. And there are again biographical relevancies. If *The Rock Garden* is about 'leaving my mom and dad', surely this play is about 'leaving the 4-H Club' of Duarte, California. It would perhaps be a mistake to look for 'development' between two short plays written so close together. But whereas *The Rock Garden* is, essentially, a dramatic anecdote of defiance and independence which clearly points to growth and escape-as-development, *4-H Club* is more ambivalent in its implications. Here, John's escape is clearly impotent fantasy, and Joe and Bob's 'escape', firmly anchored in the trashy and trashed environment, is merely one of primitive, sadistic game-playing. If *4-H Club* is a protest at 4-H Club pieties, it seems also about stasis – for here, verbal fantasy is not really a breakthrough to personal development, as it can be in other Shepard plays.

In the diachronic development of the model's sign-systems in both plays, then, some major Shepard themes and images are clearly in evidence. These include that of escape/transformation set against entropic stasis (text images versus stage images); the imaginative release of monologue set against the banality and miscommunication of dialogue; healthful food imagery transmogrified into, or set against, images of decay and putrefaction; a 'domestic' order suddenly exploded by violence; male bonding veering back and forth into competitiveness; the need to establish or redefine identity through solitariness and rumination.

The value of the performance text model here advanced, however, is just as much related to potential staging of the plays as it is to an interesting way of re-reading (and re-understanding) Shepard. Pavis rightly insists that any critic or potential director should be sensitively aware of the 'polyphony of emission' of all the sign-systems, that is, the diachronic tempo/rhythm characteristics of the play in performance; and only if this awareness is present can one do full justice to the analysis of play text as potential performance text.[17] This is especially pertinent to the plays of Shepard, and especially to the early plays, with the synchronic 'bunching' of the sometimes antithetical and disparate stimuli accruing from the scenic and performative sign systems, on the one hand, and the dialogue-based sign-systems, on the other. It is this 'tracking' tension, and the variegated patterns in 'foregrounding' and counterpoint that it produces, that gives the distinctive characteristic of what director Robert Woodruff has called the 'unity in pieces' of a Shepard play,[18] which is something apart from the conventional 'unity' of plot and character development or, for that matter, that of literary and thematic explication.

Notes

1. See Patrice Pavis, *Languages of the Stage: Essays in the Semiology of Theatre* (New York: Performing Arts Journal Publications, 1982), pp. 149–52; 203–6.
2. Ibid., p. 128.
3. Ibid., pp. 147; 127–8.
4. See Jindrich Honzl, 'Dynamics of the Sign in Theatre', in *Semiotics of Art: Prague School Contributions* ed. Ladislav Matejka and Irwin R. Titunik (Cambridge: MIT Press, 1976), pp. 88–90; and Pavis, p. 137 and p. 144.
5. Umberto Eco, *A Theory of Semiotics* (Bloomington: Indiana University Press, 1976), pp. 32–47; Dudley Andrew, *Concepts in Film Theory* (Oxford: Oxford University Press, 1984), pp. 187–90; and Pavis, pp. 199–200.
6. Pavis, pp. 28–30.
7. Honzl, p. 91; Pavis, pp. 28–29.
8. Pavis, pp. 188, 203.
9. Kier Elam, *The Semiotics of Theatre and Drama* (London: Methuen, 1980), pp. 47–51; and Martin Esslin, *The Field of Drama: How the Signs of Drama Create Meaning on Stage and Screen* (London: Methuen, 1987), pp. 102–5.
10. As outlined in Manfred Pfister, *The Theory and Analysis of Drama*, trans. John Halliday (Cambridge: Cambridge University Press, 1988), pp. 171-76.
11. Elam, pp. 138–54.
12. Sam Smiley, *Playwriting: The Structure of Action* (Englewood Cliffs: Prentice-Hall, 1971), pp. 152–57.
13. Sam Shepard, *The Rock Garden* in *Angel City and Other Plays* (New York: Urizen Books, 1976), p. 222. All quotations are from this edition; page numbers are given in the text.
14. Kenneth Chubb and the Editors of *Theatre Quarterly*, 'Metaphors, Mad Dogs and Old Time Cowboys: Interview with Sam Shepard', in *American Dreams: The Imagination of Sam Shepard* ed. Bonnie Marranca (New York: Performing Arts Journal Publications, 1981), p. 193.
15. Sam Shepard, *The Curse of the Starving Class*, in *Angel City and Other Plays* (New York: Urizen Books, 1976), p. 118.
16. Sam Shepard, *4-H Club*, in *The Unseen Hand and Other Plays* (Indianapolis: Bobbs-Merrill, 1972), p. 203. All quotations are from this edition; page numbers are given in the text.
17. Pavis, pp. 77, 188.
18. Robert Coe, 'Interview with Robert Woodruff', in *American Dreams*, p. 152.

3

The Desert and the City: *Operation Sidewinder* and Shepard's Postmodern Allegory

Leonard Wilcox

I

Two loci inform Shepard's imagination and provide the geographical poles of the landscape of his plays – the desert and the city. For example, Shepard's screenplay for *Paris, Texas*, and Wim Wenders's cinematography use the desert and the city as pivotal images around which the narrative action revolves. Travis, initially seen wandering the landscape of the desert like some burned-out Natty Bumpo traversing the barren frontier, is later taken by his brother Walt into the city with its landscape of concrete freeways and enormous billboards. Indeed, the movement back and forth between desert and city constitutes the narrative movement of the film: Travis's recuperation in Walt's house in Los Angeles is only a prologue to a journey with his son back into the huge expanses of the southwestern desert in search of his wife Jane as well as his own personal history – and this journey takes him back into the concrete mazes and imposing overpasses, the impersonal electronic drive-in banks, as well as the sleazy back alleys of prostitution that lie in the dark heart of the city.

Paris, Texas also suggests something of the sixties sense of the desert as the 'last frontier', as space and freedom of movement, the last region where one can go 'on the road', searching, as Kerouac's heroes once did, for the genuine, the authentic, the original. For the desert landscape of the tiny Texas town of Paris represents the point of origins, the place where Travis returns in the search for his own past. The city on the other hand is the realm where origins – both personal and cultural – are occluded. The city represents the image, simulacrum and the discontinuous play of the signifier. Not only does Walt work for a company that manufactures billboards, but he is at home in this world of circulating images and in his house which is a kitsch combination of Spanish 'ranch' style and stucco box. The cityscape signifies an omnipresent Americana which is the postmodern condition – a simulated or hyperreal world comprised of commodified and fetishised images (the peep-show whose exterior is appropriately decorated with a mural of the Statue of Liberty) and a world of pop and film culture references. Travis's son Hunter – beside whom the desert-saturated Travis looks like a relic of the lost frontier of the old west – wears a miniature Nasa suit, talks about space travel and time dilation, and is completely at home in his urban environment with the instruments of modern communications like the walkie talkie and the tape recorder.

In Shepard's plays, too, there are suggestions of the desert/city polarity, the desert associated with imaginative space and room to dream, the city with the corruption of dreams and the perversion of artistic creativity. As the quintessential West, the desert is perforce (as Rabbit Brown's Indian medicine wheel in *Angel City* indicates), the 'looks within place', a place of introspective discovery, the location whose corresponding bundle on the medicine wheel is the only one which is truly authentic. On the other hand the urban world threatens the wellsprings of the imagination. Cody, in *Geography of a Horse Dreamer*, protests that he belongs on the great plains of Wyoming, not held captive in the Beverly Wilshire or the motel room he now occupies, and that his manager, Fingers, has 'poisoned my dreams with these cities'.[1] In *Mad Dog Blues*, Kosmo declares that 'the city's getting me down. Too many tangents. It's no place to collaborate'.[2] And in *Angel City*, Wheeler exclaims that 'The city is eating us alive. Can't you see my skin? . . . It's turning us into snakes or lizards or something'.[3]

Yet as the 'looks within place', an arena of authentic impulses from the depths of the self, the desert has a darker side. As a symbolic inner or psychic terrain, it is often associated with an anarchy of spirit, with rootlessness, drunkenness, disorder, and the inability of men to form stable relations with women. If the desert is associated with an imaginative root force, it is also the father's country, where the law of the patriarchy dominates the inner landscape and demands allegiance to the world of men. The desert is haunted by the spirit of the 'dead father'; in *Fool For Love*, for example, the desert motel is presided over by the spectral father, a patriarchal superego who insists that the son maintain at all cost an allegiance to the world of male desire, to the order of the phallus. 'I want to hear the male side a' this thing' he demands when it appears Eddie is about to defect from the 'master' narrative justifying male rootlessness ('I was gone . . . But I wasn't disconnected', the father says of his perpetual absence from both his families).[4] Moreover, the desert is the site of oedipal struggle: in *True West*, Lee, the 'desert rat', embodies the reclusiveness and tendency to violence and drunkenness of his desert-dwelling father, and because he is a surrogate for the Old Man, the struggle between Austin and Lee takes on oedipal proportions. And in *A Lie of the Mind*, a drunken bar-hopping contest between father and son results in what amounts to an act of patricide on a lonely stretch of desert just south of the Texas border.

A symbolic psychic terrain of patriarchal mandates and oedipal conflict, the desert is also the site of the search for lost origins. In *Paris, Texas*, for example, Travis carries with him a photograph – of a vacant lot in Paris, a town on the Texas desert where he was born – because, as he says, 'this is the place where I began'. But curiously, this originary moment, this 'primal scene' is a representation, a photograph, a mere snapshot, and the picture itself is virtually blank – all one sees is sand. Around this absence, the representation both of origins and their loss, Travis constructs a narrative of how his father met his mother and how he 'began'.

Travis's picture of the desert sand in *Paris, Texas*, tells us something about the significance of the desert in Shepard's *oeuvre*. Like the unconscious itself, the desert is a landscape of the play of representation, in Derrida's terms, a 'scene of writing'. Rather than being a single term in a paired existence, a stable and determinate opposition to the city, Shepard's desert is often a 'postmodern' landscape, one in which origins are foreclosed, where the natural and original is always implicated in the play of the signifier. In this sense the desert is represented as a textual space rather than a natural one, a figurative and tropological space which defers essence, presence, and disclaims the authentic. In its occlusion of origins, it thus displays a formal affinity with the unconscious. Like the Freudian primal scene, the original moment – often pursued on the desert – is never distinguishable from primal fantasy, never available as 'full presence', never recoverable apart from the narrative that constitutes it; like all primal scenes it must be displaced to the recesses of narrative account, myth, and allegory.

Shepard's 1971 play *Operation Sidewinder* provides an uncomfortable test case for this hypothesis, uncomfortable because of the contradictory elements in the text. The play is specifically about the search for origins both personal and cultural: for the lost frontier of America, with its mythic archetypes and historical figures, and for a lost sense of personal authenticity – a major preoccupation of the sixties decade. Indeed the play has been read as the triumph of the authentic over the counterfeit, of spirituality and a sense of sacredness manifest in the desert Hopi Indians over the materialism of contemporary American urban society.[5] In that sense the play might be seen as exhibiting an attraction to alternative non-western cultural values so characteristic of the American sixties; like Carlos Castaneda who ventures out into the Southwestern desert to be initiated into pure vision under the tutelage of the Yaqui Indian Don Juan, the characters in *Operation Sidewinder* are brought to an epiphany of enlightenment, a direct apprehension of origins under the tutelage of the Hopi Spider Lady. And the trajectory of the action seems to move from a postmodern landscape of textual and popular references toward some basic myth of origins that can heal the divisiveness of the contemporary world and somehow rejuvenate the imaginative dimension of the American West.

Yet *Operation Sidewinder*, like a number of Shepard's other plays, is a postmodern text lacking the modernist assurance that literature can anchor itself in its own fullness, can contain or recuperate an originary moment or primal unity within an over-arching mythic framework. Rather than constituting an organic world, it is splayed across a variety of discourses and codes, constructed out of discourses that display a pluralized otherness. Lacking 'deep structures' and constitutive symbols it must be read in terms of some 'extrinsic' significance. Moreover, like all allegories at some level it pursues origins, presence, the 'primal scene', while simultaneously acknowledging the impossibility of apprehending or representing them directly.

II

John Larh is the only critic to have hinted at the allegorical dimension of the play in likening its scenes to a 'medieval triptych'.[6]
Lahr's analogy suggests the emblematic character of the play's
scenes and central images. Like medieval allegory, Shepard gives
us an almost dreamlike desert landscape populated by figures who
are representatives, types and forces: the hippie Everyman Young
Man, suggesting the estranged, confused, and narcissistic youth of
America, and Honey, his counterpart, a 'young woman' of America
in the sixties who embodies a shallow innocence and optimism.
General Browser, Captain Bovine, Colonel Warner and Cadet, are
all representatives of America's mindless military might, and the
scientist Doctor Vector who, having built a computer in the form of
a snake in order to communicate with extraterrestrials, suggests a
paranoiac strain in American technorationality. Billy the prospector,
and Mickey Free, a halfbreed Indian, are emblematic figures of the
western frontier. The allegory in *Operation Sidewinder* involves the
confrontation of warring principles – those of materialism and
spiritualism – embodied respectively in the military as well as
the young countercultural radicals, on the one hand, and the Hopi
Indians with their shaman the Spider Lady on the other. The play
follows the allegorical pattern of a trek through hell to the vision
of the holy city that we find in Dante and Bunyan, and this
pattern is played out in Young Man, the central character of the
play, who moves, almost in spite of himself, from self-absorption
and materialism to spiritualism.

The play opens in an allegorical mode, offering visual images
as a script to be deciphered. The house lights come down, and a
mammoth sidewinder rattlesnake emerges from the darkness. Its
ruby red eyes 'blink on and off', and it 'measures over six feet
and looks like it weighs thirty pounds'.[7] A couple from the city
next appears, Dukie, the man, wearing 'bermuda shorts and hush
puppies', Honey, the woman, wearing 'tight pants and high heels'.
The two city innocents are armed with a camera and knowledge of
the desert obtained from a tourist manual. The man, the woman,
the snake, and the desert 'garden': Shepard's version of the Garden
of Eden now begins to take shape. The man is confident in his
self mastery (Dukie assures Honey he can deal with the snake
because he has spent time in the Philippines); the woman is equally
confident that the snake means no harm: 'I mean he's just out here

trying to get a suntan or something. There's nothin' awful about
that. He looks kind of tense but I'll bet he'd loosen up in no
time at all if he got the right kind of attention. You know what
I mean Dukie? Little mice and stuff' (200). Yet Dukie's smug
assurance and Honey's domestic platitudes fail to account for the
sidewinder's threatening movements and its blatantly sexual and
phallic appearance. 'I've never seen one so huge' (200), Honey says
about the sidewinder just before it leaps out, coils itself around her
body, ravishes her, and brings her to orgasm.

Shepard's version of the Garden of Eden is outrageous and playful; while Honey lies entrapped in the snake's coils, the Holy Modal
Rounders sing a paean to sexual desire, 'Every time I see you wanna
do it girl/right out in the street I want to do it girl' (201). But the early
scenes in the play also have serious resonances. Original innocence
in Shepard's Garden is more specifically American innocence, the
obliviousness of the two tourists, urban 'innocents abroad', to the
dark forces the sidewinder represents. Like the Biblical Garden,
Shepard's desert setting is evocative of lost origins: the first scene
suggests the lost Eden of the west, the desert frontier, if not the
loss of imaginative and mythic vitality suggested in Honey's facile
sixties therapeutic terms. The Sidewinder itself, usually associated
with the open spaces of the west and the desert frontier, is mechanized; not only do its eyes blink on and off like beacons, but it
'undulates in a mechanical rhythm' (199). The Biblical myth is thus
transformed into the pivotal American myth, the snake in the garden into the 'machine in the Garden', suggesting technorationality
in which nature itself has been colonized by and transformed into
tools for military and scientific domination. The sidewinder is not
only a computer, but the name is readily associated with another
phallic and technological object – the Sidewinder guided missile.

Indeed, Shepard's play depicts a fallen world severed from origins
and dominated by a technology of death. The play is a dark
vision of the American sixties with alienation, violence, paranoia,
the oppressiveness of society's war technology on the one hand
and desperate, crackpot radical schemes to overthrow the military
industrial establishment on the other. It depicts a world in which
radical hopes have turned to despair. Young Man is obsessed with
a scheme to drop drugs into the reservoir of a nearby military base
and seize its planes, while the black militants see the Young Man as
a pawn in their own plan for occupying the base and overthrowing
white society. The military, with the assistance of Dr. Vector, has

created the sidewinder computer in an effort to control the universe, while the revolutionaries want the sidewinder because of their own desire for power. All around there is a sense of loss and lost promise. Young Man reminisces on the sense of unity and community fleetingly experienced at a countercultural gathering:

> I walked through the crowd. I saw my best friends there. Real friends. I felt such a warm bond between us. Like we were all in the same place at the same time for the same reason . . . . And suddenly I felt free, my mind was lifting up, up, up in flight. Not like a thirteen year old wild, crazy, out-of-the-house-on-Friday-night feeling but something much deeper. Like nothing could hurt me. Nothing could touch my peace. (225)

Such fleeting epiphanies of communal feeling are overshadowed by an atmosphere of political deception and violence. In a quiet moment under the desert stars, Young Man tells Honey about the 'election oppression' of 1968:

> . . . Nixon, Wallace, Humphrey. The headline oppression every morning with one of their names on it. The radio news broadcast, TV oppression. And every other advertisement with their names and faces and voices and haircuts and suits and collars and ties and lies. And I was all set to watch 'Mission Impossible' when Humphrey's flabby face shows up for another hour's alienation session. Oh please say something kind to us, something soft, something human, something different, something real, something – so we can believe again. (225)

Yet if belief has been lost irrevocably, the impulse to retrieve a sense of promise, to recover innocence, to 'get back to the garden' through shallow panaceas prevails. In the song 'Synergy', the Holy Modal Rounders satirise a puerile sixties enthusiasm: 'Kick that gong, ring that bell, synergy will save us all from hell/ . . . We can have paradise right now at a bargain price' (220). And Young Man and Honey shoot up under the desert stars, while the band plays 'Euphoria' which comments satirically on the resulting state of nirvana emptied of any sense of evil:

Pinched Eve on the bottom, patted Adam on the back

Smiled at the serpent and it winked back
Took a bite of the apple with two bites gone
And Hollered 'Euphoria'.

(217)

And yet Young Man's quest to recapture the promise, to achieve
a transcendental sense of self and being is a characteristic sixties
preoccupation, one to which Shepard is by no means unsympathetic.
Young Man seeks in the purity of the desert night a space of
authenticity, a moment of self presence and unmediated vision. As
he proclaims to Honey 'I am! I am! I am! Iam! I am! I am! Iam! I am!
I am! I am! I am! Tonight. In this desert! In this space. I am' (226).
Young Man's impulse to recover origins, transparent meaning, and
perfect presence is an impulse to recover a logocentric world. On
a certain level the play acts on this impulse, seeking ontological
self-presence as it moves toward ceremony and pure incantation
in a conclusion which ritualistically enacts the Hopi Indian myth
of origins.

The Spider Lady enters the terrain of lost origins, this phallocentric, mechanized world, with the Hopi tale of two original clans,
the Lizard and Snake Clans, the former of which was to harvest
the crops, the latter of which was to see to the spiritual needs of
the people. The latter group was given a giant 'spirit snake' to
communicate with the gods and keep peace in the hearts of the
people. Yet the Lizard clan, 'soon grew jealous' and engaged in a tug
of war to make the giant snake their own, splitting the serpent snake
into two parts. But now the 'chosen ones' live on the high mesas of
the desert and nurture a visionary prophecy of the severed halves of
the snake being rejoined. According to the prophecy, this occurrence
will produce a supreme moment of revelation and transcendence in
which the chosen will apprehend their origins and be swept from
the earth by a star, thus saving them from the destruction that will
reign on earth.

This prophetic vision narrated by the Spider Lady is realized in an
uncanny way, for Young Man, hoping to turn the high-tech snake
over to the black radicals and the revolutionary cause, seeks out
Mickey Free, who has the snake's severed head. But Mickey, now
under the influence of the Spider Lady, has embraced his Hopi origins and renounced his collusion with the violent revolutionaries. A
solemn Hopi ceremony is performed on stage, in which the severed
halves of the snake are joined.

The ceremony in the last section of the play, Shepard insists, should be *'spiritual and sincere and should not be cartooned or choreographed beyond the unison of the rhythmic patterns'* (251). Honey and the Young Man are *'calm, spiritual, totally accepting of the whole ritual'* (252). The two are baptized, their heads doused with oil by the snake chief and the antelope chief. When the desert tactical troops attempt to stop the ceremony with machine guns, their bullets have no effect. The Indian participants in the ceremony – as well as the Young Man and Honey – vanish after the desert tactical troops grab the sidewinder causing the body to separate from the head, thus fulfilling the Spider Lady's prophecy that 'once the two halves were joined the people would be swept from the earth by a star', and that 'soon after the spirit snake would again be pulled in half by the evil ones and the Fourth World would come to an end' (235).

As an allegory of warring forces, a kind of cultural psychomachia, the play ends, ostensibly, with the defeat of the phallic, militarised and death-driven impulses by a spiritual and feminine force represented by the Spider Lady. Yet this victory of the spiritual and feminine does not provide a 'myth of deliverance' or an unproblematic resolution to the play. Rather it implies, ultimately, an unfulfilled yearning, a longing to recapture the lost totality of being, and this is partly manifested in an undercurrent of oedipal desire that characterises the play. Hints of an oedipal motif occur in the early scenes. On his journey into the desert Young Man kills Dukie, an older man who has fought in the Second World War in the Philippines. Wearing Bermuda shorts and Hush Puppies, Dukie represents the middle-aged 'establishment', the far side of the generation gap, toward whom radicals like Young Man direct their oedipal hostilities. Suggestions of an oedipal dynamic are underscored when Young Man initiates a sexual relationship with Honey and later discovers he has killed her husband. He usurps Dukie's position, for Honey is now his possession which he alternatively ignores, manhandles, and recruits to assist in his drug fix.

In a larger sense, the oedipal yearning in the play has to do with the quest for the lost object, a maternal figure in a society where the paternal phallus dominates. One of the striking things about this landscape dominated by the phallus/computer is that it is, like other Shepard deserts, an allegorical landscape of male desire and patriarchal culture utterly devoid of the feminine. In this imaginative and discursive space of the desert, woman is symbolically a captive of the phallus and the patriarch; Honey literally lies on the ground entrapped in the snake's coils for the duration of the first scenes of the play. In spite of this bizarre situation, the men scarcely respond. Billy the prospector encounters the entrapped Honey in scene three and instead of helping her escape, sits on his haunches, rambling and ruminating about the decay of old mining towns. When Young Man enters he simply ignores the fact that Honey is completely encircled in the snake's coils, and when Billy asks him 'what about the lady?', the Young Man's response is 'What lady? She's got nothing to do with me' (207). Billy and the Young Man exit to carry out their revolutionary plan at the end of the scene, indifferent to Honey's predicament.

Honey's situation suggests that if women are an absence or a captive in this phallic order they are also objectified and fetishised in representation. Like Miss Scoons in *Angel City*, Honey dreams of being in the movies: her fantasy revolves around the fetishising of her hair:

> I never cut it because my Mama said that sometime . . . someday I'd make my living from my hair. That's what she told me. That I should come to Hollywood and the very next day, just from walking around the streets and everything, that someone would see my hair and ask me to come and get a screen test. And before very long I'd be famous and rich and everything. (224)

Moreover, women are represented as an absence in the discourse of the male cultural process or associated with the world of nature. In a drunken conversation between Colonel Warner and Captain Bovine, women are implicitly conflated with dogs and dog breeding.

> COLONEL: Trouble with that bitch was you just didn't get her out in the world enough, Henry. A young bitch like that's gotta come in contact with a whole lotta' people and noise. Otherwise you'll just never get her cured. There's a world of difference between your dog and your bitch. A lot of breeders forget that. Just like people. Now a woman's just naturally gonna' be more sensitive than a man. No two ways about it. Same with a dog.

> (208)

The desire of the text to move beyond this utterly phallic land-scape and return to an archaic, instinctual, maternal territory, is manifested allegorically in the movement toward the Spider Lady and Hopi ritual. Yet if Maureen Quilligan is right, allegory is always ultimately about language and signification.[8] And *Operation Sidewinder* is in some sense an allegory of the quest for presence and self presence, originary unity and transparency of meaning in language, and a fundamental impulse in this desiring quest is to move from the realm of image, simulacrum and pure signifier to some maternal 'semiotic' (to use Kristeva's term) language of poetic incantation,[9] or in dramatic terms, from verbal narrative to pure ritual. Indeed, the realm of ceremony and ritual which ends the play is beyond or anterior to language and to the paternal 'symbolic order'. It seems significant that when Young Man gives himself over to the 'feminine' order associated with the Spider Lady and walks into the Indian Wiaku, he voices the Lord's Prayer – an utterance based on the 'name of the father', on the symbolic order with its phallocentric law. Yet when he reemerges he is silent; language itself has given over to ritual and incantation. This realm prior to the symbolic order is the realm which also precedes sexual difference and sexual identity (Young Man and Honey are joined by tying their hair together, symbolically united in the ritual baptism of oil), as well as the realm that precedes the Lacanian 'castration' that accompanies insertion into the symbolic order: the severed head of the phallus or snake is joined with the body as if to imply the mending of this primal wound. Thus coextensive with the search for the lost promise of America, or for an authentic culture, the play conducts an allegorical search for 'origins' in language itself, and in the prelinguistic elements at language's origins – the 'maternal semiotic', rhythm, and, incantation.

III

Operation Sidewinder leaves us with a central problem. As a quest for the lost object of desire, the play might be seen as a trek from the postmodern 'textual' space (most often associated in Shepard's plays with the city) to some authentic terrain of myth and incan-tation based on the indigenous Hopi culture of the Southwestern desert. *Operation Sidewinder* might then be viewed as grounding the play of signification in the framework of ritual, resolving desire in the still centre of myth. Indeed it might be viewed as the logical outcome of Shepard's own search for 'words as living incantations and not as symbols'.[10] The desert, with its indigenous cultures – or as a symbolic inner landscape, the locus of origins and essence – could then be viewed as an alternative to the city with its chimeric play of images and signifiers, as a space where origins can be found in both culture and language.

Speculation on this problem of origins should begin by acknowledging the cross-grained and ambivalent nature of Shepard's text. As Craig Owens suggests, allegory may be the mode that promises to resolve contradictions, or like Lévi-Strauss's myths, maintain them in paralogical suspension. Thus on some level Shepard's allegorical impulse might arise from the need to balance opposing worlds represented by the desert and the city. Yet if Owens (following Walter Benjamin) is right, allegory is fundamentally attracted to the fragmentary and incomplete, with decay and ruins on the landscape which imply an irrevocable break with origins.[11] Indeed in Shepard's play there is the sense of a crisis of civilization resulting in the detritus of urban culture being dumped on the desert. Early in the play the urban Young Man pulls into a garage to have his Volkswagen fixed and the Mechanic observes 'I suppose what with all the earthquake scares and riots there's gonna' be a lot more folks movin' out here in the desert' (202). But the play depicts not simply the urban world come to the desert; it portrays the fragments and refuse of American history itself on the desert suggesting dissolution and decay, a progressive distancing from origins. Billy the old prospector, a relic of the old west, and Mickey Free, a half-breed Indian, are emblematic of the disappearing frontier and the vanishing native American. But distancing origins are further suggested in the fact that Billy, like Dr. Vector, is a construction of popular culture, a media figure. Billy's derivative status is emphasised by the fact that he looks and talks like the old prospector from television and film, Gabby Hayes, while Doctor Vector is obviously patterned after Dr. Strangelove. Thus we get the sense of simulacra and a popular cultural collage, the fragments of which may cry out for a modernist constitutive myth to shore up the ruins, but which also imply the absence of such a unifying thread or organising myth in contemporary culture, or an originary moment of perfect presence and transparency that can be recovered.

Allied to this is the fact that Shepard's particularly indeterminate and unstable allegorical approach might be termed 'postmodern allegory'.[12] The play contains elements of a number of genres and styles – the Indian captivity narrative, science fiction, western, musical, comic strip, so that its very form is undecidable. Not only are characters drawn from popular culture and film but there is a kind of 'sliding' between metaphorical and literal created by the fact that historical figures – such as the halfbreed Mickey Free – occupy the same stage with figures drawn from popular myth and film. It is as if in this textual space we get the interpenetration of two possible worlds: one a more recognisable literary world of allegory, the other a play between the codes of the B movie, the comic strip, media images, and rock and roll. Thus the two-level hierarchy of allegory, the metaphorical and literal, oscillates and opalesces. The text takes on a parodic, whimsical indeterminacy on the one hand, and a sense of the 'overdetermined' in its scenes and images, on the other. There is even a sense of 'mock allegory', a parody of the allegorical process itself, insofar as Shepard's text plays on a kind of basic allegorising which must be done by the reader of comic strips. Indeed, the text has a 'comic strip' character, with fantastic beings such as the computer snake and fantastic events like being spirited off the planet. All this contributes to a sense that the allegorical meaning of the play is not univocal – and that the allegorical text itself cannot point back to its source in a moment of pure self-authorised meaning.

Furthermore, if the play is a postmodern allegory of the desiring quest for the lost object, it is also, by extension, an allegory of desire in language. The sidewinder, like the Lacanian phallus, assumes the role of pure signifier – that which 'represents a subject for another signifier',[13] and thus is 'the mark of desire'.[14] The phallic sidewinder, emblem both of desire and the signifier itself, of desire in signification, strongly suggests a continual displacement of meaning in language which makes impossible the restoration of the lost object. The sidewinder functions as mobile and migratory signifier whose relation to the signified is always shifting, provisional and elusive. It is utterly commutable, oscillating and wavering in its significance, constantly undergoing transformations of form and meaning. In scene one the 'mechanical rhythm' of the snake is associated contiguously with a plane's sonic boom and thus with military technology; meanwhile in scene one other associations are developed such as the Old Testament implications of the snake in the garden. In scene two the snake's blinking red eyes *'turn to yellow and slowly rise ten feet off the ground'* (202) and metamorphose into the headlights of the Volkswagen on the mechanic's rack, where they become associated with the evil of gratuitous murder which will later take place – the murder of the mechanic by Young Man. Later the sidewinder's decapitated body becomes a tourniquet for Young Man's drug fix and thus is associated with other forms of destructive behaviour in the fallen American garden; still later it becomes the pivotal signifier in the Hopi myth of origins. Its Old Testament associations are transposed as the snake is transformed from a signifier of evil and death to its Hopi meanings of rejuvenation and rebirth. It is not so much the presence or absence of a particular meaning or 'essence' that characterises its signifying, as its position in a chain of substitutions and differences. The sidewinder's transformations and transpositions as signifier contribute to the play's spontaneity and whimsical character, yet they also suggest the ceaseless movement of desire, a function of the differential movement perpetually at work in language, of the endless substitution of signifiers in which origins are constantly receding, displaced and irrecoverable.

Moreover, as signifier, the sidewinder suggests the world of the symbolic order in which nature can only be approached through representation, in which origins have been foreclosed, in which nature and culture, the desert and the city, are irrevocably implicated in the signifying process. The sidewinder itself – both nature and technology, both snake and computer – blurs and destabilises the difference between nature and culture. And as signifier in which both nature and culture are co-implicated, it puts the polarity of the two realms into question. This problematising of the division between nature and culture is underscored in particular scenes where there is a playful blurring of their difference. For example, in order to subdue the snake which has Honey pinned to the ground, Mickey Free 'strokes the head of the sidewinder with his left hand very gently and makes a soothing sound in his throat' (211). After mesmerising the snake in this fashion he quickly decapitates it. But this wily western natural lore, the ability to hypnotise snakes, is directed at a computer, not a snake, or rather a computerised snake, a snake as computer.

Operation Sidewinder suggests that like the primal scene in psychoanalysis, origins can be represented only in the mode of narrative myth – such as that recounted by the Spider Lady, or represented in the referentially indirect mode of allegory. Indeed Shepard's version of the Garden of Eden which opens the play is Eden 're-written' with its two American tourists and the computer snake: the original is inaccessible except as writing and allegorical reading. And the conclusion of the play implies the problematic relation between primal scene and primal fantasy. The foretold discourse of origins is rendered with all the extravagant fabulation of a Captain Marvel comic strip. The Indians, Young Man, and Honey, chanting in ecstasy, are suddenly swept into the sky, having seemingly arrived at an epiphany of transparent meaning, the disclosure of origins promised by the Spider Lady. Yet like Bunyan's *Pilgrim's Progress* in which Christian enters the Celestial City we are left behind and cannot share his viewpoint. The primal scene, the knowledge of origins which the Hopi legend holds forth, has eluded the audience; the vision has burned out in a flash, its unmediated and transparent nature beyond representation. The desert tactical troops are left on stage *'holding their ears and shielding their eyes'* against the deafening whine and blinding brilliance of some unearthly force. Then *'everything goes black'* and the play lapses into significant silence, thereby prolonging its desire ad infinitum.

Shepard's text attempts to resolve desire in the still centre of myth but allegory must forever defer, must forever yearn. As Joel Fineman observes, 'allegory will set out on an increasingly futile search for a signifier with which to recuperate the fracture of and at its source, and with each successive signifier the fracture and the search begin again: a structure of continual yearning, the insatiable desire of allegory'.[15] Shepard's postmodern allegory – with its play of simulacrum and historical figures, with its continual displacement of meaning – is a drama precisely about such a search for a signifier which will somehow recuperate the fracture, locate the lost object of desire, disclose origins. Yet the sidewinder – whether signifier of evil, America's lost promise, its fall into technorationality, whether signifier of sexual impulse, spiritual renewal, or simply desire – nevertheless functions ultimately as a signifier to which the signified is provisional and elusive; the 'operations' of the sidewinder exhibit continual movement and the continual yearning that characterise allegory itself.

Shepard's desert, then, is not – even in this ambivalent text written in the wake of the romantic and essentialist sixties – some realm of original presence, the site of recuperative originality or eschatological salvation. It is not a landscape of organic or constitutive symbols that might lead to origins, but rather one that calls attention to the void that underlines signs, the yawning gap between signifier and signified.

Notes

1. Sam Shepard, *Fool For Love and Other Plays* (New York: Bantam 1984), p. 287.
2. Sam Shepard, *The Unseen Hand and Other Plays* (New York: Bantam, 1986), p. 258.
3. *Fool For Love and Other Plays*, p. 70.
4. Ibid., pp. 54, 55.
5. See, for example, John Lahr, 'Spectacle of Disintegration: Operation Sidewinder', in *American Dreams, The Imagination of Sam Shepard*, ed. Bonnie Marranca (New York: Performing Arts Journal Publications, 1981), p. 56.
6. Ibid., p. 49.
7. Sam Shepard, *The Unseen Hand and Other Plays* (New York: Bantam, 1986), pp. 199–200. All quotations are from this edition; page numbers are given in the text.
8. Maureen Quilligan, *The Language of Allegory: Defining the Genre* (Ithaca: Cornell University Press, 1979), p. 155.
9. Julia Kristeva, *Desire in Language: A Semiotic Approach to Literature & Art*, ed. Leon S. Roudiez, trans. Jordene, Gora, Roudiez (New York: Columbia University Press), p. 195.
10. Quoted in Ron Mottram, *Inner Landscapes: The Theater of Sam Shepard* (Columbia: University of Missouri Press), p. 83.
11. Craig Owens, 'The Allegorical Impulse: Toward a Theory of Postmodernism', in *Art After Modernism: Rethinking Representation*, ed. Brian Wallis (New York: The Museum of Contemporary Art, 1984), p. 206.
12. For a discussion of postmodern allegory see Brian McHale, *Postmodernist Fiction* (New York: Methuen, 1987), pp. 140–47.
13. Barbara Johnson, 'The Frame of Reference: Poe, Lacan, Derrida, in Literature and Psychoanalysis', in *The Question of Reading: Otherwise*, ed. Shoshana Felman (Baltimore: Johns Hopkins University Press, 1977), p. 497.
14. Jane Gallop, *Reading Lacan* (Ithaca: Cornell University Press, 1985) p. 145.
15. Joel Fineman, 'The Structure of Allegorical Desire', in *Allegory and Representation*, ed. Stephen J. Greenblatt (Baltimore: Johns Hopkins University Press, 1981), p. 45.

4

Memory and Mind: Sam Shepard's *Geography of a Horse Dreamer*

Gerry McCarthy

These days I wonder about leaving. But I've seen myself when I leave. Already seen myself.

Sam Shepard, *Motel Chronicles*

I

Shepard is a master of theatrical imagination, and to an audience schooled in the predominant American realism, he may seem a magician, or even a priest. Yet he is, in the fullest sense of the term, a stage dramatist with an extraordinary instinct for the imaginative modalities of the theatre. Shepard is not a visionary, but an artist concerned with ways of seeing and being within theatrical space and time.

> When you talk about images, an image can be seen without looking at anything – you can see something in your head, or you can see something on stage, or you can see things that don't appear on stage, you know. The fantastic thing about theatre is that it can make something be seen that's invisible, and that's where my interest in theatre is – that you can be watching this thing happening with actors and costumes and light and set and language, and even plot, and something emerges from beyond that, and that's the image part that I'm looking for, that's the sort

58

of added dimension.[1]

Shepard's statement rests on the relationship between actual and virtual properties of theatre which are dependent in turn on the nature of mind and perception in the audience: the sensual and mental experiences of drama which correspond to the 'something beyond'. For all his commentators, and for Shepard himself, his work is first approached in terms of images, and visual effects. The effects of the visual image in Shepard's drama, as Shepard himself suggests, are more the result of operations of the mind than actual visual image on stage, however spectacular. Indeed Shepard's account of his fascination with the theatre stresses the power of symbolic experience: the use of objects, persons and performances to stimulate playful mental experience and celebrate the power of the human mind. His plays confirm Gilbert Ryle's contention that 'the concept of make-belief is of a higher order than belief'.[2] Thus when we speak of the images of Shepard's theatre we should be clear that they are created through the operations of mind and perception which are natural to the medium. They are not actual but virtual.

This relationship of the actual and virtual is, however, felt by the spectator in any medium of art as the primary creative tension of her experience. In the case of acting, the performer is a living symbol, aware of her own function as a signifier, and all too aware of her *actual* life. The actor always experiences the dependence of the *virtual* life of character and action on the actual, but coincident, forms of physical and mental life organised in performance. This sense of significance is fundamental to acting, but always carries with it the shadow of a threat. The material life of the performance may invade the consciousness of the performer and destroy the significant structure of the symbolic performance. This danger contributes its own vitality to the process of acting, and when it is entirely absent the security of the routine is cold comfort.

Shepard challenges his performer to examine this crucial relationship of actual and virtual life on stage. As well, he intuitively challenges his performer to examine the critical relationship of bodily experience and the forms of mental life which he inhabits in performance. His earliest work demonstrates this fascination with the nature of the medium and its characteristic tensions. *Teleported Man*, written for Joe Chaikin and the Open Theatre, stresses the relationship between mental and physical being:

A sound travelled down the tube from the top to the bottom. A
line of green light. I'd never seen sound before. It weaved and
bobbed as though it were looking for me, like a thin green snake
with its tongue spitting. It found me. The top of my head then
right in the center of my forehead, like a third eye burrowing
in. It felt like an eye at least. A new sight. I could see with my
brain. My whole head lit up with sound. My body became the
sound. Pulsing to the vibrations. All the way down my spine
and into my rectum. I could feel myself going away. The body.
I didn't look down to see because I wasn't afraid. I knew it
would work. The epidermis, the tissue, the muscle fibre, the
veins, and blood, the bones, the heart, intestines. Each piece
growing away from me until there I was, left alone. Hanging
in mid air like a ghost. Just my spirit, my brain, no not my brain
but something that knew I was there even though I wasn't, in the
flesh.[3]

Teleported Man depends on a virtual creation of those sensations
of mind and body which can often threaten to become actually and
distressingly disordered to the actor in performance. The image
of the character 'teleported' out of his own physical body comes
perilously close to the actual experience of stage fright, which many
actors will characterise as an 'out of body' experience. Laurence
Olivier provides a particularly vivid account of his difficulties
playing Shylock in 1970, particularly the sensations of divorce
between mind and body: 'So you treat the body and the brain
with more respect, and you always remain conscious of the shadow
in the corner.'[4] Olivier's account raises the question of closeness of
the threat of collapse, 'the shadow', and the vitality of the medium.[5]
The exposure of the performer is inevitable if the primary tensions
and excitement of the medium are to be explored.

II

This exposure of the performer's 'self' is fundamental to the conception of Shepard's *Action*. The play represents a set of characters,
uncoordinated as a social group, and incomplete and disconnected
as individuals. They have a fragmentary memory of past time and
of the civilisation they once inhabited. In the present they exhibit an

inability to interact with any coherent purpose, and grapple with the very terms in which the self can be structured. At the same time the performances given by the actors involve a diminished sense of personal identity and a disturbing lack of objective and throughline. The integration of personality, and thereafter the creation of the society of persons, is examined through a series of self-reflective performances, which exist at the frontiers between actor and character, cast and society. Shepard composes roles where the actor insistently addresses her own actual circumstances as the matter of the virtual crises of the play. The writing requires the actor to come dangerously close to a contemplation of the mental and physical structures of her/his own performance. Thus the actor playing Jeep (this is a play in which one may not employ the shorthand terminology whereby character and actor are synonymous) pours water over his hand 'as though hypnotised by his own action'[6] and enquires about an earlier moment when the character Shooter was scared:

> JEEP: Shooter, I remember. I remember you were so scared you couldn't go up to take a bath.
> SHOOTER: Naw. That's not me at all. That's entirely the wrong image. That must've been an accident.
> JEEP: Oh.
> (JEEP *keeps pouring the water over his hand.*)
> SHOOTER: I've never been afraid of baths. I've always been brave in those situations. I've plunged right in.
> JEEP: Oh, I thought it was you.
> SHOOTER: I knew a guy once who was afraid to take a bath. Something about the water. Stank to high heaven. "High Heaven". That's a good one. He stank, boy. Boy, how he stank. Boy, did he ever stink.
> JEEP: Was it the water? . . .
> SHOOTER: Yeah. The water. The way it warped his body.
> JEEP: But that's just the way he saw it. That was him, not the water.
> SHOOTER: Then, he began to fear his own body.
>
> (137)

I have discussed elsewhere Shepard's use of the actor in this play and his dislocation of the various dimensions of the acting performance in order to create a powerful sense of the 'zero degree

of performance'.[7] Here I would point out how close he brings the
actor to the examination of the potentially disastrous disjunction
of mind and body in performance. There is a reminiscence of a
Beckettian dualism in the examination of the possible types of
congruence of mental experience and the way in which they are
tested in the crucible of performance. Physical self-consciousness
is the result of the loss of appropriate integrating mental objectives,
and is a pitfall the actor avoids. Shepard obliges his actors to court
disaster in pursuing 'hypnotic' physical actions and in imagining
simultaneously the grotesque story of 'the guy who was afraid to
take a bath' who then begins to feel 'like a foreign spy. Spying on
his body' (137).

The conscious mind, especially in performance, needs an ordered
set of focuses, appropriate to the range of ingenuous mental experience. If it is called upon to intervene in the subliminal area of
sensory/motor experience, the integrity of physical and mental
action is threatened. The contemplation of the physical body in
action produces a level of introspection which risks the loss of
the conventional actor's secure set of imagined objectives. The
objective mind is brought uncomfortably close to the consideration
of the automatism of physical actions learned in the lower nervous
system, but never directly the product of conscious choice.

In *Action* the security of mental objectives is crucial to the stability
of the characters' 'situation' (Shepard's term), as it is vital to the
continuation of the actors' performance. This is all the more urgent
as in this play the characters lack a consistent memory of past
events:

> SHOOTER: Naw. I don't remember that. Better to leave that.
> People are washing dishes now. Lupe's looking for the place
> again. Things are rolling right along. Why bring that up?
>
> (137)

For Shooter the haziness of past events conceals images most of
which recall to the conscious mind states of fear and insecurity.
The escape from these for the character (virtual agent) as for the
actor (actual performer) is to concentrate on the progress of present
events which intend future outcomes.[8] Here Shepard shows himself
acutely aware of the two capital modes of mental experience as they
must engage the actor in performance: recall and intentionality, or
memory and mind.

The success of Shepard's work derives from his exploitation of the metaphorical potential of the medium, and specifically of tension and rhythm in the thought of the actor. He shares the great dramatist's feeling for the interconnection of mind and memory as part of both theatrical and human experience of time and action. It is an experience which is woven into the very fabric of Shakespeare's *Hamlet*:

> Remember thee?
> Ay, thou poor ghost, while memory holds a seat
> In this distracted globe. Remember thee?
> Yea, from the table of my memory
> I'll wipe away all trivial fond records,
> All saws of books, all forms, all pressures past,
> That youth and observation copied there,
> And thy commandment all alone shall live
> Within the book and volume of my brain
> Unmixed with baser matter.[9]

The sensory value of acting performance must precede its moral and emotional effects. Thus the audience experiences physically the tension in the actor between past time (memory), unalterable but perpetually reviewed and repeatedly re-expressed; and present time, as both the drag on and the spur to future action (intention). Without the sensory effect (the product of strain between two experiences of mental life, mind and memory), the moral understanding of situation, and still less the concomitant emotional response to it, is impossible.

The familiar strain of performance arises from the need to govern these operations of mind, and suppress the sensations of disintegration and physical alienation which threaten to disorder the actor, if she, through a reversal of the normal process of empathy, adopts the audience's viewpoint and mental objectives. At such points she knows only too well that there is a fine balance between the objective sense which directs a performance and the necessarily free and expansive examination of the images of memory. The actor must trust that the mind will be guided by the essential rhythms of performance established in rehearsal and which propel the actor through time. In this sense text must be played but not remembered. This is the aspect of 'remembering' which Gilbert Ryle characterises as 'not-forgetting'.[10] Text is the condition for a rhythm of action triggering a succession of images which arise in the memory and which are freely available for a spontaneous consideration in performance.

Henry Hackamore in *Seduced* is one role among many in Shepard's plays which presents the elements of mental experience as they are manifest in performance:

> RAUL: (Pause) Would you like something to eat, sir?
>
> HENRY: (Pause) Why do you always do that? Food is not on my mind. Food has nothing to do with what's on my mind. Pictures are on my mind and you put food there. They don't mix! Pictures of food don't mix!
>
> RAUL: I'm sorry, sir.
>
> HENRY: You have to be more sensitive, Raul, to the subtle shifts in my intellectual activity. The mind covers a wide range of territory. Sometimes simultaneously travelling several different hemispheres in a single sweep and then diving suddenly for the prey.
>
> RAUL: I understand, sir.
>
> HENRY: You do? You understand what the prey is? The prey is an idea. A single, lonely, fleeting idea trying to duck into a rabbit hole and the mind comes sweeping in for the kill.
>
> RAUL: That's a beautiful idea sir.
>
> HENRY: That's not an idea! It's a description. An idea is something useful.[11]

Shepard's sophisticated comedy underscores the play of mind on mind within the drama, which in turn foregrounds the significant processes of the acting performance itself. The mind which contemplates one image cannot accept another simultaneously. The two do not mix, except by creating new images. Here 'pictures of food' are created where the character is arguing pictures *and* food cannot coexist. They can only mix in the sense that the mental image, equivalent in terms of activity to the basic imaging effect of memory, can adapt to the interference and produce new, unwanted, even rejected, images.

Shepard understands very well the dubious relationship of the conscious inquisitive mind to the images which litter the memory. These images may be the product of actual experience or the creations of art, but in the realm of play-acting the two come together. Shepard's creation, the text, is laid down as a complex of abstracts in the memory of the actor which is then reviewed in obedience to the structures and rhythms of performance.

In this scene the second actor attends to the description of memory in the first and is inevitably brought into a shared experience. He, and the audience, have 'seen' the image and recorded the memory. They are also stuck with it. In this sense it is 'a description', and 'useless', because it cannot inform the purpose of the performer. A memory is to be suffered, and cannot be pursued. Shepard's Hackamore is manifestly a study in the loss of action and purpose in a character who has a Howard Hughes' power in, and fear of, the world. The character is the victim of memory, unable to maintain the intentionality which preys on ideas, and unable to avoid falling back on the reviewing of past experience.

The balance between purpose and memory is crucial in all drama. The past is brought to bear upon present dilemma and future decisions. In Shepard the range of memory is devoted to a freer examination of effects in time. Different tenses can be used to address the memory. When events are examined in past tenses they are 'remembered' or 'surmised' (as in *Suicide in B♭*). However when the memory is addressed in the future tense the events have the virtual effect of the mind looking forward. Indeed this may be the fashion in which the prophetic or prognosticating mind actually operates: by assembling past events to project possible futures. This is the quality which we normally term imagination, particularly since the constructive capacity of the mind is apparent. The relationship to memory is not so evident, but nonetheless unfamiliar images are the product of the stored elements of experience and are seen in just the way that actual events and scenes are recalled. Commonly they are reviewed in terms of a virtual past, the fictive past of narrative.

The phenomena of performance include the basic data that the images of memory derive from a virtual past, while they are clearly encountered as actually presenting and being seen in present time. The structures of experience locate memory as the trace of past events, but virtual memories, the product of the actor's rehearsal, may operate just as powerfully. The actor has not experienced these events, but they come to exist as memory images as they are recalled in present time. Indeed at the point that experience is artfully suggested to the mind it is recorded by the memory as effectively as the events of life experience.

III

This mutability of the memory experience is at the centre of Shepard's *Geography of a Horse Dreamer*. The simple action of the play presents a dreamer, Cody, kidnapped to exploit his ability to dream winners in horse races. The gift has started to fail Cody, and his two captors, Santee and Beujo, have taken him abroad, clearly to England, where he turns to dog racing for a renewal of inspiration.

The metaphor of *Geography of a Horse Dreamer* has been seen as so transparent as to invite term for term 'translation'. Ross Wetzsteon sees it as:

> the work of art which ostensibly deals with another subject but which is actually an extended metaphor for the personal dilemma of the artist himself. I think of this kind of work as a translation play. Instead of translating the text from French, say, into English, the audience has to translate the plot into its meaning.[12]

This critic disarmingly confesses the pleasure of this exercise, but fails to realise its essential superficiality. It is clear that *Geography of a Horse Dreamer* is a comparatively simple work, with the allegorical clarity that might be expected of a modern morality play. (Shepard calls it a 'mystery'). Its meaning is, however, much greater than the perception of the simple action with its Western melodramatic coda. The representation of the artist by the dreamer would be small satisfaction if an audience had an experience of no greater consequence. In fact the play, characteristically for Shepard, makes its meanings at the level of sensation and in the particular forms of experience it procures for the audience. The morality which treats on one level the value of artistic creation and its vulnerability in a materialist world also presents characters with vastly different mental experiences and with different understandings of the function of mind. Its subject is the experience of time and the uses of memory, and if the play fails to satisfy to some degree it is because as a drama it fails to develop a satisfactory scheme of action and intention, hence the *deus ex machina* conclusion in which figures from the dreamer's private dream of the Great Plains come to his rescue.

The idea of the dreamer is a fascinating instance of Shepard's intuitions on the life of the mind. The linking of memory with the future is natural in terms of brain function, since all actual prediction must come from the accumulated experience of the past. Cody has a gift which extends beyond the normal inductive relationship of past and future in the rational mind. Yet while mental experience can be sustained on the basis of long-term memory, new experience cannot be accumulated save through immediate sensory interactions with the outside world. Although Cody's 'dreams' are images projected into the future, the essential mental activity is memory. Memory fossilises as a component of human identity if it is deprived of the short term store based on the sensory memory. As an element in creative thinking and experience it atrophies. Here Shepard employs memory for its function in creative experience, essentially a sensitive passive reflection of the world:

> CODY: It's very delicate work, dreaming a winner. You can't just close your eyes and bingo! it's there in front of you. It takes certain special conditions. A certain internal environment.[13]

Shepard deepens the effect of the drama through the acuity of an action centred on the processes of performance. The linking of memory (and imaging) with the sense memory has been long intuited by actors, and notably developed by Stanislavsky and the practitioners of Strausberg's Method. Here the physical and mental experiences of characters are once more disturbingly close to the habitual strains of acting. The actual forms of 'performance thought' create the virtual interaction of the characters. This is particularly clear as Santee insists that instructions must be followed to prevent Cody establishing a sense relationship with the outside world:

> SANTEE: We might arrange some fresh air. Maybe. He's gotta be blindfolded though. He can't know where he is. That's the chief thing that Fingers impressed upon us. He can't for a second know where he is outside the room he's locked up in. Otherwise it spoils the dreaming. He can't know the time either . . .
> CODY: . . . Fingers' theory was good for the beginning but now it sucks dogs.
> SANTEE: How's that?
> CODY: He don't understand the area I have to dream in . . . Not this area. The inside one. The space inside where the dream comes. It's gotta be created. That's what

Fingers don't understand. He thinks it's just like it was when
I started.

SANTEE: What's so different now.

CODY: He's blocked up my senses. Everything forces itself
on the space I need. There's too much chaos now. He'll never
get a winner out of me till the space comes back.

(124–25)

Memory experience, as the actor is first to know, cannot be
forced, linked as it is to and deriving from the rhythms of sensory
experience. Here Cody pleads to be able to listen to his record,
an unrelated but 'inspirational' aural experience, but the record,
according to Beaujo, 'drives Santee crazy'. Shepard imagines characters with disturbingly contrasted mental lives; Santee is a man
who does not dream:

SANTEE: I don't dream. I'm one a' those rare dreamless
sleepers. I got no worries, no troubles to work out. Everything's hunky-dorey.

CODY: I dream about the Great Plains.

SANTEE: Well that's your whole damn trouble! That ain't
what yer gettin' paid for. Yer paid to dream about racehorses.
That's all.

(125)

On one level the conflict between Cody and his captors can be
seen as an allegory of the artistic imagination and the forces which
threaten its survival. But much deeper is the sensation of forms of
dramatic life disturbingly and vitally re-created on stage. Santee is
dead to experience which is vital to wholeness of being, but Beaujo
is aware of the forms of memory and the necessary link with the
senses:

BEAUJO: I know you got something against art, Santee, but
maybe he's right ya'know. I mean maybe his dreaming does
take on a kind of an art form. It might need special stuff to get
him back in top form.

SANTEE: Like what special stuff?

BEAUJO: Like a decent bed for one thing.

(124)

Beaujo links the physical and sensory deprivation of their captive to the loss of range in his dreams. He describes a fundamental relationship of mind and body keenly felt by actor and audience at the point of performance:

> BEAUJO: I figure it's more like a game of pool. You know, the way sometimes you got the feel. You got the touch. All the practice and technique in the world can't beat ya' 'cause you got magic. There's no trace a' tension. Then it goes. Just like that. No way to pin it down. It just slides away from ya'. I figure that's how it is with Cody here.
>
> (123)

This sensitivity to the wholeness of mental and physical performance experience is fundamental to Shepard's writing, and is manifested in *Geography of a Horse Dreamer* most clearly in the role of Beaujo. The visions of the horse dreamer are recreated by the actor as he 'sees' Beaujo's images. These are, as ever, memory images which are shared by the audience as part of the action, and examined within the real time of the performance:

> CODY: I used to wake up and not know where I was. As long as I can remember.
> BEAUJO: It'll be all right now. It'll all come back to you. (*melodramatically*) You'll find that special area. A huge blue space. In the distance you'll see 'em approaching the quarter-mile pole. The thunder of hooves. Whips flying. The clubhouse turn. You'll get a sense of it again. It'll all come back just like it used to. You'll see. You got magic Cody. You'll see.
> (CODY *falls into a deep sleep.* BEAUJO *gets up and walks around. He comes to a stop and looks around the room*).
> BEAUJO: (*to himself*): Huh, for a second there I thought I was lost.
>
> (129–30)

The audience not only follows the struggle between the characters but is drawn into the creation of the images, and experiences directly the mental life of the performance. The audience 'sees' this image, as does the actor playing Beaujo, and so too the audience 'sees' the character Beaujo effectively 'lost'.

The tension between the roles of Beaujo and Santee depends on different moral and emotional projections of future time, corresponding to different comprehensions of Cody's dreaming. For Beaujo, the faculty of dreaming is wonderful: he calls it art. For Santee, dreaming has no intrinsic value. The fundamental moral conflict of the play is between the free exercise of memory across time, and the objective desire to compel particular ends from the exercise of memory seen as a simple resource for the projection of particular future events. Beaujo can imagine Cody's restoration and its true value. For Santee the future exists in terms of threats and results:

> BEAUJO: I got faith in him, Santee.
> SANTEE: Faith? What good is that gonna' do us? We need results!
>
> (131)

This is the sphere of action and intention, what is desired rather than seen in the future. Shepard engineers the conflict of intentionality and memory in an intriguing way since here both memory and intention are to work in the future. Santee demands only results, and even his projects are abstract, unvisualised:

> SANTEE: This better be it, boy or . . . The Doctor's on our back. The pressure's there. It comes from the outside. Somewhere out there. We wind up with the effects. I don't understand how you work, Beethoven, that's how come I got no patience. To me it's a lot of mumbo-jumbo. Like I said, I don't even have no dreams.
>
> (133)

The action depends on roles which develop different areas of mind and memory, and consists in an extended cross examination. Beaujo explores the possible landscapes of the horse dreamer without real comprehension, while Santee looks only towards objectives: the instrumental mind despising the imagination:

> SANTEE: . . . He's off his cake, Beaujo.
> BEAUJO: Lucky for us.
> SANTEE: What do ya' suppose happened to him?
> BEAUJO: You got me. Some kinda weird mental disorder.

I told ya' he was a genius. There's a very fine line between madness and genius ya' know.

SANTEE: Yeah, yeah. Cut the baloney. He's gone bananas and that's all there is to it. It just happens to coincide with our needs.

(137)

These conflicting attitudes are further explored when Fingers and the Doctor intervene in the second act. Fingers is violently affected by Cody's condition, whereas the Doctor silently watches the literal images of the television. Fingers' determination to take Cody home leads swiftly to the recollection of the 'High Mountain Country' where they seized him. Thus the climax of the play is structured out of the memory of Cody's birthplace and its sacred values, against the exploitative and violent outburst of the Doctor who proposes to kill Cody for economic gain. Fingers' recollections go back through historic into mythic time:

BEAUJO: We hit the Wind River Reservation about noon. We had lunch in the Silver Star. Fingers bought a cowboy hat and a pair of spurs.

FINGERS: Yes! I remember that! I remember thinking this is the West! This is really The West! Then we got to that town where Buffalo Bill lived. I forgot the name of it. Oh what a town! Saloons with Winchester rifles tacked up on the walls. Real cowboys in leather chaps. Indians shuffling through the dusty streets. Buffalo Bill's name was plastered on everything. And at night. At night it was magical. Like praying. I'd never heard such silence as that. Nowhere on the earth. So vast and lonely. Just the brisk cold night blowing in through the hotel window. And outside, the blue peaks of the Big Horn mountains. The moon shining on their snowy caps. The prairie stretching out and out like a great ocean. I felt that God was with me then. The earth held me in its arms.

(*A short pause as* FINGERS *reflects*).

BEAUJO: That was the town.

(143-44)

Two ideas of the West are carefully interwoven in this speech which is as much a dream as anything in the play; a tissue of fantasy and insight. The contrast is one which Shepard works out very specifically in his later *True West*. Here in this play written and first performed in England, Fingers remembers a West which, while initially conceived as commercial fiction, still arouses inner sensations of a mythic past.

The final images of the play develop the dream of the West against the background of the Doctor who has watched television throughout the act. The character is given no live memory experience, and is seen intending a single brutal purpose in the future. At this point Cody's dreaming is a particular exercise of memory to link past and future: prophecy. Cody's visions create a totemic image from the mythic past of the West:

> CODY: The white buffalo. Approach him in a sacred manner. He is Wakan. The ground he walks is Wakan. This day has sent a spirit gift. You must take it. Clean your heart of evil thoughts. Take him in a sacred way. If one bad thought is creeping in you it will mean your death. You will crumble to the earth. You will vanish from this time.
>
> DOCTOR: Santee, hand me my scalpel please.
>
> (148–49)

Without question there is something perfunctory about the conclusion to the play. As the Doctor prepares to excise from this dreamer/artist, as from others before, 'the dreamer's bone' (147), two enormous dust-covered cowboys, Cody's brothers, enter, blasting three of the captors with shotguns. They take Cody away, still in his sacred dream, leaving a 'whimpering' Fingers listening to the record which was the captive dreamer's inspiration.

Shepard appears anxious to avoid the problems inherent in the physical presentation of figures drawn from the West, stating that they should avoid stereotypical images: 'costumes . . . well used and authentic without looking like dime-store cowboys' (149). His desire for authenticity within the actual stage image indicates his concern for its symbolic value and for what is 'seen', or what he terms 'the added dimension'. The appearance of these authentic American figures in the context of a play written and (loosely) set in Britain creates a striking juxtaposition within the theatrical set. Precise symbols of the historic American past confront the group of drifting characters in an action preoccupied with the nature of mental experience within time, and with the significance of the relationship of mind and memory in the construction of the theatrical imagination. The spectator 'sees' beyond this image into the historic and then mythic time which the play suggests.

> DOCTOR: You see how we're each on our own territory right now. Each of us paralyzed within certain boundaries. We'd do anything to cross the border but we're stuck. Quite stuck.
>
> (148)

Shepard goes beyond highlighting a particular allegory. The two approaches to mental experience intuited by the dramatist are contrasted in the dramatic image. On one hand there is the purely functional and objective experience of those who see the dreamer as a source of material profit, and whose inner psychic selves are dead, not dreaming but watching the literal images of television; and on the other there are the varieties of inner life which place the self in the context of a mental landscape of myth, memory and image.

The conclusion of the play shows these possibilities in a melodramatic confrontation. Dramatically the device is insubstantial, but theatrically it has all Shepard's characteristic daring, realising these two areas of experience in the imaginative space of the theatre. Shepard's concerns relate closely to the primary function of theatre as a playing space and drama, as the integrated play activity in which the life of the personality and of the group can be freely explored. This is the 'third space' described by D. W. Winnicott as absolutely necessary to healthy individuation, and lying between object-related and dream-related experiences:

> The two areas do not lose significance because of this that I am putting forward as a third area. If we are truly examining human beings, then we must be expected to make observations that can be superimposed, the one on the other. Individuals do relate to the world in ways that involve them in instinctual gratification, either direct or in sublimated forms. Also we do know the paramount importance of sleep and the deep dreaming that is at the core of personality, and of contemplation and of relaxed undirected mental inconsequence. Nevertheless, playing and cultural experience are things that we do value in a special way; these link the past, the present, and the future; *they take up time and space.* They demand and get our concentrated deliberate

attention, deliberate but without too much of the deliberateness of trying.[14]

The integrated nature of dramatic play allows both the inner and outer experience of the individual to be characterised (rendered in terms of assumed persons) and brought into the third space. Thus inner and outer experiences of personality can be successfully interrelated if only in terms of creative hypotheses, that is imagination. The third space is quintessentially one where dramatic play mediates between the two states of mind and two representations of reality; object-related intentionality, and psychic memory.

The value of Shepard's writing lies in the serious play he makes of the life of the theatrical imagination. It is fundamental to the art of the theatre that the actor symbolically reintegrates the human personality in terms of what we conventionally call a character. In the nature of the medium this can be done only through the actor's thought, and in the face of the tensions and risks which attend the unguarded personality as it attempts the artistic reconstitution of identity within the imagined parameters drawn in the space and time of the theatre, and within the 'mental environment' of the drama. This value, it may be said, grows more profound in the recent works, notably *A Lie of the Mind* or *Fool for Love*. Shepard grows more successful in developing the capacity of the actor within a more tightly organised dramatic form. In *A Lie of the Mind*, intentionality is powerfully experienced by the audience through the presentation of mental dysfunction, and the interplay of characters is developed by a subtler and richer use of the constructions of mind and memory. In the case of *Fool for Love* memory creates the energies which power the ambiguous relationship of the lovers. While these plays assume more familiar forms, and are clearly more accessible to audiences than Shepard's earlier work, they create, like the masterpieces of Beckett and Pinter, extraordinary and moving metaphors out of tensions and sensations of shared performance.[15]

In a Barthesian fashion the most vibrant effects are those where the innate metaphorical value of the actor as human sign is fully used and in some sense acknowledged. For while the actor is the medium he is also the locus of the questions which are characteristically asked in drama about the nature of the self and the significance of human thought and action. The drive in Shepard, as in all great dramatists, is to compose works which deal directly in the forms of human life. The great critical lesson which Shepard teaches us

is that acting creates direct experience and its narrative processes
are to do with direct knowledge in the audience, as opposed to
reports and descriptions offered by actors, (or indeed critics). The
primary rhythm of drama is the rhythm of thought, promoting the
more obviously sensed rhythms of movement and breath. Nothing
is more basic to the creation of the dramatic experience than the
flux of the actor's thought in time, and the balance of reflective and
intentional mental experience, memory and mind.

Notes

1. Sam Shepard, quoted in *American Dreams: The Imagination of Sam
    Shepard*, ed. Bonnie Marranca (New York: Performing Arts Journal
    Publications, 1981), p. 197.
2. Gilbert Ryle, *The Concept of Mind* (London: Penguin, 1981), p. 197.
3. Sam Shepard, *Motel Chronicles and Hawk Moon* (London: Faber, 1985),
    pp. 185–86.
4. Laurence Olivier, *On Acting* (London: Sceptre, 1986), pp. 117–18.
5. 'It was during the run of *The Merchant* that I suffered badly from the
    actor's nightmare – *stage fright*. I wonder if that had anything to do
    with my performance becoming fresh, open and naked again? It's
    always possible'. Ibid., p. 113.
6. Sam Shepard, *Angel City and Other Plays* (London: Faber, 1976),
    p. 136. All quotations are from this edition; page numbers are given
    in the text.
7. Gerry McCarthy,'"Acting it Out": Sam Shepard's *Action'*, in *Modern
    Drama* 24, no. 1 (March 1981), 1–12.
8. The role of Shooter repeatedly avoids the fictive past of the play by
    contemplation of the present, or by a Beckettian creation of stories.
    These invest the memory with an extra-dramatic past. It is notable
    that it is only when Shooter is 'safe' in his armchair that Shepard
    writes these excursions into memory, manifested as 'pictures' of
    escape from the chair where Shooter is now 'stuck', or as images
    of a narrative past:

    > SHOOTER: Nope. This is it for me. I'm never leaving this chair.
    > I've finally found it . . .   This is more like it. This is more in line
    > with how I see myself. I picture myself as a father. Very much at
    > home. The world can't touch me. (137)

9. William Shakespeare, *Hamlet*, I, v. 95–104.
10. Ryle, p. 198.
11. Sam Shepard, *Buried Child, Seduced*, and *Suicide in B♭* (London: Faber,
    1980), pp. 79–80.
12. In Marranca, *American Dreams*, p. 133.

13. Sam Shepard, *Geography of a Horse Dreamer* in *Four Two-Act Plays*, (London: Faber, 1981), pp. 126–27. All quotations are from this edition; page numbers are given in the text.
14. In *Playing and Reality* (London: Penguin, 1973), p. 128.
15. The reader will probably have recognised the similar concern with the nature of performance and the dramatic medium in the works of Pinter and Beckett. I have in mind particularly examples such as Pinter's *Old Times* and Beckett's *Not I*.

5

Shepard's Challenge to the Modernist Myths of Origin and Originality: *Angel City* and *True West*

Sheila Rabillard

MOM: You boys will probably never guess who's in town. Try and guess.

(*long pause, brothers stare at her*) . . .

LEE: Somebody very important?

MOM: See if you can guess. You'll never guess.

AUSTIN: Mom – we're trying to uh – (*points to writing pad*).

MOM: Picasso. (*pause*) Picasso's in town. Isn't that incredible? Right now.

(*pause*)

AUSTIN: Picasso's dead, Mom.

MOM: No, he's not dead. He's visiting the museum. I read it on the bus. We have to go down there and see him.[1]

I

When 'Picasso' enters the dialogue of *True West* the audience is perhaps as startled by this apparent example of staring irrelevance as the two auditors on stage. The mother of Austin and Lee has just returned unexpectedly from her vacation trip to Alaska because, she says, she started missing all her plants. She discovers her kitchen a shambles and mysteriously full of toasters. Her son, Austin, who was supposedly minding the house while he wrote a screenplay in solitude, is taking dictation at his typewriter from his shirtless and beer-soaked ne'er-do-well brother Lee who, she is informed, has improbably sold his own story idea to a producer. The solid citizen Austin announces his intention of scavenging a living with Lee in the desert – not the desert where his derelict father subsists, but another one. And the beloved plants are dead of neglect. At this final discovery Mom remarks, 'Oh well, one less thing to take care of I guess. (*turns toward the brothers*) Oh, that reminds me – You boys will probably never guess who's in town. Try and guess' (54). Peculiar as this shift of topic may be, 'Picasso' isn't a minor digression merely illustrative of Mom's mild dottiness. I take him as the point of departure for this paper because Picasso seems to me to serve as a lightly sketched but telling contrast for the challenges to modernist myths of authorial originality presented by *True West*. Together with *Angel City*, Shepard's other drama dealing with West Coast movie making, *True West* explores the scene of writing, problematising the modernist search for grounding and presence in the artistic medium and offering above all a theatrical experience disturbing to modernist myths of origin, originality, and the unified authorial self.

Picasso serves as an emblem of the complex of ideas that surround the modern artist and the work of art, particularly those that validate the product and the producer as bearers of artistic worth: ideas of the unique art object; of the originality of the work which is expressive of particular genius and marks an overturning of previous standards and practises. And, further, in addition to these valuations based on myths of originality and origination, the figure of Picasso focuses the related modernist notion that the work should speak of its origins, should ground itself in an expression of the nature of its own materials. I do not wish to suggest that Picasso ought to stand for all of these modernist myths.[2] Yet Picasso does in fact serve this purpose in the general cultural imagination as perhaps the most renowned modern artist. He is also, as the exchange quoted above comically underlines, very definitely dead, and Shepard uses the fact of his demise to illustrate the mythic status and strength of the ideas of authorship and origination here explored.

Picasso, then, is a kind of tutelary spirit of this drama: a paradigmatic modern artist as creator whose originality, personality, self-expression, and unique style are enshrined and warranted by museum exhibitions. Mom, in other words, is not entirely off the mark in her eagerness to meet the great man; for the Los Angeles museum she has read about will undoubtedly do its best to display him. It will market to its patrons the opportunity to see the paintings of a modern genius, the very value of which is invested in the idea that these are original works, both in the sense of works unique, and in the allied sense that they are sprung from and testify to the personality and private inspiration, the essential being and spirit, of one man, their creator and originator. It will be, as they say, a *Picasso* show.

It is not coincidental that Picasso, and through him an increasingly explicit exploration of the culture's modernist myths of art and artist, should be brought into play by Mom. For it is a fairly typical Shepard ploy to associate the female with the standard views, even the clichés of the culture: consider Halie in *Buried Child* and her reliance upon the priest; Shelly in the same play with her Norman Rockwell expectations; Emma's devotion to her 4H project in *Curse of the Starving Class*; Meg's concern with domestic order and etiquette even in the midst of *A Lie of the Mind*'s almost ludicrous violence and disarray. This association of the female with the accepted cultural order (especially when it is seen as limited and potentially restrictive of a free male spirit) is, indeed, almost a characteristically American connection. As Richard Hofstadter has shown in his *Anti-Intellectualism in American Life*, there is abundant evidence of 'the American masculine conviction that education and culture are female concerns'[3] and are thereby devalued. Mom's rather stereotypical and 'feminine' adulation of Picasso, then, is an additional indication that Shepard is confronting us with a challenge to received ideas.[4]

With a typically ironic deflation, this disorienting moment in *True West* focuses a central concern of the playwright with the construction of author and authority. Such plays as *True West* and *Angel City*, by presenting scenarios in which scriptwriters labour at their craft, challenge the ideas of the originality of the author and the role of the author as originator, both thematically and in the implications of their dramatic construction. It is the latter aspect of the plays – the authorial role implied by the borrowed and patchwork fabric of the drama, and its challenge to myths of authorial origination – which is perhaps the most rewarding to explore. The following discussion is concerned, then, not with Shepard's 'authorship' in the traditional sense but with the 'author function' of the dramatic discourse of these two plays, the authorial subject as 'a complex and variable function of discourse'.[5] *True West* and *Angel City* will be explored thus not as expressions of Sam Shepard's profound inner being but as dramatic discourse that intriguingly and playfully implies a particular authorial position and, perhaps, a corollary shift in the auditor's role. As some dramatic discourse may construct a Romantic position for the author, and other plays may imply a modernist avant-garde creator, these two dramas of Shepard's construct their own authorial roles, ones that challenge modernist assumptions.

But in making this argument for dramatic words, I face a considerable difficulty; namely, that the discursive construction of authorial role in drama is not often discussed except perhaps in the most oblique terms. With drama, one frequently encounters not the myth of authorial presence and self-expression, but what initially seems its opposite: a myth of authorial absence. The prime example here would be the prevailing critical response to the plays of Shakespeare, which from the time of the Romantic critics, at least until very recently, praised their demonstration of the supposed invisibility of the authorial role: 'Shakespeare's genius alone appeared to possess the resources of nature . . . His plays have the force of things upon the mind'.[6] Even a contemporary critic such as Denis Donoghue can castigate T. S. Eliot for failing to submerge his voice completely in the voices of his characters, thereby (it is implied) making an incomplete transition from poetry and variations on the dramatic monologue to true dramatic art.[7]

My hesitation is a little disingenuous, for what I really want to argue is that this lack of discussion of the discursive construction of the authorial role bears witness to what is in fact the operant modernist myth of dramatic authorship: the powerful creator everywhere present and nowhere visible in creation – a maker who, like the Almighty, makes his or her presence felt in the very perfection, wholeness, and apparent independence and self-direction of the created world. Such, at least, seems to me the authorial role implied by the height of modernism's realist theatre, where the spectators gaze through an invisible fourth wall at a constructed world very like their own. The more embedded in and responsive to a detailed social and economic environment realised on stage, the more psychologically realistic in mood and motive the characters of such dramas are, the more their actions are read in keeping with a powerful cultural paradigm as being like the autonomous actions of humankind. Realistic characters, like free-willed humankind, are seen to speak of a creator who gave them this self-determination. The less like puppets manipulated by the visible strings of dramatic artifice the characters are, the more they seem to imply a hidden creator whose power is to be measured by the degree of seeming independence with which he or she is able to endow them. There are, of course, deeply held cultural assumptions at work, creating an implicit analogy between the relation of playwright to dramatic characters, and the Divine Creator to the world. One need not search too far in modern drama's past, after all, to find Émile Zola writing of the fictional creations of his stage almost as if they were organic creatures, subjects for study in the effects of environment: 'I am deeply convinced . . . that the experimental and scientific spirit of the age will win over the theatre'.[8] And T. S. Eliot states quite explicitly in 'The Three Voices of Poetry', his language significantly tinged with theological overtones,

> The work of a great poetic dramatist, like Shakespeare, constitutes a world . . . If you seek for Shakespeare, you will find him only in the characters he created, for the one thing in common between the characters is that no one but Shakespeare could have created any of them. The world of the great poetic dramatist is a world in which the creator is everywhere present, and everywhere hidden.[9]

The position I have just sketched takes its most straightforward form in the instance of realistic modern drama but, although considerably more complex, the case for the implied power of the absent author could still be made regarding a playwright such as Beckett, with his stylised exercises in withheld, even taboo, sources of authority (Godot, like the dramatist, continually refuses to bring his play to its awaited close); or Pirandello, whose characters search for an absent author. For these dramatists too, one could argue, the power of the authorial role is greatest, most god-like, almost paradoxical when it is apparently most absent.

Herbert Blau has written compellingly of the operations by means of which 'the gaze itself becomes the most concealed object'[10] – the residual taboo surrounding watching, and the power of the hidden presence of the spectator for whose gaze drama in the realist tradition broadly considered focuses its narrative and visual

lines of perspective. But surely the author is equally concealed in
realist drama and almost equally taboo; if, as Blau suggests, the
concealment of the gaze arises in part from the desire for and
resistance to the primal scene which must not be seen, one can
speculate that perhaps the god-like creator is precisely the most
forbidden object of the gaze, the father-figure whose nakedness –
like the patriarch Noah's – is not to be looked upon.[11]

Shepard's drama removes both the concealment and the mystification from authorial power. The author's role is, in fact, blatantly
displayed in the form of the drama: no original, originary creator
here, hidden god-like in the seemingly independent life of his creatures, but a borrower and arranger of familiar material. We recall
Patrice Pavis' comment that 'one must take into account, in the new
postmodern art, a new totality, not of utterances, but of their enun-
ciation and arrangement in artistic discourse'.[12] The authorial role
becomes precisely the opposite of the autonomous and unified subject, located at the source of meaning and controlling the ensemble
of signs which is the drama.[13] The destabilising of authorial power,
then, is two-fold: a disruption of the concealment which endows the
author with mysterious authority; and a discursive construction of
authorial function as conduit rather than source or well-spring.

The two destabilising impulses are, of course, closely related; but
perhaps, as it is the more subtle effect, the means and implications
of the breaching of authorial concealment and mystification should
be examined first, and the argument for the authorial function of
this dramatic discourse allowed subsequently to add corroborating
evidence. To begin with, I suggest that the self-advertising borrowing and arrangement of material – the collage-like quality of
these texts which will be explored below – breaches the mystery
and invites the audience to be aware of an overt construction of
authorial role. This same overtness meshes with other tendencies
in the dramas (exaggeration, conscious play with stereotyping,
self-reflexive qualities, and the like) to disrupt the broadly realist
premises which grant the concealed author's power and bring the
position of the author into the foreground of attention. Bound up
with these anti-realist tendencies is the thematisation of authorship
within the plays, both of which present characters in the throes of
composition. Moreover, *True West* presents a provocative contrast
between the myth of artistic creation playfully invoked by the name
of Picasso and the inglorious process of selling to a producer and
then writing a marketable script.

Finally it seems to me that *True West* (if not, perhaps, *Angel City*) affronts the decorum of the concealed authorial figure by alluding to Shepard, the public persona. Certainly Austin and Lee, the opposite and to some extent interchangeable brothers, correspond to two sides of the Shepard known to the audience: the photogenic and much described playwright from California (he had won the Pulitzer prize just the year before *True West* appeared on stage), and the rough-hewn character familiar from the films he had appeared in at this point in his career – the wheat farmer in *Days of Heaven*, the psychotic Cal Carpenter in *Resurrection*. This is not to suggest that the drama somehow reveals Shepard's being and voice to the audience; quite the opposite – the role of author created by hints and reminiscences of Shepard's appearances in print and film give us the author as a character, a creature of the available discourse; we recall that even his name (he was born Sam Shepard Rogers) is shaped for an audience. In sum, if in a play where authorial role is obsessively concealed the entire drama becomes, in a sense, the sign of the absent author, then these plays decisively disrupt the operation of that sign.

II

When we examine the specific construction of authorial role in *True West* and *Angel City* (a construction which I have argued is markedly overt and playful), we discover that it is achieved in large part through the clearly-signalled implication of an agency arranging elements drawn from the extant cultural and dramatic discourse, rather than the shadowing forth of a concealed originator of utterances. *True West* and *Angel City* alert us to one of the chief sources of their borrowing through their settings: California, in the various economic and cultural orbits surrounding the film industry. *Angel City* evidences in its plot a collage of Hollywood-on-Hollywood motifs familiar from films, insider biographies, and memoirs. There are the aspiring and ever hopeful actress; the embittered and exploited scriptwriters, musicians, and artists; the enslaving influence of potential fame and fortune; the power of the studio bosses who soullessly manipulate the fortunes of their writers and artists, and the dreams of multitudes. It might be objected that even if there are numerous reminiscences from that trove of American popular cultural motifs which includes *The Day of the Locust*, *A Star is Born* and like riches, it is another matter to claim that *Angel City* presents itself *as* a collage, a compilation of borrowing. The self-advertisement of the lack of originality (in its mythic and mystified sense) is conveyed in the play's cartoon-like exaggeration. Even the title emphasises and underlines the familiarity of the territory: Angel City, Los Angeles. The Hollywood dream-machine – that descriptive cliché – is literalised: the aim proposed among the artists is to create the ultimate disaster movie, the perfect nightmare which will in actual fact drive the audience mad. 'Leave them blithering in the aisles. Create mass hypnosis. Suicide. Autodestruction'.[14] One of the characters, the musician Tympani, works on the hypnotic rhythm which will provide the chief mechanism to mesmerise the audience. Not only do the situations and characters in their crude and exaggerated outlines draw attention to their mass distribution familiarity, but at frequent intervals the dialogue itself seems to aspire to cliché, to build up toward lines that sound as if they must be quoted from some well-known treatment of Hollywood:

> LANX: Well, let's get down to brass tacks, shall we? I mean, in my book a bundle's a bundle. To cut it short, my partner, Wheeler, and I are in a kind of a jam. A little bit of a fix. We've got ourselves in over our heads in this one particular project and uh – we're looking for an ace in the hole.
>
> (71)

The effect is doubled and redoubled, as characters within the fiction markedly 'quote' stereotypical dialogue, sometimes reading from a script (as Miss Scoons does, when she delivers a monologue on the power of money that she 'cooked up in the commissary during my lunch break' (74), a monologue more stereotyped in content than in its style which borders on the bizarre) and sometimes simply extemporising as in the first act sequence when, at the signal of a saxophone screech, the darkening of the stage and the lighting of a neon rectangle upstage, Rabbit and Tympani speak in the voices of little kids at the movies, then Rabbit assumes the role of newscaster and Lanx the role of a boxer being interviewed. Here, not just sentiment but every phrase seems an echo:

LANX: Yeah, I love fightin' in this town. There's somethin' about the atmosphere here. The people. The people love me here. They go bananas. This town is crazy.

(80)

These speeches repeated from a script or quoted from the storehouse of cliché are marked off from the rest of the dialogue by the lighting of the neon rectangle that evokes the frame of the cinema screen. In the sequence just described, the 'boxer' crosses into the lit rectangle to do his 'interview', as Miss Scoons has also done for her monologue.

If the film-frame rectangle is sometimes lit and sometimes dark, however, much of the drama's playful affront to originality springs from the equally exaggerated and clichéd quality of the play's dialogue whether it be framed or unframed. *Angel City* gives us play as playful reshuffling of the plot, character, and dialogue of a 'dark side of tinsel-town' exposé: by the close, of course, not only is the boss, the Wheeler dealer, a monster of manipulative greed ('*His skin is a slimy green. He now has two fangs and extra-long fingernails*' (91)), but the newcomer to town, Rabbit, has undergone a similar corruption:

Suddenly RABBIT *whips the swivel chair around so it's facing* WHEELER. RABBIT's *skin has turned slimy green; he has fangs, long black fingernails, and a long, thick mane of black hair. He remains seated.* WHEELER *is the only one who notices the change in* RABBIT's *appearance.* (108)

True West, similarly, advertises its status as a kind of collage, a selection and arrangement of familiar elements from American popular culture. Lee's speech, for example, is filled with technical terms – with the jargon that alludes to a masculine ideal life of machine and land: goosenecks, 'Tornado Country', flathead Fords that 'haul ass'. Austin talks the language of freeways and Safeways. One scarcely needs the visual prompting of heaps of consumer goods – the stack of stolen toasters – in the realistically dressed kitchen of an older California tract house, scene of so many television sit-coms, to recognize how oft-repeated are the motifs of the struggle of a brother with his evil fraternal double (this is the stuff of soap operas, of Dallas where Bobby battles J.R.) or the internecine struggle to 'make it' in the entertainment industry. And if Mom with her colour-coordinated clothes and matched luggage set, her senior- citizen jaunt to Alaska, has stepped out of the pages of a *Ladies' Home Journal* advertisement, Dad is a figure from B. Traven or Zane Grey, a reclusive, semi-derelict wanderer in the desert.

In an added twist, the structure of *True West* presents itself as a copy of the clichéd stories written by the characters within it. Lee invents a tale of endless chase across the Texas Panhandle, pursuer and pursued switching from trucks to horses when their gas runs out; and one can see the play itself as a species of extended pursuit, a contest between the rival brothers that switches its 'vehicle' from rivalry over macho thievery, to a script-writing contest, to physical combat. Like Lee's story, the play ends with the two rivals still locked in competition. The parallels between the plot of *True West* and that of Lee's script for Saul Kimmer are underlined by a good deal of heated discussion of the fictional truck running out of gas, and the amount of gas in Austin's car. Austin's proposed script, in contrast, is a love story; and one can also see the drama as structured around the two men's rivalry for the love of their father and, in a sense, of Kimmer the producer who will accept or reject their opposed versions of a true story of the west – cowboy combat or California romance.

As both *Angel City* and *True West*, with their familiar plot elements, their character types, and (especially in the case of *Angel City*) even large stretches of what sounds like dialogue quoted or echoed from elsewhere signal their status as re-writings, selections and re-workings of an extant discourse, the authorial role created is very different indeed from that of the originary creator. Not only is the playwright's position perhaps shockingly exposed when we see him as the borrower and arranger, rather than as the creator concealed behind the supposedly unique and independent lives he has placed on stage but, further, we are made aware of the dramatist as consumer of the culture's signs. Curiously, then, the author-as-consumer approaches the position of the audience: and this surely constitutes a demystification of the modernist myth of authorship. Neither spectator nor playwright is figured as source of origin; both are participants, instead, in an ongoing cultural system. Indeed Shepard has described his dramatic art in a fashion that suggests he may be quite self-conscious about his 'unoriginal' authorial role:

> I feel that language is a veil holding demons and angels which the characters are always out of touch with. Their quest in the play is

the same as ours in life – to find these forces, to meet them face to face and end the mystery.[15]

Despite its romantic rhetoric, Shepard's statement implies that the author is at work within an extant system, rediscovering what is already there. Characters, audiences, or playwright (the statement may be taken to include them all) explore the veil of language, the continually-woven social fabric which they construct and which constructs them, their angels and demons both familiar and strange.

Fredric Jameson has suggested that, as the position of the author becomes jeopardised, mass culture and especially popular music respond to this crisis with a glorification of the artist, producing the mythicised figure of the balladeer like Dylan or the martyr/Christ figure embodied in several of David Bowie's stage personae and the hero of the rock-opera *Tommy*.[16] Shepard, of course, has explored the struggle between popular reaction against the decline of the myth of the artist and the postmodern forces that promote such decay in *The Tooth of Crime*[17] and has done so using characters suggestive of rock stars-cum-gangsters. Certainly one of the playfully recycled elements of pop culture 'quoted' in *Angel City* is just this martyred artist figure: Rabbit engages in a doomed but heroic battle against corrupting influences. The play in fact has sometimes been considered, along with *Geography of a Horse Dreamer*, as an example of Shepard's recurrent concern with the artist in opposition to a materialistic society. I am suggesting, however, that we might regard Shepard as more of a postmodern than a late romantic and read *Angel City* as quoting ironically and with a certain self-advertising emphasis and exaggeration – witness the green slime and fangs – from pop culture's nostalgic glamorisation of the authoritative and originary artist figure now threatened with displacement.

If the collage-like and 're-written' surfaces of these plays evoke an authorial figure very different from the modernist creator of the realist tradition, so too do the scenes of writing depicted within them. Both dramas present us with characters who write for consumption (by studio bosses, producers, the film industry and ultimately the public). In other words, they write what is already desirable – what is already written. Saul Kimmer, the producer in *True West* whom the script must be designed to please, is a virtual embodiment of this system of re-production and consumption. Writing as part of this system (rather than original creation) is underscored by the dominant motifs in the play, bread and words, along with toasters for the bread and typewriters, telephones, and television sets for the words. The visual equation between the slices of toasted white bread Austin produces in heaps on the floor when he abandons scriptwriting, and the wrecked sheets of white paper that surround Lee as he attempts to take up the writer's role, is quite clear. And, of course, it provides a cynical revision of an ancient association between words as divine Truth, endowed with meaning by the ultimate authorial Creator, and the sustenance of bread. Here we have bread that is not for eating and words that sustain no image of authorial power.

The critique of the modernist myth of authorial originality is, if anything, even more explicit in *Angel City*. Rabbit and Wheeler engage in a dispute, for example, with Rabbit claiming that an artist such as himself is distinct from a producer like Wheeler. Wheeler insists that they are the same: 'There you go again, dreaming you're different. Setting yourself apart' (102). In his view – and it is the one that seems to prevail, since Rabbit takes on the same monstrous colouring and features as Wheeler in the end – both are part of the system of the reproduction and consumption of signs. Repeatedly, the characters discuss their scriptwriting in terms of choices from a storehouse of what has already been done:

> TYMPANI: That went out with Raymond Chandler.
> RABBIT: Yeah, he's right. Ayn Rand sorta' did it to death too.
>
> (75)

Perhaps even more disturbing, the characters discuss their own lives in similar terms:

> TYMPANI: Fun? What is this supposed to be? Mickey Rooney and Judy Garland get their big break and move to Philadelphia with the Dorsey brothers?
>
> (82)

There is no setting apart of the artist-creator. In fact, the system, the discourse, may be seen to create him or her rather than the reverse. When Rabbit tries to insist upon his status as an artist ('You don't know a thing about creation'), Wheeler replies 'I was created without my knowing. Same as you. Creation's a disease' (102). One character remarks, 'Without the public we are nothing but a part of the public' (71); and this definition of the artistic role solely by means of position leaves little room for the notion of individual and completely originary genius.

A further aspect of Shepard's sly mockery of the myths of authorial originality is suggested by Derrida's reflections upon the playwright's peculiar slavery under the rule of representation. In his essay 'The Theatre of Cruelty', he points out the paradox of the authorial role in traditional, realistically representational drama: while the playwright in such a context claims the complete authority of the creator and absent master of all that appears on the stage, the notion of representation itself at the same time requires that the dramatist be a merely passive imitator and transcriber of the 'real':

> The stage is theological for as long as its structure, following the entirety of tradition, comports the following elements: an author-creator who, absent and from afar, is armed with a text and keeps watch over, assembles, regulates the time or meaning of representation, letting this latter represent him as concerns what is called the content of his thoughts, his intentions, his ideas. He lets representation represent him through representatives, directors or actors, enslaved interpreters who represent characters who, primarily through what they say, more or less directly represent the thought of the 'creator'. Interpretive slaves who faithfully execute the providential designs of the 'master'. Who moreover – and this is the ironic rule of the representative structure which organizes all of these relationships – creates nothing, has only the illusion of having created, because he only transcribes and makes available for reading a text whose nature is itself necessarily representative; and this representative text maintains with what is called the 'real' . . . an imitative and reproductive relationship.[18]

While I do not suggest that Shepard succeeds in breaking free from the structure of representation, he does heighten something of the irony Derrida describes until it begins to reach the level of our conscious notice. The slavery of the author who transcribes a text which far from being an original creation in any absolute sense must be a representation of the 'real', seems one of the implications of the title of *True West* and of its protagonists' ludicrous pursuit and critique of a true west story. The slavery of representation is comically etched in the literal enslavement of one brother by the other, the dictator of the text to the transcriber. Austin, who is by profession an author, is forced to record what the stereotypically 'real' western man – the rebel, the loner, who can survive in the desert and knows the ways of the coyote – tells him. He is allowed to put it in his own words, of course, though he supposedly remains merely the transmitter of Lee's tale:

> LEE: 'The back a' my hand'. That's stupid.
> AUSTIN: That's what you said.
> LEE: I never said that! And even if I did, that's where yer supposed to come in. That's where yer supposed to change it to somethin' better.
> AUSTIN: Well how am I supposed to do that and write down what you say at the same time?
> LEE: Ya' just do, that's all! You hear a stupid line you change it. That's yer job.
>
> (51)

In Lee's aggressive and perhaps somewhat insecure insistence upon the primacy of his own role as source of the story and the relative triviality of the professional scriptwriter's tinkering with language, one can hear an ironic reflection upon the disempowerment of the author that is implied by the logic of representation. To be sure, in the realist text this essential authorial passivity and impotence is always repressed and concealed behind the image of the masterful creator – as in realist drama where the playwright assumes an authority almost reminiscent of the divine. But language under the rule of representation is indeed supposed to be transparent, a mere glass for reality, and the authorial manipulator of words a slavishly faithful transcriber of the 'real'. Lee's domination of Austin and scorn for his facility with language literalise the contradictions of the authorial role in representation as the subject-matter seemingly holds the author prisoner. Shepard's *True West* thus comments obliquely on the comedy of authorship traditionally conceived.

III

I have suggested that Shepard presents us with a critique of modernist myths of origin and originality; and perhaps the argument can be clarified by means of a brief comparison with a classic modern drama, a comedy of authorship that in its wit and complexity ought to ensure that the power of the myth being challenged is not underestimated. Further, this is a drama that at first might seem to be engaged in a questioning of the unified self that brings it close to the postmodern interests of Shepard's work. The play is Pirandello's *Six characters in search of an author*; and though it more often inspires reflection on the nature of dramatic character and its relation to reality, it has much to suggest about the sought-after author as well.

Far from being postmodern in spirit, Pirandello's play seems to me an example of what Lyotard has called the modernist sublime; and comparison will show that Shepard shares little of this particular sublimity. In Lyotard's words, 'I shall call modern the art which devotes its "little technical expertise" (son "petit technique"), as Diderot used to say, to present the fact that the unpresentable exists'.[19] Pirandello has written that the central conflict of this play is between the Characters and the Actors and Stage Manager;[20] it is a conflict brought about, in large part, by the contrast between the 'outrageous unalterable fixity' of the Characters' form,[21] and the ungraspable fluidity of real human selves (for whom, of course, the Actors are the representatives). Pirandello insists above all upon the flux of the human self; one is not even the same self from moment to moment. In his capacity as occasional *raisonneur*, the Father Character says to the Manager, 'All this present reality of yours – is fated to seem a mere illusion to you tomorrow'.[22] And later in the play he remarks (speaking of himself as if he were a real person) 'We have this illusion of being one person for all, of having a personality that is unique in all our acts. But it isn't true'.[23] The contrast between Characters and Actors, then, reveals a kind of modernist sublime in Lyotard's sense of the term: a species of celebration of the inadequacy of language and art to capture the mystery of the human self. The 'sublime' effect of failure is twice repeated, for the Actors, of course, are in fact characters too; and Pirandello thus makes mock of the poor devices by which we try to indicate reality as if it were somehow merely the opposite of high and tragic artistic forms: the conventions of dullness, vanity, triviality, self-absorption, and the like, with which a playwright may try to depict the formless marvel of a real human being: 'Leading Man [To Manager] Excuse me, but must I absolutely wear a cook's cap'?[24]

The author holds a position congruent with this modernist sublime of inadequacy: it is his role to fail to depict. And yet in a
sense he still centres the play, for he is the elusive being sought by
the Characters, a kind of Godot. His position is telling for, sought
after and never found, he becomes in the end almost an emblem
of the author as powerful and hidden point of origin. (Though
the Characters supposedly 'came' to him it is the power of his
being that keeps them in anguished orbit.) Moreover, since it is
he who can tell their story for them, as the Characters think, we
see that the absent author is figured as one who, in the flux and
chaos of his true humanity, will somehow make the proper use
of their 'outrageous fixity'. With Shepard, we recall, the contrast
between person and character is gone; there is no comic lament
over the inadequacy of language because there is nothing but
language against which to measure it. One might argue that the
fade at the close of *True West* leaves us with no end to the plot
(the two brothers remain locked in combat); and as there is no
signal of a shift of attention to a level other than that of the art
displayed, there is nothing against which these shadows should be
judged.

There is one other, and related, myth of origin: the modernist
seeking of a grounding, a presence, a point of origin in the medium
itself. In the field of visual art Rosalind Krauss has brilliantly
analysed the operations of this myth of origin and the way in
which collage evades its boundaries. Krauss writes, 'Modernism's
goal is to objectify the formal constituents of a given medium,
making these, beginning with the very ground that is the origin
of their existence, the objects of vision'.[25] Although Krauss in this
passage is discussing a specifically visual medium – the ground
of the canvas – one can, perhaps, hazard the same generalisa-
tion of modernism's verbal productions. The following lines from
T. S. Eliot's *Four Quartets*, for example, indicate one of the ways
in which that poem objectifies its formal constituents, making
its verbal textures and poetic strategies the essential objects of
attention:

> Words strain,
> Crack and sometimes break, under the burden,
> Under the tension, slip, slide, perish,
> Decay with imprecision, will not stay in place,
> Will not stay still.[26]

And one could offer similar examples of such grounding in *The Waste Land* with its allusions, quotations, and interpolations in foreign tongues. One need only return to the influential example of Pirandello to acknowledge the centrality of this impulse in modern drama. Here too the medium is objectified and the machinery of the theatre is in many senses the object of our gaze – as it is, one can argue, in the work of Brecht, Genet, or Beckett.

But Krauss is interested in the challenges to this modernist ideal, the seeking of an origin and grounding in the medium itself. Collage, she writes, 'problematises that goal, by setting up discourse in place of presence, a discourse founded on a buried origin, a discourse fuelled by that absence'.[27] When we turn to Shepard's drama we find that it likewise challenges the modernist desire to objectify the formal constituents of a given medium, though not in any literal sense as a dramatised staging of the complex surfaces of collage. Rather, Shepard's drama, with a strategy analogous to that of the Picasso collages Krauss analyses, problematises the modernist search for presence in the medium itself by presenting as its base not the essential, material foundation of the theatrical medium, a fixed point of origin and reference, but discourse, a continual staging of what is *not* there. If we can think of an actor's performance and the character which is presented within it as related to one another rather like ground and figure in a collage, then perhaps we can see Shepard's playful evasion of the desire for grounding in the presence of the medium. Chiefly what we discover is that, though the actor's performance is in a sense the essential material of theatre in Shepard's drama – like the canvas ground upon which the visual collage is assembled – this performance is not presented as a point of origin. Instead, the actor's performance and character define one another as polar opposites in a discursive system, a system of signs signifying precisely what is not present. Thus, *Angel City*'s Miss Scoons, as an angry young woman spouting an anti-Hollywood diatribe – framed by a lit neon rectangle that signals 'actress at work' – defines by contrast Miss Scoons in her everyday character of aspiring actress; conversely, the performative effort of the fictive Scoons – visibly throwing her energies into presenting the character who speaks the jeremiad the actress has just written – forms the ground against which the figure of this critic of Hollywood is outlined. There is neither origin nor stopping-point here, only endless mutual definition; and it is seemingly the system of representation, discourse itself, that is represented. Nor is there any secure grounding in the reality and presence of the 'real' actress's performance, the stage work of the woman whose name will appear on an *Angel City* playbill; for it too, I suggest, becomes represented.

Picasso, in Krauss's analysis, buries the ground of his collage beneath the representation of a ground: 'The collage element obscures the master plane only to represent that plane in the form of a depiction'. Collage, then, does not give us a heightened experience of the picture surface, the material support of the image, but rather something quite opposed to this modernist ideal of origin; we experience the ground, according to Krauss, 'not as an object of perception, but as an object of discourse, of representation'.[28] In much the same way, Shepard obscures the 'ground' of the actor's performance – the ground against which we expect to see the 'figure' of the character displayed – with a *re*-presentation of performance.

In what sense, then, is the actor's or actress's performance not present but re-presented? (The performance is, of course, there on stage every bit as much as Picasso's collage elements are indeed glued to some supporting material.) It is something of a common-place of Shepard criticism to observe that his characters, like pro-fessional actors, 'live by performing various fragments of them-selves',[29] and that in Shepard's drama, performance rituals are continually undertaken 'to affirm, sustain, or amplify the image of the self by exerting control over others'.[30] It is not too much to say that Shepard's characters in *True West* and *Angel City* (as in many of his dramas) are representations of actors: what is displayed to the audience is a representation of acting, performing, doing a star turn. When in *True West* Austin begins to play the wild man that his brother has been from the opening of the drama, it is a 'real performance', so to speak, an emotional exhibition. Austin's role at this juncture forms a strong contrast with his playing the ideal suburban son and husband earlier in the drama; but in both cases performing is represented. As a result, the performing that belongs to the actor himself enters a curious vacuum; it is absent, obscured, buried beneath the character's representation of an actor's performance. In less abstract terms, the audience never seems quite to observe the actor's performance but always the fictive performance enacted by the character. We find no grounding in a direct and unmediated experience of the essential element of the dramatic medium, but a sign of the actor's performance gesturing towards that always-absent, ungraspable, point of origin. In this respect, too, Shepard's dramas explore and refuse the myths of modernism.

Notes

1. Sam Shepard, *True West* in *Sam Shepard: Seven Plays* (New York: Bantam, 1981), pp. 54–55. All quotations are from this edition; page numbers are given in the text.
2. Rosalind Krauss, for one, presents a compelling argument against reading Picasso's collages as examples of the modernist tendency to objectify the constituents of a medium and make these the formal origins of the object of vision; see her essay 'In the Name of Picasso', in *The Originality of the Avant-Garde and Other Modernist Myths* (Cambridge: MIT Press, 1987), pp. 23–41.
3. Richard Hofstadter, *Anti-Intellectualism in American Life* (New York: Vintage, 1963), p. 320.
4. Suggesting that Picasso's name evokes (even if perhaps undeservedly) a popular paradigm of modernism and its attendant myths of origin risks the censure of a number of critics who have justifiably protested against facile categorizations of modernism and whatever might be considered post-, subsequent, or opposed to it. Among the warnings, Susan Suleiman's is perhaps most helpful in reminding us that 'modernism' conceived of as singular, canonical, and something against which to rebel, is for the most part Anglo-American and largely the product of academic influence. 'It is only in the Anglo-American context that literary Modernism came to be seen as a solidified, monolithic tradition against which reactions or "renovations" needed to be played off'. Suleiman, 'Naming and Difference', in *Approaching Postmodernism*, ed. Douwe Fokkema and Hans Bertens (Amsterdam & Philadelphia: John Benjamins, 1986), p. 265.
5. Michel Foucault, 'What is an Author?' in *Language, Counter-Memory, Practice*, trans. Donald Bouchard and Sherry Simon (Ithaca: Cornell University Press, 1977), p. 138.
6. William Hazlitt, *Characters of Shakespeare's Plays* (London: Oxford University Press, 1916), p. 12.
7. Denis Donoghue, *The Third Voice* (Princeton: Princeton University Press, 1959), pp. 136–37.
8. Émile Zola, Preface to *Thérèse Raquin*, in *Oeuvres Complètes, Théâtre 1* (Paris: Fasquelle Editeurs, 1969) 33, p. 51. 'J'ai la conviction profonde . . . que l'esprit experimental et scientifique du siècle va ganger le théâtre.'
9. Eliot, 'The Three Voices of Poetry', p. 112.
10. Herbert Blau, *The Audience* (Baltimore: Johns Hopkins University Press, 1990), p. 327.
11. Genesis 9:23. 'And Shem and Japheth took a garment, and laid it upon both their shoulders, and went backward, and covered the

nakedness of their father; and their faces were backward, and they saw not their father's nakedness'.

12. Patrice Pavis, 'The Classical Heritage of Modern Drama: The Case of Postmodern Theatre', *Modern Drama* 29 (1986), 8.

13. See Patrice Pavis, 'Le jeu de l'avant-garde théâtrale et la sémiologie', *Revista Canadiense de Estudios Hispánicos* 7 (1982), 40.

14. Sam Shepard, *Angel City* in *Fool for Love and Other Plays* (New York: Bantam, 1984), p. 71. All quotations are from this edition; page numbers are given in the text.

15. Sam Shepard, 'Metaphors, Mad Dogs, and Old Time Cowboys', interview with Kenneth Chubb and the editors of *Theatre Quarterly* (1974), in ed. Bonnie Marranca, *American Dreams: The Imagination of Sam Shepard* (New York: Performing Arts Journal, 1981), p. 208.

16. Fredric Jameson, '"In the Destructive Element Immerse"', *October* 17 (Summer 1981), 105.

17. See Leonard Wilcox, 'Modernism vs. Postmodernism: Shepard's *The Tooth of Crime* and the Discourses of Popular Culture', *Modern Drama* 30 (1987), 560–73.

18. Jacques Derrida, 'The Theatre of Cruelty', in *Writing and Difference*, trans. Alan Bass (Chicago: University of Chicago Press, 1978), p. 235.

19. Jean-François Lyotard, 'What is Postmodernism?' in *The Postmodern Condition: A Report on Knowledge*, trans. Geoff Bennington and Brian Massumi (Minneapolis: University of Minnesota Press, 1984), p. 78.

20. Luigi Pirandello, Preface to *Six characters in search of an author* in *Naked Masks*, ed. Eric Bentley (New York: Dutton, 1952), p. 209.

21. Ibid., p. 367.

22. Ibid., p. 265.

23. Ibid., p. 261.

24. Ibid., p. 213.

25. Krauss, p. 38.

26. T. S. Eliot, "Burnt Norton", *Four Quartets* (London: Faber and Faber, 1944), p. 19.

27. Krauss, p. 38.

28. Ibid., pp. 37–38.

29. Gay Gibson Cima, 'Shifting Perspectives: Combining Shepard and Rauschenberg', *Theatre Journal* 38 (March 1986), 80.

30. Florence Falk, 'The Role of Performance in Sam Shepard's Plays', *Theatre Journal* 33 (1981), 195.

6

True Stories: Reading the Autobiographic in *Cowboy Mouth*, 'True Dylan' and *Buried Child*

Ann Wilson

I

Sam Shepard is an anomaly among American playwrights: one of the most critically acclaimed playwrights of his generation who has been honoured with a number of awards (including Obies, a Pulitzer Prize for *Buried Child* and the New York Drama Critics Circle Award for *A Lie of the Mind*); he is popularly known as an actor in commercially successful American movies, including *The Right Stuff* (for which he received a nomination for an Academy Award). He is a celebrity whose face is so recognisable that it is not uncommon for photographs of him to grace the covers of mainstream publications such as *Newsweek* and *Esquire*. The terms of Shepard's celebrity are interesting, not just because he is a celebrated playwright who is probably better known for his movie roles, but because the recurring comment made about him is that he is a private man who shuns publicity.[1] If Sam Shepard is so publicity-shy, why has he granted interviews to magazines ranging from *American Film* to *Vogue*? Why, when the evidence seems to counter the contention that Shepard is a recluse in the order of Pynchon and Salinger, does the image of him as a private, inaccessible figure persist? These questions address the problem of Sam Shepard's identity as a public figure which is, in Shepard's case, particularly complex. His persona is composed by the media

97

of an intertextual weave of biographic details, set against his writing which critics insistently read as autobiographic.

Casting Shepard as a figure who is as wary of the media as J. D. Salinger may be somewhat hyperbolic, but the sense that Shepard is guarded in interviews is not unfounded. 'I don't want certain aspects [of myself] to be public', he told Kevin Sessums. 'They are not for public consumption. They're private, they belong to me, they don't belong to everybody and I refuse to let them out there'.[2] Shepard's desire for privacy does little to diminish the public's curiosity about his personal life, a curiosity which is aroused in some small part by his relationship with Jessica Lange, a leading American movie star. Inevitably, the public is interested in the domestic lives of two people who are talented, respected, successful – and hence powerful – within their fields. As understandable as the public curiosity is, so too is Shepard's desire to guard his privacy and that of his family. In an age when celebrities and their families are often subjected to relentless scrutiny by the media, when the adoration of fans can become obsessive to the degree that adoration becomes pathological (occasionally even violent), Shepard's reluctance to expose his children to the invasive glare of publicity is not unusual. What distinguishes Shepard's case is not his refusal to disclose details about his family life, but the way that refusal is read.

Shepard's silence about his private life creates the personal as a site onto which meaning can be imposed by the interviewer. Interviewers who create an identity for Shepard take their cue from his unabashed love for horses and for all that he calls 'horse culture' (including rodeos, the frontier, lore about cowboys and Indians – in short, the West), suggesting that Shepard is a modern cowboy.[3] For Shepard, riding is more than a pleasurable pastime, more than an acting out of child-like fantasies about the frontier; it is an experience which connects him with the roots of American culture. In an interview with Kevin Sessums, Shepard remarks:

> From the very origins of the horse culture in this country – which was ancient, it went back to the Spanish stuff – there's been a big distinction between men on horseback and men on foot . . . If you get up on a horse and see what kind of ground you can cover, there is a completely different feeling from being earthbound. There's just an amazing *sense* – not so much of power, but you're just in a different relationship with the earth.[4]

This love of, and connection with, Western lore not only facilitates the construction of Shepard's persona as a contemporary cowboy, but explains his silence, because what are cowboys if not laconic men, more given to action than to talk?

What emerges in these profiles is a circular argument: if cowboys are by nature silent, somewhat enigmatic figures, then Shepard is silent because he is a cowboy. That Shepard is at heart a cowboy becomes the key to decoding his silence and gaining a fuller understanding of the man. Because the West and its various aspects recur as themes in Shepard's work, and because Shepard is seen as a cowboy, then the conclusion drawn by many writers is that Shepard's work is autobiographic. The apparent assumption is that while Shepard may refuse to disclose the intimate details about his life in the course of an interview, he does not hesitate to do so in his writing.

Reactions to *Fool for Love*, written at roughly the time he left his marriage to O-Lan Johnson to pursue his relationship with Jessica Lange, serve as examples of this tendency by many writers to read Shepard's work as autobiographic. Writes Don Shewey,

> What he [Shepard] doesn't acknowledge is how much the story of *Fool for Love* – a movie stuntman who's run off with a rich cover girl has it out in a motel room with his childhood sweetheart – sounds like the final blowout in his thirteen-year marriage to O-Lan. And who else could the Countess be but Jessica Lange?[5]

Shewey's sentiments are echoed by Ellen Oumano who speculates that in *Fool for Love* Shepard 'was also working out some of the pain regarding his feelings for his wife and for Jessica Lange'.[6] Jennifer Allen notes that the 'love story of a half brother and half sister' seems 'to parallel Shepard's leaving his wife for Jessica Lange, whom he met while playing opposite her in *Frances*'.[7] My intention is neither to support nor to refute the contention that Shepard's work is autobiographical; rather I want to suggest that the eagerness with which Shepard's work is read as revealing, apparently unproblematically, the 'real' Sam Shepard indicates the writers' desires to 'know' Sam Shepard. The desire cannot be confused with the satisfaction of that desire; in other words, the 'real' Sam Shepard is not necessarily revealed in his work simply because critics believe this to be the case. What these accounts tend to elide is the problem of identity, a concern to which Shepard returns throughout his work. If Shepard's plays are going to be read as autobiographic, then surely this can be done only in the context of his formulation of the problem of identity within those plays. To begin to explore the problem of identity in Shepard's work, I want to look at three plays, *Cowboy Mouth*, 'True Dylan' and *Buried Child*.

II

Ellen Oumano asserts with assurance that *Cowboy Mouth*, which Shepard co-wrote with Patti Smith, is 'frankly autobiographic'.[8] Certainly, the play does have elements of autobiography. Shepard married O-Lan Johnson on November 9, 1969; in May of the following year Johnson gave birth to their son Jesse Mojo. During that year, Shepard began an affair with Patti Smith, a punk-rock star of the early seventies, leaving his wife and infant son. 'Their affair', notes Don Shewey, 'looms large in legend'.[9] As becomes legends, the couple lived for a brief time in the Chelsea Hotel, which has been home to cultural figures such as Tennessee Williams, Dylan Thomas, Bob Dylan and, after Shepard's and Smith's tenancy, Sid Vicious. In *Cowboy Mouth*, Cavale has kidnapped Slim *'off the streets with an old .45'* because she *'wants to make him into a rock-and-roll star'*.[10] At one point, Slim exclaims, 'I should just leave and go back to my family. My little family. My little baby' (200). Later he tells her that 'you've stolen me away from my baby's cradle! You've put a curse on me! I have a wife and a life of my own! Why don't you let me go! I ain't no rock-and-roll star' (205). The striking correspondence between the lives of Cavale and Slim and those of their creators seems to invite reading *Cowboy Mouth* as autobiographic, an invitation made all the more attractive because Smith played Cavale and Shepard Slim, in the American premiere of the piece at the American Place Theatre in April 1971. Yet, despite this enticement, reading *Cowboy Mouth* as autobiography is made problematic by its theme of the outlaw.

The theme is established by the disorder of the set, a room which has *'a fucked up bed is centre stage . . . Scattered all around on the floor is miscellaneous debris'* (199). Visually, the disarray establishes an air of menace because the incongruous elements of the set do not suggest any obvious meaning to the audience. Slim's first speech in the play reinforces this sense of threat. He charges around yelling, 'Wolves, serpents, lizards, gizzards, bad bladders, typhoons, tarantulas, whip snakes, bad karma, Rio Bravo, Sister Morphine' (199).

The aggressive cadence of this list of nouns culminates with Slim's explosive 'go fuck yourself' (199). As Slim darts erratically around the room, Cavale *'is rummaging through junk, yelling with a cracked throat'* (199). The scene, both visually and aurally, is one of manic chaos.

What becomes clear is that Cavale and Slim actually personify this disorder inasmuch as they see themselves as contemporary outlaws who live outside the rules of society. Cavale, who has 'stolen' Slim from his 'baby's cradle' in the hope of transforming him into a rock-and-roll star, imagines herself to be a type of thief (205). Her actions are in the spirit of her heroes, François Villon and Jean Genet, two figures notorious in literary history not only because of their writing but because they were convicted thieves. Celebrating thievery, Cavale says, 'A marvellous thief like Villon or Genet . . . they were saints "cause they raised thievery to its highest state of grace"' (207). In Cavale's mind, stealing is more than the act which violates laws of ownership; it has redemptive qualities. This sense of redemption is associated with her ambitions for Slim, not simply because she has kidnapped him, but because she envisions that 'the rock-n'-roll star in highest state of grace will be the new saviour . . . rocking to Bethlehem to be born' (208).

In many ways this remark establishes that within their world, that is, within the room, Cavale is the consummate outlaw. Not only has she stolen Slim using the gun of the old West, the '.45', adopted a borrowed persona of thief for herself and assigned Slim the similarly borrowed persona, that of saviour; but she does so using a phrase borrowed from Yeats' 'The Second Coming'. The theme of stealing continues when Slim loses his place as her protegé upon the return – literally the second coming – of the Lobster Man:

> Let the lobster man be the new Johnny Ace. It's the Aquarian Age. Ya know it was predicted that when Christ came back he'd come as a monster. And the lobster man ain't no James Dean. (213)

When Slim realises that the Lobster Man has stolen his place (and has done so because Cavale has assigned to him the stolen persona of Johnny Ace) he says, 'Now what rough beast slouches toward Bethlehem to be born?' (213).

This misquoting of the lines 'And what rough beast, its hour come round at last,/Slouches towards Bethlehem to be born?' from 'The Second Coming' is not a casual literary allusion because in many

ways *Cowboy Mouth* is a parody of Yeats' vision in that poem. 'The
Second Coming' provides an accurate description of the world of
Cowboy Mouth:

> Things fall apart; the centre cannot hold;
> Mere anarchy is loosed upon the world,
> The blood-dimmed tide is loosed, and everywhere
> The ceremony of innocence is drowned;
> The best lack all conviction, while the worst
> Are full of passionate intensity.
> Surely some revelation is at hand;
> Surely the Second Coming is at hand.[11]

Florence Falk adopts a literal reading of Cavale's speech about
'the rock'n'roll star . . . rocking to Bethlehem to be born'. She writes:

> In other words, forged of pain and loneliness, rock and roll is the
> only creation one can trust as genuine. Cavale's neo-romantic
> cant recapitulates nineteenth century transcendental gestures to
> the experience of the godhead. Her vision of sainthood, pure and
> selfless as the holy flame, is drawn of pain and inspiration. Cavale
> whispers stories about the martyrdom of performance into her
> lover's ear; to the brooding reluctant Slim she is the angel of
> darkness at his side urging him to be the new saviour.[12]

I quote Falk at length because I think that her earnest efforts to
find meaning in the text, and to locate *Cowboy Mouth* within a
tradition of American transcendentalist writing, ignore the obvious
playfulness of the text. This is, after all, a play which represents
the new saviour as a Lobster Man, so that whatever else *Cowboy
Mouth* is, it is not an apocalyptic vision. An important moment
in the script is Slim's misquoting of the lines from Yeats, because
the punctuation of the line in the script suggests that he quotes
directly from the poem, when in actual fact he omits some of
the lines. At issue is not the accuracy of the quote but the fact
that in quoting Yeats, in effect borrowing from him, the original
is lost. The vision of 'The Second Coming' is manifest in the very
quoting of the text: things have fallen apart; the centre has not
held.

The parody in *Cowboy Mouth*, by drawing our attention to the object of parody, 'The Second Coming', makes us aware of the transmutation which the original text has undergone. This should make us cautious of reading the play as Shepard's and Smith's revelation of their relationship, because their lives, as 'original' texts, are subject to the same processes of permutation as the text of 'The Second Coming'.

Arguably, *Cowboy Mouth* is a pastiche of texts which are transformed to the point where they are virtually beyond recognition. A case in point is the title of the play which echoes a line from Bob Dylan's song 'Sad-Eyed Lady of the Lowlands': 'And your cowboy mouth and your curfew pluses'. The enigmatic lyrics of the song tempt the listener into speculating about the identity of the lady who, in popular lore, is assumed to be Joan Baez, who was involved with Dylan during the sixties when he became a powerful force in popular music. In two of her songs, 'Diamonds & Rust' and 'Winds of the Old Days', Baez reflects on her involvement with Dylan during that period. In the latter song, she describes Dylan as being cast as a rock and roll saviour: 'Singer or Saviour, it was his to choose. Which of us knows what was his to lose?'[13]

In the context of Cavale's project to transform Slim into a rock and roll saviour, the popular mythology which surrounds Baez's and Dylan's relationship is of particular interest. In an interview with Anthony Scaduto, Baez spoke about her relationship with Dylan. She recalls,

> I really loved him. I wanted to take care of him and have him sing. I mean, brush his hair and brush his teeth and get him on stage . . . I wanted to have as many people hear him as possible. I asked him to appear with me because he was brilliant. I loved him, I loved his music, I wanted people to hear him.[14]

Later in the interview she remembers her response to Dylan's suggestion that they perform in Madison Square Garden: 'I think what it means is that you'll be the rock-and-roll king and I'll be the peace queen'.[15] The image of Dylan as the pretender to the throne of Elvis Presley, the king of rock-and-roll, is made clearly in the line of Don McLean's song about the period, 'American Pie', in which he describes Dylan as the 'jester' who steals Presley's 'thorny crown'. What is evident is the process of mythologising figures of popular culture, and in particular, the lexis relating to Christ which is used to effect the transformation of individuals into myths. If Shepard and Smith envision themselves as becoming larger-than-life figures of popular culture, they do so within an established frame of reference. In short, they 'steal' the personae of Dylan and Baez and so are engaged with elaborate role-playing in which they assume identities.

Role-playing is a key to *Cowboy Mouth* because Slim and Cavale perform throughout: Slim *'growls like a coyote and howls'* (201); Cavale and Slim *'walk through the room as though it were the city'* (202) and pretend to shop for shoes; *'Cavale plays dead'* (204). All through the play Cavale tells stories, and Slim plays the electric guitar and sings. Are these 'real' identities, or are Cavale and Slim simply creating characters for their mutual amusement? The room is a place of representation, a scene of fantasy for the two characters who, at least in the case of the first American production, may be the actors staging themselves. How can we claim with any certainty that Shepard and Smith grant us a glimpse of their 'real' selves when any sense of what is 'real' and 'authentic' seems so lost?

III

The problem of 'true' and 'real' identity is posed again in a one-act play called 'True Dylan',[16] which promises a depiction of Shepard's attempt to interview Dylan 'as it really happened one afternoon in California' (59). Apparently 'True Dylan' is autobiographic, the transcription of an interview which Shepard conducted with Dylan, whom he first met in the fall of 1975 when he joined The Rolling Thunder Review as the screen-writer for a film about its tour.[17] Shepard's involvement with the project was minimal because Dylan favoured improvised scenes over scripted ones. Despite some acrimony over this project, Shepard and Dylan have maintained a relationship and have collaborated creatively, co-writing 'Brownsville Girl' which Dylan recorded on his album *Knocked Out Loaded*. The account of their meeting in 'True Dylan' is not just the meeting between interviewer and interviewee, but a glimpse at the friendship between two men popularly represented as fiercely private. We might wonder whether this interview in fact does represent a betrayal of that privacy by revealing the friendship, or whether with a certain slyness, Shepard is mocking the pretence that interviews reveal the 'real' and 'true' subject. By choosing to write the interview as dialogue, Shepard points to what is true of this or any other interview: interviewees stage their presentation of themselves.

Exchanges between friends and between interviewer/subject frequently rely on the same medium, conversation, but the structure of the conversation differs. When two friends talk, communication circulates between them, whereas an interview with a celebrity always implies a third party, the audience. The interviewer is, in effect, a surrogate asking the questions on behalf of the absent audience. The subject, conscious of this dynamic, bifurcates her replies by responding to the immediate presence of the interviewer but, at the same time, speaking beyond her to the absent addressee. The subject of the interview can reach the audience only through an elaborate structure of mediation: the taped exchange which is transcribed, published, bought by the audience and then read. Frequently celebrity interviews minimise this structure of mediation by suggesting that the subject reveals her inner-most self to the public by speaking beyond the interviewer to her true addressee, with whom she feels intimacy and trust.[18]

Given that the expectation of a celebrity interview is that the subject's 'true' or 'real' self is revealed, then Shepard's decision to write the interview as a play which transcribes (or at least appears to transcribe) the conversation between himself and Dylan, emphasises that an interview is always the staging of the self for an audience. This structure, which allows only the *representation*, never the presentation, of self, makes it difficult to imagine that the 'real' person is ever revealed. In such a context, Shepard's staging of his interview under the title 'True Dylan' rings with irony which is sustained within the piece itself.

Shepard, the anxious interviewer, enters the scene *'carrying a tape recorder, several notebooks and a six pack of beer'* (60). Despite his appearance of being at the ready, Shepard tells Dylan that he isn't sure what 'this thing [is] supposed to be about' but, nevertheless, he has prepared some questions:

> BOB'S VOICE: [*off*] Are we supposed to have a theme?
> SAM: I got a buncha questions here.
> BOB'S VOICE: [*off*] You brought questions?
> SAM: Yeah.

> BOB'S VOICE: How many questions?
> SAM: Couple.
> BOB'S VOICE: What if I don't have the answers?
> SAM: Make it up.
>
> (60)[19]

Shepard's instruction to 'make it up' casts doubt on the truth of
Dylan's answers: perhaps all, most, some of the answers are made
up. The problem of the 'truth' of the exchange is raised again
when BOB goes off stage to answer the phone. Alone on stage,
SAM rewinds the tape searching for the interview. When he plays
the tape what is heard is the Jimmy Yancey piano solo which was
heard at the beginning of the show. BOB returns and listens to the
tape:

> SAM: Well, our voices ain't on here.
> BOB: Don't matter.
> SAM: Well, I can't remember all this stuff. How am I gonna
> remember all this stuff?
> BOB: Make it up.
>
> (66)

Finally, SAM finds the interview, although how it was lost remains
a mystery. The instruction to 'make it up', this time coming from
BOB, like the earlier one from SAM, casts doubt on whether the
dialogue is really a true and accurate account of the conversation.
Perhaps the original was lost and SAM reconstructed BOB's answer
which may have been fabrications in the first place. In other words,
despite the title's claim that what is revealed is 'true' Dylan, the
whole thing may be a fabrication, Dylan's and Shepard's staging of
themselves.

The self-conscious creation of identity is as evident in 'True
Dylan' as it was in *Cowboy Mouth* where Shepard assumed the
persona of Dylan, although in the case of 'True Dylan', it is BOB who
assumes a persona. At the beginning of the interview, BOB tells SAM
that he recently visited the highway near Paso Robles where James
Dean died in a fatal car crash, and 'the place where he died is as
powerful as the place where he lived' (60). He tells Shepard that he
initially went to New York City ' 'cause James Dean had been there'
(62). Twice, the interview is punctuated by the sounds of screeching
brakes and a car crash (60, 68), clearly an allusion to Dean's accident

but also to Dylan's near-fatal motorcycle crash outside Woodstock in July 1966 which ʙᴏʙ discusses in the final speech of the play. He claims that during his recovery, he could 'feel the steady thrust of death that had been constantly looking over its shoulder at me' (68). The parallels between James Dean and Bob Dylan are not unique to this play but recur throughout the early part of Dylan's career, particularly with regard to the motorcycle accident.[20] Shepard does not simply pick up on these parallels by casting ʙᴏʙ as a James Dean-like figure, but in this way insists that Dylan, like Dean, is a legendary figure of popular culture. Dylan becomes a figure whom we see in the context of James Dean. The (pseudo) interview of 'True Dylan' points to an aspect of identity which emerges in other works by Shepard: identity is not necessarily a 'true' story of the self but might be a ruse which may – or may not – be believed. It is clear from 'True Dylan' and *Cowboy Mouth* that identity is mutable because it involves assuming roles, a performing of the self. This problem is evident in *Buried Child*[21] when the prodigal son, Vince, returns to his family's home where initially no one from the family will acknowledge him.

IV

In *Buried Child*, Vince stops by his grandparents' home on his way to visit his father, whom he believes still to be living in New Mexico. The visit, explains his girlfriend Shelly, is precipitated by Vince's desire to become reacquainted with his family. As Shelly explains to the grandfather, Dodge:

> I mean Vince has a thing about his family now. I guess it's a new thing with him. I kind of find it hard to relate to. But he feels it's important. You know. I mean he feels he wants to get to know you all again. After all this time. (86)

What Shelly doesn't tell Dodge, but what seems evident, is that Vince expects to be welcomed by the family as the returning prodigal. This expectation is not met because neither his father nor his grandfather recognise him. 'Look, Grandpa', Vince pleads, 'Don't you remember me? Vince. Your grandson' (87). When Tilden similarly fails to recognise Vince, Shelly says, 'This is supposed to

be your son! Is he your son? Do you recognize him! I'm just along
for the ride here. I thought everybody knew each other!' (92)

Eventually, Vince is recognised by the family, although the circumstances of that recognition are ironic. Earlier in the play, Vince
attempts to gain his grandfather's favour by going off to buy him a
bottle of liquor. During his absence, Halie, his grandmother, returns
from her tryst with Father Dewis and bemoans the sorry state of
the men in the family: 'What's happened to the men in this family!
Where are the men!' (124). As if these lines were a cue, Vince,
who is very drunk, returns to the house, his condition verifying
Halie's complaint. Ironically, at this moment, Vince is recognised
as a member of the family, but he, assuming the family's earlier
attitude, forgets who he is:

> SHELLY: (*after silence*) Vince?
> (VINCE *turns towards her. Peers through screen*).
> VINCE: Who? What? VINCE who? Who's that in there?
> (VINCE *pushes his face against the screen from the porch and
> stares in at everyone*).
> DODGE: Where's my goddamn bottle!
> VINCE: (*looking in at* DODGE) What? Who is that?
> DODGE: It's me! Your Grandfather! Don't play stupid with
> me! Where's my two bucks!
> VINCE: Your two bucks?
> (HALIE *moves away from* DEWIS, *upstage, peers out at* VINCE *trying
> to recognize him*).
> HALIE: Vincent? Is that you Vincent?
> (SHELLY *stares at* HALIE *then looks out at* VINCE).
> VINCE: (*from porch*) Vincent who? What is this! Who are
> you people?
>
> (125–26)

Vince's acceptance by the family is formalised when Dodge names
Vince as his heir, bequeathing the house and its contents to him
(129).

Buried Child, on its simplest level, is an exploration of identity.
The strangeness of the family in *Buried Child* makes it difficult
to imagine that Shepard might be exploring his own family. Yet
the autobiographic component of *Buried Child* is suggested by the
correspondences between the play and a piece in *Motel Chronicles*,
a collection of poems, prose, reflections and photographs which

are Shepard's recollection of his own life – or so we are told on the book's jacket. In this piece, Shepard writes about visiting his grandparents who lived near Chicago:

> My grandfather sits as he's always sat – in a hole of his sofa wrapped in crocheted blankets facing the T.V. He's like a skeleton now . . . He smokes and drinks continuously and spits blood into a stand-up brass ashtray like you see in lobbies of old hotels. Sometimes he coughs so violently his whole body doubles over and he can't catch his breath for a long time. His world is circumscribed around the sofa. Everything he needs is within a three-foot reach. The T.V. is only on for the baseball. When the game ends my Grandmother comes in and turns it off. She does it right on cue. She can hear when the game ends from any room in the house. She has great ears.
>
> When everyone's asleep I wander around in the room upstairs staring at all the photographs of my Uncles. The Uncle who dies in a motel room on his wedding night. His wife who died with him. The Uncle who lost a leg at the age of ten. The Uncle who married into the Chicago Mafia . . . All the Uncles who carry the bones of my Grandpa's face.[22]

Certainly Dodge and Halie are recognisable in Shepard's description of his grandparents while Bradley and Ansel (who married into the 'Mob') seem similar to Shepard's description of his uncles. Shepard's nocturnal viewing of the family photographs reminds us of Shelly who goes upstairs at night and looks at the photographs of the family which are hanging on the wall. The comment that the uncles carry the bones of their father in their faces is developed fully in Vince's speech about his vision of the family, which comes to him as a reflection in the windshield of the car as he drives towards the Iowa border (130). These correspondences create links between the two works and, at the same time, call into question the status of *Motel Chronicles*: is it document or fiction?

Shepard, in his interview with Kevin Sessums, is clear about the status of *Motel Chronicles* as a work of fiction. When asked by Sessums whether he will write a novel, Shepard replies, 'Oh man, I've tried it and tried it. The only serious attempt I really made, I guess, was with *Motel Chronicles* but it just broke into a million pieces. A novel just seems beyond me'.[23] Yet despite Shepard's claim that *Motel Chronicles* is fiction, it reads like a series of his notes on, and recollections of, his life. Many of the pieces, particularly those recounting specific moments with his family, seem extremely intimate, and hence authentic, because ours is a culture which equates the dropping of the public persona with the revelation of the private, real, and therefore, authentic, self.

The veracity of the pieces in *Motel Chronicles* is not simply reinforced by the use of photographs but depends on it. Most of the photographs show Shepard with his family and indeed, the volume is a sort of family album. The use of these photographs is more complicated than simply being illustrative because they direct us to read the written text in a particular way. Photographs, Roland Barthes informs us, record 'the scene itself, the literal reality. From the object to its image, there is of course a reduction: in proportion, in perspective, in colour. But this reduction is at no point a *transformation* . . . '24 In other words, what a photograph creates is an apparently unproblematic relation between the object and its image because the photograph is a record, unmediated by the photographer's selection of elements in the scene. In contrast to a painting in which the painter selects what is to be included in the work, the photograph records whatever is in range of the lens. In short, a photograph is supposedly a record of reality, not a rendering.

Because *Motel Chronicles* is composed of photos, poems and bits of prose, an intertextual network is established within the volume itself: photographs and writing are read in relation to one another. The proximity of the photograph (which seems artless) to writing, which we normally consider to be artifice because of the mediation of the writer, creates a spill-effect so that writing, read in the context of the photograph, becomes similarly artless – or at least less artful. In the words of Roland Barthes, language is 'made innocent' by its proximity to the photograph. The authenticity of Shepard's apparently intimate revelations about his family is reinforced by the inclusion of the photographic record of family. Both seem to be the true, unmediated representation of reality.

And yet, are they? Several of the photographs, including the shot on the cover, are clearly posed. In the cover photograph, for example, Shepard stands next to a car with Texas license plates. All the clothing he wears is black: pants, t-shirt, jacket and stetson. He holds a bottle of Coca-Cola. In the background is what looks to be a country store, complete with a porch. This portrait creates a persona for Shepard as the dark figure on the landscape of mythic America metonymically marked by Coca-Cola, cars and cowboys. The scene seems staged, the photograph designed to create a particular effect: the mythologising of Sam Shepard. Yet, as staged as the scene is, it does seem to allude to the actual world: the license plates on the car permit the vehicle to be driven on public roads. The car, the Coke, the clothing, and general store, while serving as props, also have use (and hence value) outside the staged scene. As James Lingwood notes, the 'mythologies photography serve to create cannot easily be separated from our knowledge that it is working with reality'.[25] This tension between the actual and the fictional is an important component of *Buried Child*.

The beginning of Act Three is the morning before Vince stages his second, and this time successful, homecoming. Shelly comes downstairs and tells Dodge that she slept in the room 'with all the pictures . . . your whole life's up there hanging on the wall' (111). Dodge denies that the figure in the photographs is connected with him: 'That isn't me! That never was me! This is me. Right here. This is it. The whole shootin' match, sittin' right in front of you' (111). Dodge's insistence that what is important is the present amounts to a refusal to remember the past. Obviously this refusal safeguards the family secret, creating the curious effect that the denial of history, and hence of identity, is in fact what holds the family together because it gives them a common purpose.

While the function of the secret as metaphoric glue which binds the members of the family together is evident, the status of the secret – whether it is true – is not so apparent. In a conversation with Father Dewis in which Halie celebrates the memory of Ansel, she comments, 'We can't not believe in something. We can't stop believing. We just end up dying if we stop. Just end up dead' (118). In this context, the secret is the belief that keeps the family alive; its veracity is unimportant and, indeed, difficult to determine. When the secret of the infanticide is told, the teller is Dodge who says of Shelly, 'See this girl, this girl wants to know. She wants to know something more' (123). Ostensibly, the story is told because Shelly wants to 'know', to hear a story by which she can verify the narrative which she has constructed for the family pictures; but to say that is not to claim that the story which is told is true. Indeed, Bradley claims that Dodge 'doesn't remember anything. I'm the only one in the family who remembers' (123).

The revelation of the secret to Shelly, the outsider, violates the structure of the family which is held together by maintaining the secret. The revelation is occasioned by Shelly's discovery of the documents – in this case, the photographs on the wall – which she reads and interprets: a process involving her creating a story, fashioned from what she knows (or at least what she thinks she knows) of the family's past, which corresponds to what she sees in the photographs. Because Shelly is a reader, her process of coming to knowledge is similar to that of readers who insist that Shepard's work is autobiographic. Like Shelly, who believes that the photographs correspond to an actuality, we, as Shepard's readers, often accept the pretence that the celebrity, when interviewed, speaks directly and truthfully to his (or her) fans, that the medium of the interview is a transparent transmitter of the celebrity's self-revelations. As Shepard rather wittily suggests in 'True Dylan', the apparatus of interviews – the questions asked by the interviewer, the responses, the means of recording the interview, the dissemination of the interview – shapes the response of the audience. Given these conditions, can we as readers ever know the 'real' Sam Shepard? This question begs another: what constitutes the 'real' or 'true' self? Both *Cowboy Mouth* and *Buried Child* seem to suggest that notion of a 'true' self is false inasmuch as an individual's identity is his (or her) narrative of self. In *Cowboy Mouth*, we see Slim and Cavale creating personae (or identities) by self-consciously assuming roles. In *Buried Child* the process is perhaps less evident to the reader because the characters are not flamboyant, self-conscious auto-performers like Slim and Cavale; rather, Vince is engaged in the fairly common attempt of renewing his contacts with his family. 'This thing about his family' (86), as Shelly phrases Vince's desire to restore his connection with his past, is a way of gaining a sense of personal history, of creating a personal narrative. In *Buried Child*, the 'true' story may, or may not be told; what seems more important is the actual telling of the story because it satisfies Shelly's desire to know, a desire which is presumably based upon her need to 'make' sense of her encounter with this family. Shelly is a paradigmatic reader because the desire to understand is common to all readers – whether reading literature, or a performance, or the text of their lives. This desire for meaning or for order, is often articulated through the ordering structure of narrative. At the same time our socialised responses to certain modes of textuality (for example, interviews or photographs) as referring in an unmediated way to an actuality – leads us to read Shepard's work as providing privileged glimpses of the 'true' Sam Shepard. To do this is to allow our desire to know the 'true' Shepard to blind us to ways in which those works which are termed 'auto-biographic' themselves explore and, in so doing, render problematic, the individual's construction of identity.

Notes

1. Jennifer Allen remarked in her profile of Shepard which appeared in *Esquire* that 'he has become a Great American Writer, and beyond that, a reclusive ala Salinger and Pynchon'. Jennifer Allen, 'The Private Sam Shepard: The True Story of a Self-Made Myth', *Esquire* (November 1988), 148.
2. Kevin Sessums, 'Geography of a Horse Dreamer: playwright, actor and movie director Sam Shepard', *Interview* (September 1989), 76.
3. Indeed, Shepard's love of horses is so pronounced that in an article on Shepard in *Time Out*, Chris Peachment recounts an incident when Shepard became impatient with a New York 'intellectual' acting as a translator for a European journalist. Peachment describes the impatient Shepard looking 'for all the world like a bad horse, watching the approach of a rider, smelling fear'. This incident is cited by Duncan Webster in 'Sam Shepard's Cowboy Mouth: Representing Masculinity', in *Looka Yonder: The Imaginary America of Populist Culture* (London: Routledge, 1988) p. 85.
4. Sessums, 76.
5. Don Shewey, *Sam Shepard* (New York: Dell, 1985) p. 149.
6. Ellen Oumano, *Sam Shepard: The Life and Work of an American Dreamer* (New York: St. Martin's Press, 1987), p. 146.
7. Allen, 148.
8. Oumano, p. 91.
9. Shewey, p. 77.
10. Sam Shepard and Patti Smith, *Cowboy Mouth, Angel City & Other Plays* (Vancouver: Talonbooks, 1976), p. 199. All quotations from the play are from this edition; page numbers are given in the text.
11. Yeats, 'The Second Coming', *The Collected Poems of W. B. Yeats* (London: Macmillan, 1955), pp. 210–11.
12. Florence Falk, 'The Role of Performance in Sam Shepard's Plays', *Theatre Journal* 33 (May 1981), 191.
13. Joan Baez, 'Winds of the Old Days', *Diamonds and Rust*, A&M Records, A&M SP-4527, 1975.
14. Anthony Scaduto, *Dylan: An Intimate Biography* (New York: Signet, 1971), p. 222.
15. Scaduto, p. 226.
16. Sam Shepard, 'True Dylan', *Esquire* (July 1987), 60–68. All quotations from the play are from this edition; page numbers are given in the text.
17. The Rolling Thunder Revue was a concert tour throughout the Atlantic seaboard and parts of Canada. The tour, which featured

(among others) Joan Baez, Joni Mitchell, Patti Smith, Bob Neurwith and Roger McGuinn, was directed by Jacques Levy who directed several of Shepard's plays, including the premier production of *La Turista* in 1967.

18. Celebrity is discussed fully by Ruth Amossy, 'Autobiographies of Movie Stars: Presentations of Self and its Strategies', *Poetics Today* 7, no. 4 (1986), 673–703.

19. To alleviate confusion between the characters in 'True Dylan' and their living counterparts, I'll refer to the characters in the play as BOB and SAM.

20. Scaduto, p. 282.

21. Sam Shepard, *Buried Child, Seven Plays* (New York: Bantam, 1981). All quotations from the play are from this edition; page numbers are given in the text.

22. Sam Shepard, *Motel Chronicles* (San Francisco: City Lights, 1982), pp. 45, 46.

23. Sessums, 78.

24. Roland Barthes, *Camera Lucida: Reflections of Photography*, trans. Richard Howard (New York: Hill and Wang, 1981) p. 5.

25. James Lingwood, 'Self-Portraits', in *Identity: The Real Me, ICA Documents* 6, ed. Lisa Appisanesi (London: Institute of Contemporary Art, 1987) p. 20.

7

Shepard's Family Trilogy and the Conventions of Modern Realism

Charles R. Lyons

The final moment of Sam Shepard's *Buried Child* holds one of the most potent theatrical images of contemporary American drama. As the off-stage (upstairs) voice of the mother, Halie, recites a litany that celebrates the miraculous regenerative power of the rain,

> TILDEN [her son] *appears from stage left, dripping with mud from the knees down. His arms and hands are covered with mud. In his hands he carries the corpse of a small child at chest level, staring down at it. The corpse mainly consists of bones, wrapped in muddy, rotten cloth. He moves slowly downstage toward the staircase, ignoring* VINCE *on the sofa. As* HALIE'S *voice continues,* TILDEN *slowly makes his way up the stairs. His eyes never leave the corpse of the child. The lights keep fading.*[1]

This visual image constitutes both a shocking surprise and the seemingly inevitable confirmation of an event within a narrative past that the text has suggested carefully in a series of allusions to the correlated transgressions of incest and infanticide. Shepard's use of the image of the sacrificed child in relationship to the cumulative revelation of the past exercises a set of conventions operative in realistic drama since Ibsen's experimentation in the 1880s.

The death of a child – as an event within the narrated past or the dramatized action – works within a particular process in which many realistic dramatic texts organize the experience of its protagonist and the social dynamics of its domestic scene. The

signal text of late nineteenth-century realism, Ibsen's *Ghosts*, ends
with the impending death of an innocent son destroyed by the
corruption of the father. *The Master Builder* includes the story of
the infant sons who died after fire destroyed Fru Solness's family
home, the incident on which Solness rebuilds his career and then
later reconstructs in his imagination as the evidence of demonic
forces that serve his will. The suicide of Arkadina's son, Treplev,
ends Chekhov's *The Sea Gull*. The revelation of the past in *The Cherry
Orchard* discloses the drowning of Ranevskaya's son, Grisha, as the
beginning of a series of incidents that she perceives as retribution
for her moral failing. The event of Eugene's death, revealed in the
retrospective structure of *Long Day's Journey into Night*, becomes
a focal point in the complex family project of assigning guilt in
O'Neill's ostensibly autobiographical drama. In Arthur Miller's *All
My Sons*, the father's crime in manufacturing flawed equipment for
military aircraft results in his son's death. In Edward Albee's *Who's
Afraid of Virginia Woolf?* George improvises upon the death of the
son conceived in the complicity of his and Martha's fantasy, and the
revelation of the young man's death coincides with the spectator's
realisation of his son's status as the illusory subject of a perverse
game.

In many of the plays I note above, the revelation of the *kindermord*,
or the discovery of critical facts related to a child's death, functions
as the significant data from the past that the dialogue eventually
reveals. The death of the child almost invariably points toward a
parent's act that the dialogue frames as a transgression. *Buried Child*
plays within that particular nexus of conventions. At critical points
the text voices the possibility of an infanticide and then quickly
suppresses it. In the final moments, the act suggested in narrative
reference becomes a tangible sign, and yet the play refuses to make
unequivocal connections between this strikingly material evidence
of a *kindermord* and a final, resolving vision of the past that would
allow the spectator to organise most of its details into a cohesive
narrative.

This ending sustains the text's unwillingness to unify the details
of the narrative of the past that it invokes. Both Tilden and his father,
Dodge, voice the revelatory statements, but at no point does the
individual predication of one elicit a confirming response from the
other. This refusal to reinforce narration complicates the strategies
of dramatic realism and relates the play to the conventions of its
own theatrical moment, organisational techniques that fragment the

possibility of narrative unity with significant disjuntions, interstices, and inconsistencies.

The relationship of the arresting final theatrical image of *Buried Child* to analogous motifs in earlier drama suggests that the play does not function as an imitation of a pattern of behaviour drawn from the playwright's observation or experience, but that it functions as a self-conscious, ironic, manipulative image that makes reference to theatrical convention itself – the earlier deaths of fictive children from modern realism. From this point of view, the object of representation in *Buried Child* would not be the dysfunctional American family or data from the playwright's autobiography but, rather, that object would be the structural paradigms in which realistic drama defines itself as a theatrical mode. This play, and the other two related texts, present problematic domestic relationships that derive principally from a particular set of relationships within the mode of realism itself. Within the terminological game of current critical discourse, the self-conscious assimilation of these modernist conventions would mark Shepard's play as postmodernist. Although, as this essay suggests, Shepard's 'family' trilogy extends and amplifies certain problems in the realistic project that many significant modernist works had already brought to the foreground.

The earlier plays of Sam Shepard display both an eclectic diversity of theatrical modes and an identifiable, idiosyncratic voice. These works respond to the kind of improvised, transformative structure that marked the *avant-garde* in the 1960s, the experimental American theatre responded to the theatrical innovation of Beckett, Genet, Ionesco, and Pinter as well as to an increasing interest in the political theatre of Brecht.[2] *Red Cross*, for example, combines an absurdist situation with elegant monologues on skiing, swimming, and drowning that seem to play out an associative logic that relates to Jerry's diatribe in Albee's *The Zoo Story*. A freedom to abandon the literal and play with an associative logic informed the *avant-garde* of the 1960s, and this emphasis upon the atemporal and the disjunctive allowed Shepard to speak in an original voice within a dramatic structure that allowed idiosyncratic improvisations. In the early 1970s, *The Tooth of Crime* appropriated the phenomenon of rock music in a curious balance of freedom and restraint. In a recent article in *The Journal of American Drama and Theatre*, Robert Baker-White deals with Shepard's assimilation of a phenomenon of popular culture in his use of rock music, an aesthetic form that offered him an apparent freedom and, simultaneously, constrained him within a certain structure and an ideology. Baker-White writes: 'The rock movement created a community with its own rules and authorities, its own taboos, and its own exclusive sense of truth. This is the paradox of self-contradiction that *The Tooth of Crime* presents . . . *Tooth*'s effect as a piece of *avant-garde* theatre is . . . self-contradictory. The play demonstrates how rock's energy of liberation is inextricably tied to a parallel energy of restraint'.[3] With *Buried Child* in the late seventies, Shepard took up another highly conventionalised aesthetic form – dramatic realism – and reconfigured its typical structure to accommodate the more open, fluid conventions of his writing. While *Curse of the Starving Class* (1978), *Buried Child* (1978), and *True West* (1980) break with Shepard's earlier dramatic writing by implementing several of the conventions of dramatic realism, these plays allow the playwright's singular voice to speak. I would contend that this shift forms another 'appropriation': Shepard's borrowing of the conventions of dramatic realism, theatrical schemes which, by this point, were also 'popular' although decidedly not ideologically radical.

Buried Child, in particular, makes use of the retrospective structure that we find operative in realistic plays since Ibsen. Shepard's exploitation of this organisational strategy produces a sophisticated variant of a theatrical scheme that both exercises convention and undercuts it with irony. Of course, as early as Ibsen's first realistic plays, the practice of combining a retrospective structure with the materialist scene of realism produced its own problematic. These texts initiated the demand for the physical realisation of theatrical images of space that presented three dimensional, unique replicas of middle-class rooms, filled with real objects and furniture, theatrical spaces that displaced the two-dimensional painted representations of typical sites used in the repertory of most theatres. Writing a text for a specifically detailed location, which would be constructed for an individual performance, imposed significant temporal demands on the action represented. The realistic dramas of Ibsen, Strindberg, Hauptmann and Chekhov focused, ostensibly, upon the kind of mundane domestic and social transactions that would take place in the ordinary domestic, middle-class rooms the stage appeared to replicate. This spatial and temporal limitation conflicted with the nineteenth century fascination with causality and a scientific model that demanded that the realistic drama present a complex and yet plausible explication of determination and consequence working through time. The exploration of biological, psychological, social, economic and political cause required a narrative, dramatised or embedded, that would be sufficiently extended to display the processes in which the network of these teleologies operates. Consequently, within the brief period of time that could be played out plausibly within these mundane spaces, the dialogue had to reveal the impact of the past upon the present. Consequently, the revelation of the past, which has presence only as the material of language, became the actual stuff of dialogue.

To make the required narrative recitation dramatically active as dialogue, conversation must reveal information that has been previously suppressed in a revelation that irredeemably alters the present circumstance. The plays of both Ibsen and Chekhov fulfill this demand in structures in which the precarious balance of a domestic group is destabilised by the intrusion of an external agent or agents. In *The Three Sisters* and *The Cherry Orchard*, that intrusion results in the underclass agent taking control of the space. In Ibsen, the appearances of Gregers in *The Wild Duck*, Hilde in *The Master Builder*, and Ella Rentheim in *John Gabriel Borkman* stimulate the revelation of the past. The presence of the outsider naturalises the discussion of the past, both by presenting a figure who questions those who inhabit the space and by the newcomer's own revelation of knowledge that the inhabitants do not possess. In *Buried Child* the arrival of Vince with his girlfriend, Shelly, forces the dialogue to confront the past, despite the energy with which the grandparents, his father and uncle expend to suppress it. The presence of the grandson, as intruder and external agent, not only provides the catalyst that provokes Tilden to exhume the corpse of the child; Vince's arrival results in the transfer of power from the inhabitants to the visitor. Here we have a conflation of structural conventions from modern realism: the *kindermord*, the embedding of the past in the dialogue, and the dispossession of the characters from the space represented.

In *Buried Child* the dialogic exposition skilfully reveals the coordinates that everyone agrees upon: the relationship of Halie and Dodge, the death of the third brother, the difference between the aggressive Bradley and the strangely passive Tilden, and Tilden's 'trouble' in Arizona that has brought him home after his imprisonment. What is not revealed are the actual circumstances of Ansel's death during the war; nor the reason why Tilden was put in jail and has become almost inarticulate; nor the identity of Vince's mother;

nor the reason why the grandson left this home six years earlier.
The statements that prefigure the visual image of the child's corpse
are terse and undeveloped, in dialogue that alternates assertion and
suppression. Consider the operation of that pattern at the point at
which Shelly confronts Tilden, trying to force him to recognise Vince
as his son.

> TILDEN: I had a son once but we buried him.
> (DODGE *quickly looks at* TILDEN. SHELLY *looks to* VINCE.)
> DODGE: You shut up about that! You don't know anything
> about that!
>
> (92)

Later, again with Shelly, Tilden provides more details: 'We had a
baby. (*motioning to* DODGE) He did. Dodge did. Could pick it up
with one hand. Put it in the other. Little baby. Dodge killed it'
(103). Here Shelly attempts to suppress the narrative, but Tilden
continues to mark, without elaboration, the circumstances of the
infant's disappearance, the search, the speculation about the child's
fate, and the fact that Dodge drowned it and buried the body at
some location unknown to anyone else.

This revelation correlates with Dodge's narrative, also directed to
Shelly:

> . . . we were a well-established family once. Well established. All
> the boys were grown. The farm was producing enough milk to
> fill Lake Michigan twice over. Me and Halie here were pointed
> toward what looked like the middle part of our life. Everything
> was settled with us. All we had to do was ride it out. Then
> Halie got pregnant again. Outa' the middle a' nowhere she got
> pregnant. We weren't planning on havin' any more boys. We had
> enough boys already. In fact, we hadn't been sleepin' in the same
> bed for about six years. (123)

Here Halie and Bradley attempt to suppress the information Dodge
discloses. He continues to detail the unattended birth, unlike the
birth of the boys he had fathered. He notes the unsuccessful pretence
that he was the father: ' . . . everyone around us knew. Everyone.
All our boys knew. Tilden knew' (124). He rationalises the infanticide as an attempt to exorcise a transgression that despoiled the

family: 'It made everything we'd accomplished look like nothin'. Everything was canceled out by this one mistake. This one weakness' (124).

Consider the conventionality in modern realism of the process in which a hidden or suppressed sexual transgression comes to the surface: Captain Alving's lascivious behaviour, and his fathering of Regine; Ranevskaya's sexual behaviour; Trigorin's seduction of Nina and the death of their child; Willy Loman's sexual adventures on the road; Blanche Dubois' promiscuity; Jimmy Porter's relationship with Helena; Martha's hostile sexuality. While *Buried Child* borrows this phenomenon of the hidden sexual transgression revealing itself, Shepard's dialogue refuses to expose unequivocally the precise coordinates of that event in the past. The play relates to the theatrical practices of its own moment by using the visual exposition of the infant's remains rather than resolving the earlier provocative textual references in a verbal narrative that would resolve and close off the image of a family history. In that sense, *Buried Child* extends or amplifies the tendency in modern realism to close the action with a shocking event – Hedvig's suicide, Treplev's suicide, or Hedda's suicide – that is only briefly mediated in the segment of dialogue that follows its enactment. In this text, Shepard replaces that brief dialogic processing with the juxtaposition of the visual image of Tilden and the infant's corpse, with Halie's ironically unrelated and sentimental celebratory monologue. The disjunction of the visual and the verbal amplifies the problematic nature of the resolution of most realist dramas, the arbitrariness and artifice of their closure.

Reading Ibsen's plays as a sequence clarifies the presence of a persistent alignment among the imaginary figures of a male: an erotic female that he denies, renounces, or sacrifices for a vocational project (ideological, conceptual, narrative, or artistic); a female whose absence of eroticism defines the hero's present alienation from physical sexuality; the failure of the vocational project; and the return of the erotic female or a substitute who offers a promise of renewed sexuality that the hero denies as he involves her in a suicidal movement that disguises itself as a marriage. The initial renunciation of the erotic female, demanded by the vocational or creative project, often aligns with a literal or metaphoric *kindermord*: the deaths of Alf in *Brand*, Solness's and Aline's infant twin sons in *The Master Builder*, Eyolf in *Little Eyolf*, the statue, 'the Resurrection' in *When We Dead Awaken*. These deaths signal the male's inability to negotiate the relationship between sexuality and his own sense of identity. When we discuss, direct, or enact Ibsen's 'characters', we need to confront the fact that while the individual text may suggest discrete conscious or unconscious motives for their behaviour, these figures perform the dynamic transformations and substitutions that this sexual triad acts out from *Catiline* in 1849 to *When We Dead Awaken* in 1899. The specific theatrical modes in which Ibsen worked, from the historical through the nationalistic dramas, from the great trio of non-theatrical dramas, through the realistic sequence to the more open forms of the last phase – all serve in turn as the means of representing an idiosyncratic, subjective, sexually-based relational structure. In other words, while realism's ideological need to articulate determining teleologies forced the dialogue into a retrospective structure, the relational dynamic among the fundamental sexual triad remained stable or, to speak more precisely, remained caught within its basic instability. The materialist detail of realism, which infuses Ibsen's dramatic figures with both conscious and unconscious motives, services the representation of Ibsen's sexual triad more than this triad serves the programme of realism. That is, the erotic triangle does not constitute a constellation of relationships that the playwright discovers and then represents as a phenomenon of nature and culture; but, rather, this persistent paradigm stands prior to the materialist details which Ibsen figured in his realistic writing. The consistent presence of the Ibsenian sexual triad through his fifty years of playwriting suggests the continuity of an obsessively demanding psychic paradigm. This idiosyncratic structure, working with the aesthetic and ideological demands of emerging realism produced the particular retrospective form that playwrights continue to find useful. Ibsen was forced to make dialogue narrative in order to embody the complex history of the shifts and substitutions of his basic triad within the temporal restraints of the realistic scene. The process of revising the image of the past with the revelation of long-suppressed details becomes, after Ibsen, one of the primary conventions of dramatic realism itself.

Even in the radical diffusion of characters in Eugene O'Neill's *The Iceman Cometh*, the dialogue reifies both the distant and immediate past and works progressively in stages of anticipation and deferral toward Hickey's extended narrative of the murder of Evelyn. As well, the significant event of Larry's suicide, obliquely represented, forms an action contrapuntal to Parritt's narrative confession of his betrayal of his mother. The present of *Long Day's Journey into Night* takes the form of the interactive retrospection of its four principal dramatic figures. Arthur Miller, also, works within realism's convention of narrative revelation; and both *All My Sons* and *Death of a Salesman* organise themselves around the phenomenon of the revelation of a revised past whose coordinates destroy the residual family structure. Williams's *The Glass Menagerie* assumes the form of a failed exorcism of the past, and the narrative revelation of *A Streetcar Named Desire* exposes the dynamics of the present. Blanche's recitation of her discovery of her young husband, a poet, with his male lover and the related story of his suicide inserts a trauma from the past that, in part, works to explain or make plausible her 'psychological' and 'moral' disintegration. The ideologies that impact the history of dramatic realism tend to blind us to the artifice of the strategies in which the past comes to the spectator's attention in these plays. The very persistence of the retrospective structure in modern realism reveals its conventionality and its usefulness in naturalising the dynamics of the relationships presented. The ideological demand to relate the present to the material and psychological conditions of the past pervades the narrative and forces us to see the represented present as the consequence of a network of those natural and cultural teleologies in which the late nineteenth century figured 'reality'.

Shepard's pseudo-realistic texts focus, with theatrical energy, on the relationship of fathers and sons; and the plays dramatise incidents in which a son negotiates the re-enactment of his father's identity in his own persona. This emphasis requires some form of retrospection in order to generate an image of the father against which the son or sons operate. *Buried Child* poses a triangular relationship between two sons and the father, disturbs that triad with the intrusion of the grandson and then, in the subsequent revelation, merges the son, Tilden, with the father, in the son's possible Oedipal usurpation of the father's sexual role with the mother.

This narrative of the past, the brief story in which Tilden, for a time, displaces his father as the sexual partner of his mother and takes on the role of father to the unnamed son, diminishes the authority of the patriarch. But the text removes Tilden from the role of father in a different sense. When Vince returns in the third act, he reports on his attempt to drive away, to escape from his failed reunion with his family. In a lyric passage, he details the reflection of his face in the rain-streaked windshield of his car:

I could see myself in the windshield. My face. My eyes. I studied
my face. Studied everything about it. As though I was looking at
another man. As though I could see his whole race behind him.
Like a mummy's face. I saw him dead and alive at the same time.
In the same breath. In the windshield, I watched him breathe as
though he was frozen in time. And every breath marked him.
Marked him forever without him knowing. And then his face
changed. His face become his father's face. Same bones. Same
eyes. Same nose. Same breath. And his father's face changed
to his Grandfather's face. And it went on like that. Changing.
Clear on back to faces I'd never seen before but still recognized.
Still recognized the bones underneath. The eyes. The breath. The
mouth. (130)

Here Shepard exploits his personal convention of the bizarre solilo-
quy and the narrative representation of the father/son relation that
fuses past and present in disjunctive illogicality. Vince's effort to
metamorphose into the figure of the Grandfather conflates the
'transformation' technique of the early plays with the familial
dynamic of the pseudo-realistic trilogy. Notice the capitalization
in the passage quoted immediately above, with 'his father' in lower
case and 'his Grandfather' capitalised.

The permutations of convention in this play also force strange
transformations in the figure of Tilden as Vince's father. Tilden's
mental incapacity, manifested most clearly in his apparent inability
to recognise and accept Vince as his son, contributes to the instability that stimulates Vince to restructure the domestic environment
and by-pass his father as he assumes the role of the patriarch
himself. At the end of the play, Vince claims ownership of the
house.

The *characterisation* of Tilden also works to diminish the power of
the image of the father – creating an absence that operates as a variant of the absent or waning authority of fathers as conventional figures in modern realism. The diminishing value attached to the theatrical presence of Tilden as Vince's father allows Shepard to establish
a more resonant presence, with the image of Tilden as the possible
father of his mother's child, the father of the child whose exhumed
corpse he carries toward her as the play ends. Shepard, with a
high degree of self-consciousness, I suggest, offers an image of
the son/father/husband that presents Tilden as a modern Oedipus,
rendered intellectually impotent in his incestuous domestic drama.

Curse of the Starving Class displays its schematic organisation by dividing up most of its text among four principal family member/speakers in a artificially symmetrical scheme – Weston/Wesley; Ella/Emma. This contrived conflation of names suggests, early in the play, that the text relates the younger figures to the older; and, as the play progresses, we see certain ways in which the children replicate or substitute for their parents. In general, *Curse* voices and reiterates a process in which self-identification takes the form of assuming aspects of the identity of another. The text also voices resistance to that process. The language suggests that the assimilation of the physical traits or behaviour of the older by the younger is either an inevitable or natural process of inheritance, a logical transfer of some substance from one person to another: the physical image of the father reproduced in the body of the son, the poison of the father inherited by the son, the curse of menstrual blood inherited by the daughter.

Curse of the Starving Class brings the problematic father to the foreground even though, at one provocative moment, the mother works with the idea of her son as the replication of her father rather than her husband in a moment that relates to the son/grandfather connection of *Buried Child*. The text demands that the actor playing Wesley urinate on the charts that the character, Emma, has prepared for an oral presentation, revealing his penis to the audience, in an exhibitionistic gesture the stage directions place 'downstage'. While this act also clarifies the hostility of the relationships among the family structure, the incident functions primarily to display the son's circumcised penis that Ella will soon identify as identical to that of her father. Here she focuses upon her dream of Wesley as the replica of her father:

> Why aren't you sensitive like your Grandfather was? I always thought you were just like him, but you're not are you? . . . Why aren't you? You're circumcised just like him. It's almost identical in fact. (143–44)[4]

This statement implies that the father, Weston, is not circumcised, and this indirect suggestion works to undermine or complicate the several processes in which Wesley attempts to present himself as the replica of his father.

Weston narrates a significant action in which he removes his clothing, refreshes or purifies himself in a cleansing bath, and walks

naked through his house in a deliberate celebration of his reconsti-
tuted identity. In Wesley's attempt to incorporate the identity of his
father, he acts out what Weston only tells us about. That is, the text
of this play presents the father's action in the less 'present' form of
narration and demands that the son enact the sequence, in a scene
that displays his body to the audience. Consequently, the imitation
has more theatrical substance – both in its dramatised presence and
exhibitionist quality than the original narration that exists only as
speech.

The language of the play – and its visual display of the narrative
field, the space in which the story plays itself out – works both to
incorporate the presence of the father and to dislocate that image.
The play opens with the son's narrative recitation of the destructive
arrival and abrupt departure of the father as an event in the immediate past; the text clarifies that the father's presence is periodic rather
than continuous; and the text removes his ownership of the land
and distances him as the sexual partner of his wife, replacing him
with a surrogate lover. Wesley's actions attempt to appropriate and
displace the presence of the father and in this assimilation to lose his
own identity.

Shepard's problematising of the father figure is conventional. In
all of Chekhov's major works, the father's absence contributes to
the deteriorating state of the immediate environment: for example,
in *The Cherry Orchard*, the death of Ranesvskaya's husband, the man
whom she married from outside her class, allows the transgressive
behaviour that accelerates the decline of the estate and its purchase
by the former peasant, Lopahin. Nora's independence is drained by
her father's behaviour toward her in Ibsen's *A Doll's House*; and in
Rosmersholm, Rebekka's recognition that Dr. West, the mentor with
whom she had a sexual relationship, was actually her natural father,
disallows her relationship with Rosmer. The problematic father
becomes a staple of American realism as evidenced by *Long Day's
Journey, All My Sons, Death of a Salesman*, and *The Glass Menagerie*.
We even see this figure in *Who's Afraid of Virginia Woolf?* in the
representation of the illusory father's weakness. The patriarchs of
Shepard's trilogy continue to play out this convention.

In more obvious instances of self-consciousness, *Curse of the
Starving Class* displays an overt symbolism that extends the kind
of metaphoric use of scene and objects that characterises the texts
of Ibsen and Chekhov. First of all, the centrality of the refrigerator
to which the inhabitants of this house go again and again, seeking

nourishment that will abate their appetite, gives this object, in repeated use, a kind of inconographic value. The refrigerator is both a failing source of nourishment and the repository for the inadequate nourishment the parents provide for themselves and their children. The function of this rather banal and obvious symbol is not as significant to this discussion as the blatancy of its use. The lamb provides a more typical symbolic use of a material object. Here the performed text presents a familiar symbol of Judeo-Christian theology: the Pascal lamb sacrificed in the Passover as a substitute for the firstborn son, as that figure is articulated by the Hebrew Bible and transformed in the New Testament into the image of the Christ himself, the lamb or son of God, sacrificed to atone for the sins of all mankind. The complex conflation of lamb, firstborn son, and the symbolic sacrifice of Isaac, which is reified in the Christian passion and the relationship between human father and son and Divine Father and Son – all these resonances amplify the living stage property of the maggot-infested lamb that Wesley nurtures and eventually sacrifices as he acts out his imitation of his father. These images also inform Weston's monologue in which he describes the fight between the tom cat and eagle that takes place while he castrates sheep. For our purposes, the mythic signficance isn't as important as the ways in which the text operates to incorporate this material, to formulate a self-conscious image of the self as a son who is the victim of the dominating presence or residual authority or constraining identity of the father. Ella assists Wesley in that project as she prompts him to re-tell his father's story of the self-destructive hostility of eagle and cat that in combat and death merge into each other to form 'one whole thing'. The unity here, of course, is the merging of mutually self-destructive acts, a unity that does not provide a figure that successfully integrates the various elements of *Curse* into cohesive narrative structure. That refusal to spell out a coherence extends the inconclusive resolution of modern realism – typified in *Ghosts'* refusal to reveal whether Fru Alving gives the fatal sedative to Oswald in the immediate future. The problematic nature of this story's assertion of wholeness, in combination with the theatrical shock of the explosion that denotes the destruction of the Packard and the apparent death of the young girl, aligns with the final shocking images that terminate many of the texts of modern realism: Treplev's suicide, Hedda's suicide, Julie's murder/suicide, the figure of the bound Captain in *The Father*.

Shepard's text merges images that are, clearly, highly resonant cultural artifacts, with the conventional representation of problematic sons who are caught within the coordinates of a role determined by their father's identity. Shifting among the conventional schemes of modern realism and the self-conscious invocation of mythical parallels, *Curse of the Starving Class* attempts to identify the father as both castrator and wastrel and tries to identify the son as both inadequate substitute for the father, and as the failed redeemer of familial guilt through his performance of a ritual sacrifice. In an ambiguous transfer of sexual roles, the menstruating young woman enacts her father's prodigality, and in being blown-up in his Packard, wired to murder him, becomes his surrogate.

True West removes the figure of the father completely except for the ways in which his character is embodied in the language and interaction of the antithetical sons. As a presence in the embedded narrative, however, the father of *True West* becomes a signficant figure, a physically and mentally disabled man in deliberate self-exile, pursuing his self-sufficient but self-destructive course. Here *True West* exercises a structural convention that is a particularly American variant of dramatic realism: the opposition of two brothers caught in a triangular relationship with a father. Consider, for example, the competitive brothers in O'Neill's *Beyond the Horizon* who, like Austin and Lee, exchange roles; the sequence of paired brothers in the plays of Arthur Miller; the ambivalent affection and hostility that marks the relationship of Jamie and Edmund in *Long Day's Journey into Night*. In *True West* the convention provides a structure in which the playwright may display the negotiation that takes place between the brothers as they attempt to define themselves through their difference or likeness to the absent and problematic father.

Shepard conflates the paradigmatic relationship of brothers with the convention of the external figure who invades the scene and attempts to dispossess the inhabitant(s). Here that space gains resonance because its comforting, if banal, dimensions belong to the mother. However, the psychic territory over which these men do battle focuses more upon the father than the mother. Lee, apparently less connected to the 'real' world than his educated brother, acts out a role that, in itself, seems to enact his father's failed western mythology. Ironically, Austin himself trades upon a more self-conscious fictionalising; and, to compound the irony, Lee is able to market his mythologising more successfully than Austin in the negotiation with Saul Kimmer, the Hollywood producer –

although he depends upon Austin's mediation of plot/myth into scenario/text. In *True West* the embedded narrative includes the ostensible biographies of its principals, the Ivy League university student opposed to the nomad – but the primary embedded narrative becomes the scenario of Lee's western drama, the compressed text-within-the-text.[5]

In summary, I would describe this group of three related texts as a theatrical attempt to articulate the processes of exorcising the presence of the father, and assimilating his energy by appropriating self-consciously both the aesthetic conventions of realism, and the archetypal paradigms in which we perceive the relationships of father and son. One of the difficulties of reading dramatic texts with the perspectives of psychoanalytic theory is the difficulty in separating the archetypal from the conventional. Reading the Ibsen canon, with the insistent repetition of the sexual triad that remains constant throughout its variety of theatrical modes, it is possible to see the ways in which theatrical convention serves an idiosyncratic and obsessive central drama. The combination of Ibsen's idiosyncrasy and the materialist demand for contemporary detail forged many of the conventions that shape the realist project. Shepard both uses those conventions and ironically foregrounds their artifice in a curious explication of familial relationships that seem to me, at this point, more conventional than archetypal, more self-conscious than unconscious, more public than private, more aesthetic than psychological, more theatrical than autobiographical.

Notes

1. Sam Shepard, *Seven Plays* (New York: Bantam, 1981) p. 132. All quotations are from this edition; page numbers are given in the text. This includes: *Buried Child, Curse of the Starving Class, True West*, as well as other plays.
2. In his introduction to *Seven Plays*, Richard Gilman discusses the influence of the 'transformation' exercises of the Open Theatre upon Shepard's playwriting. These improvisatory games, in which the actors shifted, without transition, from one character and situation to another, were themselves informed with the arbitrariness and shifting nature of *character* in absurdist drama.
3. Robert Baker-White, 'Rock/Poetry: Popular Theatricality in *The Tooth of Crime*', *The Journal of American Drama and Theatre*, 2 (Winter 1990), 69.
4. Note the continuation from *Buried Child* of the practice of referring to 'father' in lower case and the capitalization of Grandfather.

5.   It would be interesting to mark out the similarities between the ways
        in which *True West* uses the 'fiction' narrated by its characters (recall
        that Austin reads out Lee's dictation) and Pirandello's use of recited
        and dramatised narrative in *Six characters in search of an author*. In
        both plays, the fiction, gradually spelled out in the performance,
        substitutes for the past in the conventional retrospective structure.
        In both texts, this variation both exploits and ironically displaces the
        conventional structure of realistic drama.

8

A Kind of Cavorting: Superpresence and Shepard's Family Dramas

David J. DeRose

During the 1970s and for most of the 80s, theatre scholars writing about Sam Shepard tended to agree on only two issues. One, that Shepard is one of the most talented and important playwrights of his generation; and two, that nobody had yet to arrive at a critical vocabulary to adequately discuss his work. Regarding the second of these points, Bonnie Marranca stated bluntly in 1981 that Shepard is 'not an easy writer to write about'.[1] In 1981, Christopher Bigsby put the case a little more eloquently, proposing that Shepard's work is 'simply not susceptible of analysis in conventional terms'.[2] Richard Gilman and Ron Mottram each added their two cents, respectively classifying Shepard scholarship as 'extremely limited' in its 'ready-made vocabulary'[3] and plagued by a 'common confusion'.[4] Yet, while each of these scholars offered their own thoughts and observations on past Shepard scholarship, no cohesive sense of his work nor any common vocabulary developed. The critics 'agreed to disagree' as it were.

Perhaps it is too obvious to say that Shepard's plays have defied reduction to any single critical vocabulary because, at any given point in his career, his work has been so full of contradictory agendas and changing dramatic strategies as to perpetually make any attempt to define it immediately obsolete in light of his next play. Shepard, in short, has been consistently inconsistent in dramatic technique, theatrical style, and thematic concerns. Critics, thus, have occupied themselves by keeping abreast of Shepard's latest theatrical innovations and shifting agendas.

131

But in the 1980s, almost as if to accommodate scholarly criticism, Shepard brought an end to his theatrical innovation. His once-rampant productivity slowed, and then came to a complete halt (temporary, one assumes) after *A Lie of the Mind* in 1985. In the void left by the lack of new work, and in the absence of performance reviews concentrating on the evolving theatrical style of each new Shepard play, Shepard's work has drawn increasing attention from literary rather than performance scholars, who have applied a multitude of theoretical vocabularies to Shepard's already existing plays. While this trend has raised Shepard scholarship to a level of sophistication seldom seen before, it has also very nearly brought an end to any discussion of Shepard's work as a theatrical event (i.e., in performance or as an evolving entity). In short, the field observer has been replaced by the lab technician, and the living, breathing theatrical event has been dosed in theoretical formaldehyde and prepared for literary vivisection.

One critical vocabulary which is increasingly applied to Shepard's work (as this volume demonstrates), and which *is* equipped to consider Shepard in performance, is that of 'postmodernism'. This vocabulary, especially as it has grown out of the disciplines of art theory and architecture, displays a vital capacity for discussing the co-existence of the scripted reality of the text and the physical reality of the performance, and thus for discussing the playscript as a performance text as well as a literary one. And yet, there is no little irony in the fact that a critical vocabulary as vague and self-contradictory as that of postmodernism is being applied to the equally vague and self-contradictory agendas and strategies of Sam Shepard as theatre artist and dramatist.

In the preface to *The Anti-Aesthetic: Essays on Postmodern Culture*, Hal Foster acknowledges the confusing mass of critical and creative voices speaking in the name of postmodernism. He sees the public perception and critical application of the term as characterized by a basic opposition between two contradictory interpretations of the term.

In cultural politics today [1983], a basic opposition exists between a postmodernism which seeks to deconstruct modernism and resist the status quo and a postmodernism which repudiates the former to celebrate the latter: a postmodernism of resistance and a postmodernism of reaction.[5]

Whereas Foster's 'resistant postmodernism' is concerned with the 'critical deconstruction of tradition' as begun by modernist artists, the contradictory concept of a retrograde strain of 'reactive postmodernism' promotes a 'return to the verities of tradition'.[6] So, postmodernism – at least as applied to the arts, both fine and popular – is seen by some as a step beyond modernism, while to others it is a rejection of the modern: a return to time-honoured pre-modern traditions.

Anyone familiar with Shepard's drama can see how applicable both of these definitions of postmodernism, however contradictory, are to his work. Plays like *Operation Sidewinder*, *The Unseen Hand*, and *The Tooth of Crime*, take place in a pop culture landscape littered with discontinuous cultural narratives and archetypes, expressed in floating ideolects, and peopled with the shadowy simulacra of fragmented characters. Yet while the cultural landscape within which Shepard's characters roam may reflect the 'postmodern condition',[7] his emotional attachment to the master narratives of an old 'true' West and the myth of a once-great America is not. Shepard's pastiche presentation of pop-historical relics is a reactive or retrograde celebration of the traditional, and a lament at its loss. In *The Tooth of Crime*, Shepard can both bring to life a cold postmodern predator like the selfless Crow, and at the same time lament the loss of the pop culture traditionalist Hoss. That retrograde lament is accompanied in Shepard's most recent writing by a regressive turn toward increasingly conventional dramatic forms and themes in the shape of family dramas.

As we move further away in time and artistic disposition from 1978 when Sam Shepard stunned the American theatrical community with *Curse of the Starving Class* and *Buried Child*, the manner in which those plays are viewed and performed becomes less and less connected to Shepard's theatrical style at that point in his career. No wonder, since we now see them in light of Shepard's most conventionally domestic work ever, *A Lie of the Mind*, not to mention his equally domesticated debut as a film director with *Far North*. What time and shifting perspective have diminished in our view of these important plays is the struggle between Shepard's potentially contradictory agendas as an avant-garde theatre artist – interested, not in plot, but in expressing a heightened state of consciousness – and as a fledgling domestic dramatist – attempting for the first time to create sustained realistic characters and a conventional dramatic action. On the one hand, *Curse of the Starving Class* and *Buried Child* indicate a new (though less innovative) direction in Shepard's work: a suddenly humanistic interest in the domestic landscape of the declining American family. On the other hand, these two plays, as well as the later *True West* (1980) and *Fool for Love* (1983), still bear the unmistakable theatrical stamp of the avant-gardist who was writing the rather surreal *Angel City* (1976), *Suicide in B♭* (1976), and *Seduced* (1978) at roughly the same time.

Shepard's family plays might rightfully be labelled postmodern in the retrograde sense that they are, cumulatively, a progression away from the theatrical innovations of his earlier, more experimental work. Shepard himself has added fuel to the fire of those who would classify his family plays as retrograde by attempting to devalue the work he did during his early period. In interviews, Shepard has dismissed his early plays and his avant-garde theatrical techniques as a 'kind of cavorting'.[8] He does not dismiss the family plays outright, but he does reject 'anything about them that smacks of the "old" Shepard', citing examples of non-representational staging from *Curse of the Starving Class*, *Buried Child*, and *Fool for Love* as sources of embarrassment.[9]

And yet, the very fact that Shepard feels obliged to reject anything of this 'old' artistic self in his family plays proves the existence of elements in those plays which share the aesthetic of Shepard's more experimental work. In particular, Shepard now appears uncomfortable with the sense of a heightened stage presence, or 'superpresence', which is so characteristic of his early work, and which, when integrated into his family plays, led one critic to call for the coining of 'a word like "nova-realism" to describe the style into which Shepard's plays have settled'.[10] This theatrical superpresence, which, as we shall discuss, reflects a resistant, not retrograde postmodernism, originally grew out of Shepard's desire to theatrically manifest altered or heightened states of perception on the stage. As Robert Corrigan noted in discussing Shepard's modernist fore-bears, the European avant-garde, such works are not interested in presenting a dramatic action, but in 'dramatizing a condition' by physically manifesting the qualities of that condition on stage.[11] Shepard himself said in 1977, 'I've always been interested in various states of consciousness . . . . Many of my plays centre around a character in a critical state of consciousness'.[12] Out of this critical state of consciousness came the sense of a heightened reality which Shepard now sees as 'cavorting', but which has been the lifeblood of his innovation as a theatre artist.

The consciousness which dominates Shepard's work – a consciousness which Shepard once attributed to his choice of drug, crystal Methadrine[13] – has been labelled as absurdist, hallucinatory, even paranoid. But Shepard's particularly heightened, sensory-specific theatricality, with its lack of temporal continuity and its intensified focus on physical reality and on the immediate present, more closely resembles what Fredric Jameson labels (in a descriptive, not diagnostic manner) as the schizophrenic qualities of the postmodern condition.[14] Jameson's description of postmodern consciousness, with its lack of a persistent reality or self and its sense of a 'perpetual present', might well be a review of one of Shepard's early plays:

> [A]s temporal continuities break down, the experience of the present becomes powerfully, overwhelmingly vivid and 'material': the world comes before the schizophrenic with heightened intensity, bearing a mysterious and oppressive charge of affect, glowing with hallucinatory energy. But what might for us seem a desirable experience - an increase in our perceptions, a libidinal or hallucinogenic intensification of our normally humdrum and familiar surroundings – is here felt as loss, as 'unreality'.[15]

Shepard's work repeatedly addresses the disorientation of the self in an environment which does not sustain the self's created vision of reality. The result is that reality fragments into a sequence of seemingly unlinked events and images (signifiers), and that these signifiers are experienced with heightened intensity. In early plays such as *Cowboys* (1964) and *Dog* (1965), it was Shepard the farm boy whose sense of continuous self and of reality were threatened when confronted with the alien sights and experiences of New York City. In *La Turista* (1967), *Blue Bitch* (1973) and *Geography of a Horse Dreamer* (1974), it was Shepard as the American abroad whose senses were overwhelmed when faced with the mysterious unreality of foreign lands and cultures. When dealing with the disintegration of the family in the face of a rapidly-changing American landscape, Shepard adapts his schizophrenic vision by juxtaposing the 'superpresence' of the early plays – the immediate material presence of actors, objects, and discontinuous actions – to the 'humdrum and familiar' world of domestic family life. Shepard thus creates a 'resistant' strain of postmodern realism: a schizophrenic 'superrealism'.[16]

Ironically, Shepard's superreal family plays suggest almost immediately that he is unaware of the appropriateness of this innovative style of representation in terms of his vision of the dysfunctional family in postmodern America. And so, Shepard's use of the superreal shrinks and changes from the very moment he begins to write the family plays. With each successive play, he attempts to tame (with varying degrees of success) his own schizophrenic vision in favour of a conventional, linear stage reality. The plays are, thus, uneven in style, showing elements of both resistant and retrograde postmodernism.

From a purely narrative perspective, there is nothing in the least schizophrenic or unreal about *Curse of the Starving Class*. A rural Southern Californian family comes under increasing pressure from mounting poverty, suburban sprawl, and personal greed. The characterizations of the four family members are all richly drawn and relatively consistent. Their story is not wholly uncommon. The mother tries to sell the family farm out from under the drunken father's nose. The children, finding themselves at the crux of this battle, look for avenues of redemption or escape.

When *Curse of the Starving Class* first appeared in London in 1977, and then in New York the following year, critics and audiences did not know what to make of this domestic drama from the master of the surreal and the 'hipster fringe'. London reviewer Charles Marowitz asked 'Is this Shepard or Saroyan?',[17] and his New York colleague, Gerald Weales, felt the play contained 'a touch of William Inge'.[18] These comparisons to two of America's great working class naturalists give some indication of the play's ability to sustain itself based on the quality of its skilful characterisations and moving family themes. In fact, *Curse* has found increasingly greater commercial and public success through productions which have emphasised the play's human qualities and downplayed or entirely eliminated any unreal or incongruous elements of temporal continuity, characterisation, or setting.[19]

Curse of the Starving Class might be considered a more carefully 'crafted' play when compensation is made in production for the play's inconsistencies in style and for the disruptions of temporal and physical continuity. But, when such compensations are made, it is not the play Shepard wrote in 1977. While Marowitz's London review noted Shepard's Saroyanesque focus on the 'spiritual consequences of economic deprivation', he was also troubled by the play's 'obligatory fantasy-riff[s]'.[20] Weales was also quick to mention that Shepard was apparently 'uncomfortable' with realism.[21] *Curse*, as Shepard wrote it, and as it was originally produced in light of his earlier work, is a family portrait, but one painted by an avant-gardist, uncertain of his tools, and working well outside his usual medium. The result is a play of mixed style and intent: a duel between the strategies and techniques of Shepard the intuitive avant-gardist and Shepard the would-be American dramatist.

The most unsettling stylistic element of *Curse* in production as envisioned by Shepard is also the first thing one encounters either upon entering the theatre or reading the play in print: the minimalist stage setting. Shepard's scenic strategy in the works which immediately preceded *Curse* – i.e., *Action*, *Suicide in B♭*, and *Angel City* – had been to place only a few significant objects or set pieces in an otherwise empty black space. Most striking of all is the set for *Angel City*, ominous and empty except for an enormous black swivel chair at centre stage. The chair faces upstage, away from the audience and toward a large blue neon rectangle which is seemingly suspended in air.

In the stage directions from the plays of this period, Shepard is certain to emphasise the look he intends: *Angel City* has a 'Basically bare stage'; in *Action*, 'the upstage is in complete darkness'; for *Seduced*, 'the stage is basically bare and empty'; and in *Suicide in B♭*, 'These are the only objects on stage. The floor of the stage is not painted but left bare'. The scenic design for *Curse of the Starving Class* pursues this same stark aesthetic:

> *Upstage center is a very plain breakfast table with a red oilcloth covering it. Four mismatched metal chairs are set one at each side of the table. Suspended in midair to stage right and stage left are two ruffled, red-checked curtains, slightly faded. In the down left corner of the stage are a working refrigerator and a small gas stove . . .* (135)[22]

Like the neon rectangle in *Angel City*, the curtains are suspended in air. They suggest only the most token imposition of a realistic space against the black expanse of the stage. The space is thus purely theatrical, not representational of a 'real' kitchen, and as such it can be exceptionally unsettling.[23]

The sense of discomfort created by the tension between the imposed, fictional 'kitchen' and the presence of the theatrical space it inhabits is a reflection of one of the central thematic concerns of the play. *Curse of the Starving Class* is about violation and invasion:

about the all-too-sudden invasion of a once-rural farming community by sprawling suburban housing developments; about the poisonous violation of one's physical being by invisible biological 'curses' like genetic conditioning, microscopic germs, maggots, even menstruation; about the impersonal invasion of uncontrollable socio-economic forces into the family unit; and about the terrifying violation of a house at night by a drunken father who smashes down the front door, leaving home and family vulnerable to even further violation.

The fragments of kitchen furniture set against the stark, open stage are, in themselves, an image of the home (and the comforting reality 'home' traditionally signifies) violated. The play opens on a further image of such violation, for in the middle of the 'kitchen' the family's teenage son Wesley fills a wheelbarrow with the shattered remains of the door to the house. As does Shepard's wall-less scenic concept, this image of a wheelbarrow in the kitchen effectively negates any sense of 'interiority'. When Wesley's father, Weston, enters midway through the play to find a live lamb in his kitchen, he ponders aloud the lack of differentiation between interior and exterior.

> Is this the inside or the outside? This is inside, right? This is the inside of the house. Even with the door out it's still the inside. (*to lamb*) Right? (*to himself*) Right. (156)

The home has been broken open by the dissolution of the family and the estrangement of the father and mother. It cannot be repaired. Even when Wesley builds and hangs a new door in an act symbolic of his desire to keep the family intact, strangers walk straight onto the stage and into the 'home'.

The peculiar characterisation of those intrusive strangers is another superreal technique Shepard uses in juxtaposition to the seeming naturalism of the members of the family and the logical narrative of the play. In 1977, Charles Marowitz commented that 'these outside characters . . . waft on in a style peculiar to themselves with no reference to the ongoing, naturalistically pitched main situation'.[24] Similarly Gerald Weales, calling the family 'Saroyanesque', noted that 'In contrast, the thugs . . . were pure cartoon'.[25] The result of these other-worldly characters is that the audience feels it is watching the intersection of two contradictory planes of reality. And indeed this is so, for Shepard employs the heightened theatrical style of the slick criminal outsiders who enter this home to represent a world entirely foreign to the family. In socio-historical terms, they embody the sudden and unprecedented penetration of super-highways, shopping malls, and mass housing into the quiet rural areas surrounding the Los Angeles basin in the post-World War II era.[26] But in terms of the collective psyche of the play, they are the invasion of the self (here, the family) by a world so strange as to permanently unfix one's preconceptions of reality.

The creation of such disparately drawn characters, here used to create the traumatic experience of one plane of reality suddenly juxtaposed to another, is subtly adapted from a technique Shepard employed frequently in his earlier plays. In *Cowboys #2*, it was the business-suited men who invade the stage at the end of the play, reading from scripts in a monotone voice, repeating lines spoken earlier by the two young cowboy protagonists. In *Geography of a Horse Dreamer*, it was the wild cowboys who invade the urban hotel room where dandyish city gangsters have been holding their brother hostage. In *Forensic and the Navigators*, it was the futuristic exterminators who crash in upon two young men dressed like a cowboy and an Indian. Later, in *True West*, it will be the rather anaemic mother, who returns to her own kitchen only to find she is now a stranger in the violent landscape created by her sons.

In *Curse*, Wesley draws attention to the 'otherness' of these intrusive characters and to their significance within the thematic structure of the play when he describes the loss of his family's rural way of life as a 'zombie invasion'.

> It's a zombie invasion. Taylor is the head zombie. He's the scout for the other zombies. He's only a sign that more zombies are on their way. They'll be filing through the door pretty soon. (163)

Taylor, a slick real estate lawyer who helps the mother, Ella, sell the farm without her husband's signature, is the first 'zombie' to stroll unannounced into the kitchen. He is followed by a bar owner, a police officer, and two moronic thugs, Emerson and Slater. These unannounced entrances become increasingly bizarre and threatening, climaxing with the off-stage explosion of Weston's car as Emerson and Slater enter holding the slaughtered carcass of a lamb.[27]

While these superreal theatrical images are unquestionably outside of the stylistic circumference of the conventional family drama, in *Curse of the Starving Class* they nevertheless serve to theatrically reinforce Shepard's naturalistically-couched thematic focus on the dissolution of the home and the family. But *Curse of the Starving Class* is also full of disruptive and superreal images and actions which offer no support to Shepard's thematic concerns in the play. They are, rather, the left-over 'cavorting' of Shepard's schizophrenic aesthetic: still extremely powerful as stage images, but finally at odds with Shepard's new intentions as a family dramatist.

Curse of the Starving Class opens, for instance, with a string of typically Shepardesque non-sequiturs which do not build upon each other, but transform the stage reality into 'a series of perpetual presents'.[28] Wesley and his mother, Ella, discuss Weston's drunken appearance the night before. Wesley suddenly launches into an extended monologue – much like the sensory-specific incantatory monologues of Shepard's early work – recounting the previous night's events as he experienced them from his bed. Just as suddenly, he leaves the stage and Ella starts speaking to the empty space. She appears to be rehearsing the lecture she will give to some (unidentified) girl who is having her first menstrual period. Perhaps a minute into this lecture, Ella's adolescent daughter Emma enters. Ella *'talks as though she's just continuing her conversation'* (139). Emma responds, in turn, as though she has been present for the entire speech.

While it is easy to smooth over the unreal edges of these individual moments and create a linear through-line, as some directors have done, the sequence of events is far too bizarre, especially coming, as it does, at the very beginning of the play, to overlook. Some productions have blocked the mother-daughter scene as though Ella is aware of Emma's presence just off stage and well within earshot.[29] But Shepard's stage directions indicate no such assumption, stressing that Ella 'speaks alone' at the beginning of the speech and that Emma does not enter, nor is she heard off stage, until later (138–39). The casual and temporal reality of the scene is thus unfixed, and the sequence of events resembles Fredric Jameson's description of schizophrenic reality: 'an experience of isolated, disconnected, discontinuous material signifiers which fail to link into a coherent sequence'.[30]

But to what end? Neither Wesley's transfixing monologue, however beautifully crafted, nor Emma's dreamlike materialisation in the middle of her mother's discourse serve to reinforce any apparent dramatic or thematic intention on Shepard's part. Such schizophrenic images are without context in this play, and these discontinuous moments seem to exist for their own sake as unqualified material images. The same is true of Shepard's startling use of the unqualified physical presence of the actor playing Wesley.

Early in the play, the actor playing Wesley must, without warning or explanation, unzip his pants and urinate on Emma's 4-H club charts.[31] Later, he is required to walk naked onto the stage, again without warning, and scoop a live lamb into his arms, carrying it off. The purely physical reality of the actor – either exposing himself to urinate, or entering naked – linked to the unexpectedness and inexplicability of his actions, is so strong that the created illusion of his character and of the fictional stage reality are shattered. In Jameson's words, 'the experience of the present becomes powerfully, overwhelmingly vivid and "material"'.[32] Such physical nudity gives a heightened quality to the stage reality: there is no such thing as a naked 'character' on stage. When the actor sheds his clothing, he sheds the illusion of character, of acting, and brings a new level of physical immediacy to the stage. This effect is intensified by the presence of the live lamb. The unqualified superpresence of the animal – that is, its immediate physical presence without the created pretence of character or performance – is far more 'real' than the fictional reality of the play. The image of the naked actor scooping the live lamb into his arms and carrying it offstage transcends the realm of scripted reality in favour of the superreal.

Had these events occurred in just about any Shepard play previous to this one, they would have been equally shocking perhaps, but vital to and an integral part of Shepard's schizophrenic stage consciousness. However, in *Curse of the Starving Class*, Shepard is both telling a conventional story and introducing sustained characters and a narrative discourse into his writing. If he is 'dramatizing a condition', that condition is the thematically anchored state of invasion in which the characters find themselves. If these instances of heightened reality have any relation to that condition, it is only to intensify the physical and psychic discomfort expressed by the characters. More likely, though, is the possibility that Shepard, without thought to the impact he was having on his dramatic intentions, turned to a stage aesthetic which had been part of his highly intuitive *modus operandi* for over ten years.[33]

It can be argued that such disruptions of the stage reality and of characterisation should be seen as postmodern deconstructions, drawing attention to the fiction or simulation of the reality being presented on stage. But, these moments, rather than exposing an absence of authenticity behind that simulation, actually highlight the material (authentic) presence of the actor. This latter interpretation is far more in keeping with Shepard's position as a child of the 1960s. The great spectacles of the 60s are a celebration of 'presence' – children of Artaud: Happenings, Peter Brook, Open Theatre, Living Theatre, Performance Group, Grotowski – all celebrate the presence of the actor.[34] Thus, the naked actor and the live lamb are not signifiers which have lost their referent, but which have been freed of the burden of significance within the narrative.[35]

With each successive family drama, Shepard makes a greater conscious effort to subjugate his impulsive use of heightened reality in order to develop his new dramatic strategies and thematic concerns. In *Buried Child*, rather than disrupt the continuity of the stage reality, the superpresent – here taking the shape of fresh vegetables and threatening, physically grotesque characters – serves to intensify the physical and visual impact of moments of heightened symbolic significance within the text, especially strange rituals of domination.

Perhaps the only noteworthy subversion of the stage realism in *Buried Child* is in the set design.[36] Unlike *Curse of the Starving Class*, the domestic setting of *Buried Child* is, at first glance, perfectly representational: the living room of an old mid-West farmhouse, with stairs leading to the second floor, and a screened-in porch outside the front door. Yet both the porch and the stairs, as described by Shepard in his stage directions, and as realized in the first New York production, create peculiarly unrealistic effects.

> In *Buried Child* it is the abrupt staircase that seems to vanish into nothingness, and the further curious nothingness of a useless corridor [the porch] at the rear of the stage . . . Anyone entering or leaving must pass through a void . . . Provocative.[37]

The use of the stairs and the porch, however bizarre, is nevertheless integrated into the thematic concerns of the play, reinforcing the isolation experienced by the inhabitants of this house. The porch, for instance, becomes a passageway linking the ghostly happenings of the household, which has escaped the passage of time for thirty years, with a frightening and unpredictable world outside. At one point, the family patriarch Dodge screams to his son Tilden, 'Don't go outside. There's nothing out there . . . Everything's in here. Everything you need'.[38] Later, Tilden's son Vince threatens his girlfriend Shelly from the porch: 'don't come out here! I'm warning you! You'll disintegrate!' (128). In truth, it seems as though the entire family might risk disintegration if they wandered too far from the confines of this house, especially Dodge who has holed himself up inside the house for thirty years, hiding from the dead child buried in the yard and the consequences of that child's death.

In *True West*, the superreal is again manifest: this time in the guise of functional toasters, burning toast, menacing golf clubs, and a much-abused typewriter. But, here as in *Buried Child*, the superpresence of these objects does not unfix the fictional reality of the play; rather it becomes more of a comic distraction, grounding the far-fetched psychological transformations of the two brothers, Austin and Lee, in the concrete physical reality of their stage occupations. If we were not so busy laughing at the smoke billowing out of the toasters, or at the gutted remains of the typewriter as Lee takes another swing at it with his nine iron, we would be far more likely to pass critical judgement on Shepard's poorly motivated characterizations. Only in the final moment of *True West* does Shepard create an image which transcends the stage reality; and here, as in the ritualistic images which concluded the three acts in *Buried Child*, Shepard is using imagery more as a means of intensifying a highly symbolic moment than evoking a schizophrenic reality.

After a violent brawl in which it appears that Austin has strangled his brother Lee to death, Lee suddenly springs to his feet. The lights change as 'the two brothers square off to each other'.

> . . . *the figures of the brothers now appear to be caught in a vast desert-like landscape, they are very still but watchful for the next move, lights go slowly to black as the after-image of the brothers pulses in the dark . . .* [39]

The pulsing of the after-image, burned momentarily into the retina, suspends the image of the brothers in time and space, transporting it beyond the realistic realm of the play. It is a post-play (in the sense of post-hypnotic) suggestion in which the brothers are transformed into archetypal figures, fighting on against the backdrop of eternity.

As Ross Wetzsteon once wrote of the final moment of Shepard's *La Turista*, it was an image which 'dramatised the themes of the play far more precisely than could any words'.[40] That description certainly applies to the conclusion of *True West* as well.

Only in *Fool for Love* does Shepard successfully blend form and content by creating a theatrical spectacle of juxtaposed realities which embodies the play's thematic concerns over illusion and the subjectivity of experience. The irony of *Fool for Love*'s success is that Shepard came to this juxtaposition almost against his own will. Shepard has said in numerous interviews that he wrote as many as sixteen drafts of *Fool for Love* before he felt he had a play which remained true to the characters and the situation.[41] What Shepard does not mention in those interviews is that it was not until the final draft of the play that he introduced the spectral presence of The Old Man who watches the reunion of his incestuous off-spring from an alcove at the edge of the stage.[42] Until that draft, the play had been a straightforward romantic confrontation between the long-separated lovers, Eddie and May. That Shepard would write well over a dozen drafts of a naturalistic play, and then finally complete a satisfactory draft only after the inspired addition of The Old Man, suggests the power of Shepard's intuitive theatricality over his conscious attempts to write within the self-imposed restraints of psychological realism. The solution to Shepard's writing problem was not a psychological or dramatic one, but a theatrical one involving the presence of a character who suspends the play between dream and reality.

The struggle between Shepard's intuition and his conscious restraint can be further felt in the published text of *Fool for Love*. In that text, Shepard states that The Old Man *'exists only in the minds of* MAY *and* EDDIE'.[43] This rationalisation of The Old Man's presence would have been totally unnecessary for the 'old' Sam Shepard, who felt perfectly comfortable with intersecting planes of reality in *Suicide in B^b*. And in point of fact, when *Fool for Love* is performed live, there is no suggestion in the play itself that The Old Man is being imagined or dreamed by either Eddie or May. One feels, on several occasions, that he may well be dreaming them. As one reviewer noted:

> The Old Man and the pair of lovers exist on two different planes of reality: one exists only as a figment of the other's imagination. The underlying question of the play is: *whose* imagination?[44]

A large portion of the theatrical energy of *Fool for Love* in performance comes from the fact that it offers no answer to this
question. And yet Shepard felt obliged, when publishing the play,
to rationalize The Old Man's existence.

While many reviewers, including myself,[45] saw *Fool for Love* as
the final triumphant resurrection of the 'old' Shepard in a new and
glorious incarnation as an innovative family dramatist, the inclusion
of this single stage direction in the text of the play should have been
an obvious death knell. Shepard's next play (and to this date his
last) is the sadly conventional, tamely self-imitative *A Lie of the
Mind*. Often teamed with *Fool for Love*, this play has gathered a
great deal of critical attention, especially from feminist scholars
discussing issues of gender in these, the only two Shepard plays
to make any attempt at three-dimensional female characters.[46] But
discussions of Shepard as a theatrical innovator have dropped off
substantially since 1985 because with *A Lie of the Mind*, Shepard's
staging has lost all traces of its earlier schizophrenia. The superreal
vegetables of *Buried Child* and the live lamb of *Curse of the Starving
Class* are here replaced by an obviously fake deer carcass which is
flung about the stage. The juxtaposed realities of *Fool for Love* are
reduced to a simple split-location set.

The only evidence of a heightened consciousness in *A Lie of the
Mind* is introduced not theatrically, but thematically. One of the central characters of the play, Beth, is a battered wife who has sustained
brain damage. She suffers from aphasia and partial amnesia which
create a typically Shepardesque state of 'critical' consciousness.
Her partial loss of speech and memory become an opportunity
for perceptual rebirth as she recreates herself, her world, and the
language which gives meaning to that world, without the enforced
preconceptions of experience and education. But Shepard does not
theatricalize Beth's fragmented consciousness as he might have in
his earlier work; unlike Austin's world in *True West*, the world in
which Beth lives does not come unfixed as does her perception
of it.

The only theatrical manifestation of Beth's consciousness is an
ineffectual shift in the set. When the play begins, the primary acting
areas on stage are surrounded by black curtains and have no walls
or doors, only isolated pieces of furniture. The extremities of the set
are filled in only gradually during the course of the play as if to
suggest that, as Beth (and her husband Jake) reconstruct their lives,
the world around them becomes more concrete, begins to order

itself, as well. By the second act of the play, walls, doors, and other touches or realistic scenic detail have appeared. While this scenic concept might be said to 'reflect' Beth's gradual reconstruction of self and reality, it does not theatrically or materially manifest it. It does not, in Corrigan's words, 'dramatise' her condition, but only timidly takes license with strict scenic realism, paling in comparison to the bold theatrical strokes of Shepard's staging in *True West* or to his visceral use of the stage as emotional signifier in either *Curse of the Starving Class* or *Fool for Love*.

As Shepard's dramatic expression of thematic concerns takes greater and greater precedence over his theatrical expression of states of consciousness, those writing on his work, or producing it, will tend to look *backward* from *A Lie of the Mind* to Shepard's earlier family dramas, focusing on the family themes and the apparent surface realism of the plays and ignoring the schizophrenic vision and the heightened realism which Shepard has gradually tried to stifle. The irony of this situation is that in a play like *A Lie of the Mind*, which adheres as strictly as any play Shepard has ever written to the conventions of stage realism, his characters are nevertheless addressing issues of the impermanence of the self and of so-called reality. So, while Shepard's plays are becoming more and more theatrically conventional, his thematic interests are still partially focused on the expression of the postmodern condition. Where he once wrote plays which appeared to have no thematic content, except as it manifests itself through theatrical form and presentation, he has now reached the other extreme, denying theatrical form and presentation any role whatsoever in the expression of theme. The tentative balance he achieved, whether consciously or not, between a resistant postmodern form and postmodern content in *Curse of the Starving Class* has been lost. Shepard does not appear to have understood or he did not wish to pursue, that balance, and so his plays have become increasingly conventional. The characters in *A Lie of the Mind* may speak of the impermanence of self and reality, but the dramatic world in which Shepard has placed them reflects that impermanence only timidly, if at all.

Thus, as we move further away from Shepard's first family plays, and as Shepard himself makes every effort to remove all traces of his 'old' theatrical self from his writing, his family plays may be confined, at least in production, to the school of retrograde postmodernism and his superrealism seen, more and more, as 'a kind of cavorting'.

Notes

1. Bonnie Marranca, ed., *American Dreams: The Imagination of Sam Shepard* (New York: Performing Arts Journal Publications, 1981), unnumbered Preface.
2. Christopher Bigsby, 'Sam Shepard: Word and Image', in *Critical Angles: European Views of Contemporary American Literature*, ed. Marc Chenetier (Carbondale: Southern Illinois University Press, 1986), p. 214.
3. Richard Gilman, Introduction to *Seven Plays*, by Sam Shepard (New York: Bantam, 1981), p. xi.
4. Ron Mottram, *Inner Landscapes* (Columbia: University of Missouri Press, 1984), p. vii.
5. Hal Foster, ed., 'Postmodernism: A Preface', in *The Anti-Aesthetic: Essays on Postmodern Culture* (Port Townsend: Bay Press, 1983), pp. xi-xii.
6. Ibid., p. xii.
7. See Jean-François Lyotard, *The Postmodern Condition: A Report on Knowledge*, trans. Geoff Bennington and Brian Massumi (Minneapolis: University of Minnesota Press, 1984).
8. Jennifer Allen, 'The Man on the High Horse: On the Trail of Sam Shepard', *Esquire*, 10, no. 3 (November 1988), 148.
9. Ibid., p. 150.
10. John Glore, 'The Canonization of Mojo Rootforce: Sam Shepard Live at the Pantheon', *Theatre* (Yale), 12, no. 3 (Summer 1981), 57.
11. Robert W. Corrigan, *The Theatre in Search of a Fix* (New York: Dell, 1973), p. 94.
12. Quoted in Bernard Weiner, 'Sam Shepard Goes into a Trance for His New Play', *San Francisco Chronicle*, 20 March 1977, p. 14.
13. Shepard: 'I was on a different drug – crystal Methedrine, which has much more of an edge; when you walk down the street, your heels sparked'. Robert Goldberg, 'Sam Shepard: American Original', *Playboy*, March 1984, 193.
14. Frederic Jameson, 'Postmodernism and Consumer Society', in *The Anti-Aesthetic: Essays on Postmodern Culture*, ed. Hal Foster (Port Townsend: Bay Press, 1983), p. 119.
15. Ibid., p. 120.
16. It should be noted here that the use of the term 'supperrealism' throughout this essay is not intended to correspond to the terminology of the 'Super-Realist' school of painting, nor to Toby Silverman Zinman's comparison of Shepard's work to that school of painting in her essay: 'Sam Shepard and Super-Realism', *Modern Drama* 29, no. 3 (1986), 423–30. While I agree with Zinman's comment that Shepard creates a dynamic on stage which is essentially one of performance rather than of fourth-wall realism, I do not agree that such a dynamic links him to the Super-Realists. On the contrary, I see the Super-Realists' emphasis on surface and on photographic detachment to be a direct contradiction of Shepard's emphasis (as I see it) on 'superpresence', that is, the heightened, immediate

17. Charles Marowitz, 'Is This Shepard or Saroyan?', *The New York Times*, 15 May 1977, Section 2, p. 3.
18. Gerald Weales, 'American Theatre Watch 1977–1978', *The Georgia Review*, 32 (Fall 1978), 523. Hereafter cited as Weales.
19. The script itself has always been criticised for its irregularities, and the reviewers have always praised the rich comic characterisations of the starring players.
20. Marowitz, p. 3.
21. Weales, 523.
22. Sam Shepard, *Curse of the Starving Class* in *Seven Plays* (New York: Bantam, 1981), p. 135. All quotations are from this edition; page numbers are given in the text.
23. Early productions of the play followed Shepard's non-representational lead.
24. Marowitz, p. 3.
25. Weales, 523.
26. The societal changes which serve as a backdrop to Shepard's play are the same as those which Fredric Jameson points to as the dawning of the postmodern era. Jameson, pp. 124–25.
27. This particular entrance is one of the theatrical images which Shepard now, in his turn toward total stage realism, finds embarrassing: 'I don't drag dead animals on stage anymore', he has declared. (Allen, 150)
28. Jameson, p. 125.
29. I make reference in particular to the 1982 Magic Theatre production, directed by John Lion, in which this scene was blocked and performed in a completely casual and realistic fashion. Lion told me later that he wanted to observe whether or not the play 'worked realistically'. The play 'worked', but in my estimation it suffered from this limiting approach.
30. Jameson, p. 119.
31. Although both the productions of *Curse* I have seen have had the actor turn away from the audience in order to 'urinate' on the charts (using, I assume, an artificial bladder), Shepard's stage directions have the actor 'downstage' and 'facing front' just moments before the event, suggesting that he expected the actor to expose himself and urinate on stage.
32. Jameson, p. 120.
33. This type of superreal presence is also manifest in Shepard's use of operative stage props, such as a functional stove and refrigerator, and of real food.
34. I am indebted to the discussion of this topic in an excellent article by Roger Copeland: 'Imagination After the Fact', *American Theatre*, October 1989, 54–57, 123–25.
35. '[T]he avant-garde sought to transcend representation in favour of presence and immediacy; it proclaimed the autonomy of the signifier, its liberation from the "tyranny of the signified": postmodernists instead expose the tyranny of the *signifier*, the violence of its

David J. DeRose 149

law'. Craig Owens, 'The Discourse of Others: Feminists and Postmodernism', in *The Anti-Aesthetic: Essays on Postmodern Culture*, ed. Hal Foster (Port Townsend: Bay Press, 1983), p. 59.

36. I refer here to the scenic realism of the play. The story, with its contradictory accounts of the past, is a subversion of the narrative realism of the well-made play.

37. Walter Kerr, 'Sam Shepard – What's the Message?' *New York Times*, 10 December 1978, Section 2, p. 3.

38. Sam Shepard, *Buried Child*, in *Seven Plays* (New York: Bantam Books, 1981), p. 80. All quotations are from this edition; page numbers are given in the text.

39. Sam Shepard, *True West*, in *Seven Plays* (New York: Bantam, 1981), p. 59.

40. Ross Wetzsteon, Introduction to *Fool for Love and Other Plays*, Sam Shepard (New York: Bantam, 1984), pp. 1-2.

41. Shepard discusses the writing of *Fool for Love* in the following two interviews, among others: Amy Lippman, 'Rhythm & Truths', *American Theatre*, April 1984, 22–29, and Jennifer Allen, 'The Man on the High Horse: On the trail of Sam Shepard', *Esquire*, November 1988, 57–59.

42. John Lion mentions that the Magic Theatre auditioned 'about a hundred actresses' for the part of 'princess' before Shepard ever showed him a draft of the script. That draft, which Lion estimated was number eleven, had no 'princess' and no Old Man. John Lion, 'Rock 'n Roll Jesus with a Cowboy Mouth', *American Theatre*, April 1984, 6.

43. Sam Shepard, *Fool for Love and Other Plays* (New York: Bantam, 1984), p. 20.

44. Mimi Kramer, 'In search of the good Shepard', *The New Criterion*, 2, no. 2 (October 1983), 56.

45. See David J. DeRose, 'Theatre Review *Fool for Love*', *Theatre Journal*, 36, no. 1 (March 1984), 100–101.

46. Most notable among feminist readings of these plays are: Rosemarie Bank, 'Self as Other: Sam Shepard's *Fool for Love* and *A Lie of the Mind*', in *Feminist Rereadings of Modern American Drama*, ed. June Schlueter (London: Associated University Presses, 1989), 225–37. Lynda Hart, 'Sam Shepard's Spectacle of Impossible Heterosexuality: 'Fool for Love', in Schlueter (Ibid.), 210–18. Felicia Hardison Londré, 'Sam Shepard Works Out: The Masculinization of America', *Studies in American Drama 1945–Present*, 1, no. 2 (1987), 12–27.

9

Speaking Without Words: the Myth of Masculine Autonomy in Sam Shepard's *Fool for Love*

Ann C. Hall

Sam Shepard's popularity has often been explained by his unorthodox dramatic methods; his experiments with form, character, and action have not only forced critics to resort to non-dramatic terminology in order to analyze his style, but they have also made him and his works, in Don Shewey's words, a 'true American original'.[1] For many critics, however, Shepard's heterodoxy does not extend to his female characters; his characterisation of women is resolutely conventional. The women in his plays are merely 'stage property', present only to uphold the privileged male performance. Lynda Hart, for example, writes that Shepard's experience with Joseph Chaikin's 'Open Theatre' may have inspired him to create characters with shifting rather than consistent identities, but his female characters remain 'naively' stereotypical.[2] Florence Falk argues that the male characters in Shepard's plays are their 'energy centres'; their roles, motives, and moods may shift, but their treatment of women is all too familiar. Men dominate the stage, its spectacle, its language, and their female counterparts. Women in his plays are cast into the roles traditionally assigned to them by culture, specifically American popular culture; they are marginalised, absent, silent, 'other'.[3] In an essay on Shepard's early works, Bonnie Marranca concurs, while offering a challenge to Shepard: 'The landscape of the female body has yet to appear, but when a language of the sexes and a female language are added to all the other "languages" he has mastered, the silent voices in the plays will tell their stories'.[4]

While the existence of a 'female language' is subject to debate, the means by which both Marranca and Falk critique Shepard's female characterization is consistent with many feminist rereadings of the literary canon: gender and language are closely aligned, and female silence is often one of the earmarks of patriarchal oppression. Yet Shepard's *Fool for Love* (1983), written after Falk's and Marranca's essays, foregrounds the relationship between sexuality and language by presenting a female character who struggles against the 'his-story' of her brother-lover, Eddie, and her father, The Old Man, and who, in the final moments of the play, in fact challenges their version of the past with 'her-story'.[5] In this play, at least, Shepard's unconventional methods, style, and content include a female character. May challenges The Old Man's, Eddie's and our culture's stereotypical representation of women. Through the course of the play, May changes from a silent, marginalised object of male desire to a speaking subject. What I would like to demonstrate throughout this essay, through the works of psychoanalyst Jacques Lacan and others, is that the play explores the complexities of language and sexual difference in order to expose the mechanism of patriarchal dominance, thereby disrupting rather than endorsing female oppression.

Shepard's comments about the play indicate that it represents a departure from his earlier work. It is the first play in which he tried to 'sustain a female character and have her remain absolutely true to herself'.[6] He told Bernard Weiner, 'I wanted to try to take this leap into a female character, which I had never really done. I felt obliged to, somehow. But it's hard for a man to say he can speak from the point of view of a woman'.[7] Judging from the sixteen drafts of the play, the task was not an easy one.[8] Admittedly, W. K. Wimsatt modified literary critics' use of authorial intention, but Shepard's claims, particularly his recognition of the perils of male authority and female representation, a recognition of sexual 'difference', as well as his continued focus on female characters, as illustrated by *A Lie of the Mind* (1985) and the *Far North* screenplay (1988), indicate that he was dissatisfied with his earlier representations and that he is currently rethinking the status of his female characters in his dramatic works.[9]

Shepard's noticeable shift from his experiments with form, character, and setting in his earlier plays to more 'realistic' practices,

coincides with this focus on female representation. The family settings of his latest dramas, traditionally the site of female oppression,
may have prompted him to reconsider the female role in such a
structure.[10] The question of Shepard's 'realism', however, is complicated by the fact that these later plays do not fully embody those
dramatic techniques traditionally associated with realism, particularly in the area of consistent characterisation, which presupposes
a wholly understandable and consistently motivated character. As
Florence Falk notes, Shepard's characters are often inconsistent,
rapidly shifting from persona to persona, from mood to mood,
desperately searching for the secure identity the realistic formula
presumes.[11] Since this technique precludes consistent characterisation, searching for a complete, fully developed and consistent
female character in the plays of Sam Shepard is troublesome at
best. The technique, however, does not preclude Shepard's ability
to create an important female character in this work. May indeed
violates the conventions of realistic characterisation, but she is the
'energy centre' of the play. This shifting characterisation, moreover,
forces both feminists and non- feminists to reevaluate the means for
defining 'accurate' or 'acceptable' means of female representation in
a manner similar to Brecht's 'alienation effect' – by presenting conventional ideologies in unusual ways, we are forced to reevaluate
those ideologies.

Lacanian theory, which also challenges the concept of a unified
self and which also challenges the assumption that both gender
and language are 'natural' occurrences in the development of the
human subject, then, is a useful approach to the works of Sam
Shepard. According to Lacan, 'man cannot aim at being whole (the
'total personality' being another premise where modern psycho-
therapy goes off course)'.[12] While the subject is inherently lacking
or 'castrated', human beings are also 'subject' to the simultaneous
yet contradictory presumption that they are, in fact, 'whole' or
'complete'. For Lacan, this paradox 'begins' with the 'mirror stage',
Lacan's addition to the Freudian stages of development. In Lacan's
words, the stage is a

> drama whose internal thrust is precipitated from insufficiency to
> anticipation – and which manufactures for the subject, caught up
> in the lure of spatial identification, the succession of fantasies that
> extends from a fragmented body-image to a form of its totality
> that I shall call orthopaedic – and, lastly, to the assumption of the

armour of an alienating identity, which will mark with its rigid structure the subject's entire mental development.[13]

The difficulty with articulating this moment stems from the fact that the stage is not a statically originary moment, a 'beginning', but instead a process, a drama, which establishes the dynamic which will determine the entire individual's existence and desires. According to Jane Gallop, this dynamic is established by the stage's temporality, 'its intrication of retroaction and anticipation. In other words, the self is constituted through anticipating what it will become, and then this anticipatory model is used for gauging what was before'.[14] What the self assumes it will become is a complete autonomous entity. Trapped by the lure of the mirror image, the subject presumes it is the image. The subject makes no distinction between the object represented, the body, and its representation, the mirror image. This oversight characterises what Lacan calls the 'imaginary'. A subject caught up by the imaginary denies difference, presumes a unified sense of self, and believes itself capable of mastering meaning, others, and existential lack.

During the mirror stage, however, the subject simultaneously enters the 'symbolic', the realm of difference, division, language, and lack. Simply, the subject begins to discover sexual difference, that there are 'others' in its world, that signifieds and signifiers often do not correspond. Stephen Heath notes:

> Caused in language, which is division and representation, the subject is taken up as such in an interminable movement of the signifier, the process of the symbolic, and in a structure of desire, the implication of the subject's experience of division, or lack, in language . . . to grasp language as the condition of the unconscious is to insist on desire in language and to make the subject the term of a constant construction and representation, outside of the expression of any unity, biological included.[15]

Faced with such challenges to the jubilant, imaginary assumption of unity and a unique self, the subject looks to its past in order to explain this difference, Gallop's retroactive process of the mirror stage. Rather than recognising the undifferentiated nature of the pre-mirror stage, the subject, who is already inscribed in the symbolic and the imaginary, perceives the difference between self and (m)other, but through the imaginary process, joins the two. Through this retroactive movement, self and other are not mutually exclusive, as the symbolic threat implies, but instead, complementary. Further, because the subject perceives this moment of imaginary as pre-symbolic, the unity takes on an even greater importance: it represents a moment in the subject's development during which self and other could communicate without the divisive function of the symbolic, a moment when self and other could 'speak without words'.

Reassured that imaginary unity is possible, a union which transcends language, the subject projects this 'imaginary' interpretation into the symbolic realm, Gallop's anticipatory element of the mirror stage. That is, from a later period of development, the subject interprets a prior stage, and then imposes that interpretation and the expectations which accompany it onto later phases of existence. Simply, subjectivity is characterized by an extreme and fallacious nostalgia for an imaginary moment which never existed. Ironically, the goal of this illusory process is to protect the subject from the realisation that the self is an 'illusion done with mirrors'.[16]

While separate processes, the opposing forces of the symbolic and the imaginary coexist throughout the subject's existence. In Jacqueline Rose's words, despite the subject's inscription into the symbolic, imaginary myths continue to haunt the symbolic, myths which Lacan attempted to indict by reminding us that meaning, sexual difference, and identity are always constructed by language, not the inevitable consequence of nature.[17] The imaginary attempts to fix meaning, thereby making signified and signifier complementary, while the disruptive reality of the symbolic undercuts such certainty. In terms of sexual difference, subjects perceive division, but in order to deactivate the threat such difference poses to the imaginary belief in autonomy, they impose meaning onto that difference which acts to support the illusion.

Specifically, the 'lack' of all human subjects is projected upon women. As a result of the castration complex and the subject's fuller participation in the symbolic, the signifier for the lost, imaginary 'Other' is the Phallus.[18] Lacan's use of linguistic rather than anatomical terminology here is important, for it clearly indicates that the Phallus is not the penis, but, instead, a signifier for the desire of the Other. In this way, Lacan argues that all subjects are castrated, not just women. The myths of the imaginary, however, equate the penis with the Phallus and elide any threats to psychic completion: the male possesses the penis-other, while the female lacks. Thus, while men and women are equally inscribed into language, the illusion of imaginary unity prompts individuals to assume that by ordering sexual difference along these lines, by prescribing sexual roles in language, by imposing meaning upon am unstable symbolic, imaginary unity is attainable. According to Jacqueline Rose, 'within this process, woman is constructed as an absolute category (excluded and elevated at one and the same time), a category which serves to guarantee that unity on the side of the man. The man places woman at the basis of his fantasy, or constitutes fantasy through the woman'.[19] As our western history demonstrates and as Lacan points out, this absolute category requires that women adapt, remain silent, and deny their desire. This process does not deny women's access to language or assume that women are inferior, but it does establish the dynamic which make such conclusions possible and, in many cases, preferable.

What Lacan's work demonstrates is that masculine autonomy requires female oppression, but, ironically, the woman, as Other, takes on the role of the Phallus, that term which will provide existential certitude. Through the function of the symbolic, however, no matter how codified the imaginary sexual prescription, the phallic or the nostalgic desire of the subject is disrupted. Lacan's task, and the function of the symbolic, is to highlight the disruptive nature of language and representation. Where, for example, the imaginary illusions of the symbolic leads the subject to presume that sexual difference is based upon the biological 'fact' of phallic possession, the disruptive aspect of the symbolic exposes the illusory nature of such conclusions. In Freudian terms, this function of the symbolic signifies the return of the. repressed, the subject's denial of lack. It is the 'reality' of signification, the often impossible relationship between signifiers and signifieds, which challenges the easy and complementary division between male and female, the 'reality' that disturbs representations intended to confer autonomy upon the subject. As Lacan's own work demonstrates, however, an exorcism of the imaginary dynamic within the symbolic is impossible; the myths may be exposed and even challenged, but they persist.[20] The desire for psychic completion coexists with the reality of its impossibility.

In terms of Shepard's play, then, May appears to represent the disruptive symbolic function. She continually challenges Eddie's imaginary myth of autonomy, confronting him with the lies he has told, the fantasies he has constructed. And to a great degree, May does fulfil this function. To view her as simply the 'symbolic' in the play, however, falls prey to the imaginary myth of sexual division. May is the irrational element to Eddie's pristine ego. As the play demonstrates, May is not merely an allegorical representation of symbolic division; she, too, struggles with imaginary fantasies and the symbolic's disturbing effects. Further, as Lacan and the play demonstrate, the imaginary cannot be purged from any subject's psyche or the structuring of the symbolic. Instead, the play, through its focus on sexual difference (admittedly largely through May) reminds us of the coexistence of both the desire for autonomy and the 'reality' of its impossibility, thereby indicting the privileged position of the 'imaginary'.

Even before the action of the play begins, conflicting audience responses are provoked. Two Merle Haggard songs, from his *The Way I Am* album (1980), frame the play. On the one hand, this device distances the audience from the stage: the play is 'Other', different from the audience. On the other hand, the choice of country western songs positions the play in the context of familiar American popular culture, thereby dismantling any difference between spectacle and spectator. The opening song, 'Wake Up', blurs difference further by presenting a relationship similar to Eddie and May's. These characters are also typical, familiar selections off an old record.

The song's scenario also confirms the imaginary sexual division the audience seeks. Like Eddie, the male speaker attempts to awaken his sleeping lover in order that she might facilitate his autonomy:

> Wake up, don't just lie there like cold, granite stone.
> Wake up, we're too close to alone . . .
> There's too many empty pages
> With so many things in store . . .
> I'm not prepared to handle the things we're going through.[21]

The song foregrounds the masculine desire for complementarity, and makes it clear that the woman will satisfy that desire.

Through the parallels between Eddie and May and the couple in the song, the play appears to endorse this pattern of male dominance: Eddie towers over the silent May, offering her food. He is the Phallus-bearer who has the power to fulfil May. She is castrated, 'lacking'. Humorously, the play quickly undercuts such an assumption through the type of food Eddie offers May. Tea,

Ovaltine, and potato chips are 'imaginary' food; they only provide the 'lure' of sustenance without providing real nourishment.

May's response to these gifts also undermines Eddie's authority. She violently jumps off the bed and begins beating her lover. Through this attack, the play quickly dispels a conventional reading of the heterosexual relationship. May is not merely a passive victim. In terms of Shepard's previous work, this female violence is a departure. As Florence Falk noted, women might manipulate their male characters, but violence was reserved for men, thereby assuring them of their status as the play's 'energy centres'.[22] While such characterisation might indicate that Shepard is merely using masculine qualities to create a female character, the shift does create a disturbance in the rigid gender codification of the imaginary myth of the symbolic, for here we have a female character using the means of confrontation traditionally associated with men.

Such shifting also occurs when May confronts Eddie about his fidelity. Despite his professions of love, his faith in their ultimate, but imaginary unity, May says she knows that he has been unfaithful because he smells like 'metal', like 'pussy' (22). This image highlights the position of women in a society which prescribes gender behaviour. As Luce Irigaray, Lacan's one-time student, notes: 'the society we know, our own culture, is based upon the exchange of women'.[23] In May's commentary, genitalia are metallic, the substance of money, the symbol of economic exchange. Whether May realises that she, too, is yet another object on the sexual marketplace is difficult to say, but when she tells Eddie that she fears he will 'erase' her, her inscription into this economy, the imaginary myths of the symbolic, is clear. Despite her attempts to subvert Eddie's fantasy of phallic mastery, she also believes that he has the power to 'erase' her. She can only attain value – even existence itself – through her relationship to Eddie. May, then, is not simply removed from the pressures of the myth of masculine autonomy; she is not 'outside' of the psychic conflict between imaginary and symbolic, but, like Eddie, she is 'subjected' to it. And while such a representation may not fulfil our expectations for a feminist hero, it accurately portrays the difficulties associated with female subjectivity. May does not only confront Eddie, she must also confront her own participation in the fantasy.

Ironically, Eddie confirms her 'imaginary' assessment when he lovingly tells May that he travelled 'Two thousand, four hundred and eighty' miles all the while imagining May's neck, a piece of her (24). While Eddie admits that he needs May, that he lacks, he simultaneously reestablishes the myth of autonomy by fragmenting May; even though she may function as the 'other' which will fulfil him, he must simultaneously and paradoxically degrade her, as well, in order to ensure the pristine autonomy he imagines himself capable of.

Eddie's responses to May's challenges also demonstrate his ego's effective defensive mechanisms against such attacks. When, for example, May confronts him about the Countess, Eddie creates yet another fantasy. He magnanimously offers May a better life, a 'piece of ground up in Wyoming' (24). Despite May's lengthy and vituperative protests, Eddie assures her that she will 'get used to it' (25). In order to retain his myth of masculine autonomy, Eddie banishes female desire. Whether trapped within a trailer or in the wilds of Wyoming, Eddie wants May to shut up, adapt, and protect his visions, no matter how often they change or how revolting they are to her. While clearly demonstrating Eddie's presumption of mastery, the play also exposes the fantastic nature of such domination. Eddie's myth of autonomy, his 'Marlboro Man' fantasies, requires a silent female.

By appealing to an image from popular culture, the 'Marlboro Man', the play highlights the dream's persistence in the American culture, a dream which, according to Annette Kolodny, founded America, a dream which both May and her foremothers suspected. In her study of frontierswomen's narratives, Kolodny demonstrates that the women's reluctance to accompany their partners to the New World was not inspired by a perversely overdeveloped respect for European civilisation; instead, the women correctly interpreted the rhetoric of the frontier which described the land as a female body. In the myth of the American Adam, 'Eve could only be redundant'.[24] Like her foremothers, May knows that there will be nothing 'out there' for her, only 'a nightmare of domestic captivity'.[25]

May's response to this offer is her most physically violent in the play. She knees Eddie in the groin, perhaps indicating where she presumes the source of the problem to be. When The Old Man appears, the play confirms that May's 'symbolic' action has punctured Eddie's imaginary illusions. Doubt, division, and a sense of lack (indeed her gesture is one of emasculation) have been established by May. Consequently, The Old Man challenges Eddie, asking, 'I thought you were supposed to be a fantasist, right'? Eddie's lapse in faith is confirmed when he answers, 'I don't know' (27). The Old Man appears in order to resurrect the benefits of fantasy and reiterates the means by which it is attained – female containment.

At the same time, however, the play disrupts this fantasy and illusion. Such resurrection is merely reconstruction; masculine autonomy is predicated upon male fantasy. The Old Man, for example, promises to show Eddie something 'real', something 'actual' – a picture of Barbara Mandrell – to whom he claims he is married:

> THE OLD MAN: That's realism. I am actually married to Barbara Mandrell in my mind. Can you understand that?
> EDDIE: Sure.
> THE OLD MAN: Good. I'm glad we have an understanding.
> (27)

By 'framing' a woman, The Old Man upholds his phallic power. In Stephen Heath's words, 'the man, perhaps the woman in place in his perspective, is assured of the sex of the woman, as of his own thereby (the look as phallus) . . . the guarantee of *the* woman, in this image'.[26] Despite the benefits The Old Man gains from his relationship to this photograph, however, it is clear that his reality is an image. As Stephen Heath points out, 'the real of the photograph is a real that is always an image'.[27] In this way, the play challenges The Old Man's assumption of mastery. Further, because the photograph is of a woman, the means by which he attains this illusion is also illustrated. Mythic masculine autonomy is attained through 'framing' the female, keeping her disconnected, silent, and 'other'. The Old Man's narrative, then, implies that he believes Eddie is failing to achieve this goal, since May is not 'framed' as neatly as Barbara Mandrell. Through the ambiguous characterisation of The Old Man, moreover – the fact that only Eddie and May can see him and the fact that he is generically defined – the play accurately depicts him as a representative of the 'imaginary' myths which haunt the 'symbolic'. Through him, Eddie denies the threat of symbolic castration. According to The Old Man, Eddie is not inherently castrated; he need only frame May further in order to achieve masculine autonomy.

May's subsequent commentaries, however, illustrate the effects such fantasies have upon the female subject. As she tells Eddie:

All I see is a picture of you. You and her. I don't even know if the

picture's real anymore. I don't even care. It's a made-up picture.
It invades my head. The two of you. And this picture stings even
more than if I'd actually seen you with her. It cuts me. It cuts me
so deep I'll never get over it. And I can't get rid of this picture
either. It just comes. Uninvited. Kinda' like a little torture. And
I blame you more for this little torture than I do for what you
did. (28)

While the narrative demonstrates that May, like Eddie, has difficulty separating the image from the reality, the symbolic from the
imaginary, it also illustrates the destructive effects such phallic
representation elicits.

The story almost moves Eddie to compassion, but because he has
been reinvigorated in his purpose by the Old Man, he continues in
his attempts to dominate May. When she, for example, tells him
that she has a 'date', Eddie wields his assumed linguistic power.
He presumes he is a linguistic master manipulator, by challenging
May's use of the word 'man' to describe her date:

If you called him a 'guy', I'd be worried about it but since you call
him a 'man' you give yourself away. You're in a dumb situation
with this guy by calling him a 'man'. You put yourself below
him. (30)

Eddie uses the control of language, the patriarchal 'symbolic' as a
strategy for controlling May.

May's initial response to this departure is to accept Eddie's
assumed power. She is devastated, literally brought to her knees
by his absence. Like Barbara Mandrell, she is framed by the micro-
phoned walls she crawls around. Like the photograph, male expectations and her participation in those expectations entrap May.
Unlike the photograph, however, May is a 'moving picture', at once
participating in the prescribed sexual roles of the imaginary myth of
masculine autonomy and serving as a reminder of the insufficiency
of those roles.

Once again, The Old Man appears in order to stabilise patriarchal
authority through another narrative. In this fantasy, he appears as a
'founding father'. He drives a Plymouth with 'a white plastic hood
ornament on it. Replica of the *Mayflower*', and he tends to the crying
May by taking her out of the car (32). Cows surround and frighten
him:

I saw somethin' move out there. Somethin' bigger than both of us put together . . . And then it started to get joined up by some other things just like it. Same shape and everything . . . And I stopped dead still and turned back to the car to see if your mother was all right. But I couldn't see the car anymore. So I called out to her. I called her name loud and clear. And she answered me back from outa' the darkness. (32–33)

The dark forms threaten his sense of mastery, and he calls out to his wife and is reassured by her presence. As a result of his wife's voice in the darkness, he 'sees', he masters, the situation. What The Old Man does not 'see', however, is that the 'phallic mastery' of the 'founding fathers' requires the presence of an oppressed female, a 'voice in the darkness'.

The incident also raises the question of the effects of female community upon this phallic illusion. As we learn later, The Old Man lived separate lives with separate women. Rather than questioning the assumption of autonomy, however, The Old Man, in a move characteristic of male subjects in the symbolic, chooses another love object.[28] The choice of two love objects, moreover, illustrates that his sense of psychic wholeness is in fact based upon division and separation.

Like his father, Eddie also lives two separate lives, so he, too, must keep the Countess and May separated. He attempts to leave May in order to ensure this division, but Martin's entrance poses another danger. He risks losing one of the units which supports his masculine fiction. In order to assure his autonomy, Eddie must keep May. Ironically, he attempts to possess her by 'erasing' her in Martin's mind. He counters, challenges, and denies all of May's excuses and explanations. He is the character in control of the truth; she lacks it. She is a 'liar'.

Eddie fortifies his credibility by educating Martin, an adopted man, an individual without an Old Man, who may not have had the benefits of such information, in the ways of masculine fiction. Eddie further believes that he alone is versed in the complexities of truth and fiction. When Martin tells Eddie that he will offer May a choice in the movies they see, thereby verifying female desire, Eddie counters citing precedent: 'the guy's always supposed to pick the movie' (45). Men choose the fantasies; women only attend. Eddie tells Martin that soon he will not even need the Hollywood-manufactured illusions:

MARTIN: What would we do here?
EDDIE: Well, you could uh – tell each other stories.
MARTIN: Stories?
EDDIE: Yeah.
MARTIN: I don't know any stories.
EDDIE: Make 'em up.
MARTIN: That'd be lying wouldn't it?
EDDIE: No, no. Lying's when you believe it's true. If you
already know it's a lie, then it's not lying.

                                                            (45)

As an *exemplum*, Eddie tells his own story, circling around the stage,
with Martin, not May, tagging along.

Like Shelly in Shepard's *Buried Child* (1978), Martin occupies the
role of confused spectator, but he, too, is subjected to the imaginary
myths which haunt the symbolic, for he, like us, searches for
an answer, a static explanation for these unusual circumstances.
Through Martin's appearance, then, Shepard leads his audience to
expect such explanations. As in *Buried Child*, however, *Fool for Love*
does not fulfil these desires, but instead, provokes the desire for
closure, an answer, just as it provokes the desire for prescriptive
gender divisions, in order to articulate and analyse such a desire. In
Buried Child, for example, Shepard offers no solutions, only images
– an empty grave and a decaying child. And in *Fool for Love*, he
points us in the direction of incest, the apparent origin of May and
Eddie's troubled relationship. But this, like the images of the earlier
play, is not a solution but yet another Gordian knot of motives and
signification.[29]

When Eddie meets the young May in his narrative, the on-stage
May reappears, slamming the bathroom door and interrupts Eddie's
tales. She tries to dismiss the narrative in the way Eddie dismissed
her: she has the truth; Eddie is lying. Eddie counters, invoking the
word of an 'impartial' listener, his initiate, Martin: 'Did you think I
made that whole thing up'? (51). Martin undercuts Eddie's version,
saying, 'at the time you were telling it, it seemed real' (51). The story
is not real, only apparently so. Since Martin will not uphold Eddie's
illusion, he attempts to goad May into compliance. This baiting,
however, results in the antithesis of Eddie's imaginary desire, for
May begins to tell her story, not his:

Okay. Okay. I don't need either of you. I don't need any of it because I already know the rest of the story . . . I know it just exactly the way it happened. Without any little tricks added onto it. (52)

While May's promise to offer the truth certainly exhibits the imaginary function of the symbolic, that function which stabilises signification, it is complicated by the fact that it will be told by a woman, traditionally the silent other in the sexual dialectic. Unlike Eddie's version of the past, May's does not contain the discovery of an 'other' (May herself in Eddie's story) which will bring jubilant completion; instead, her version contains painful loss. In effect, May's narrative returns the repressed 'absent' woman in order to confront the imaginary myth of autonomy. The entire family history is based upon a 'forgotten' female corpse, a woman literally 'erased', a lack.

The Old Man's interruptions confirm the subversive power of May's narrative. He tells Eddie, 'Boy is she ever off the wall with this one. You gotta' do somethin' about this' (53). The phrase 'off the wall' echoes the earlier scene in which May could not escape Eddie or The Old Man. This shift marks May's departure from the family's phallocentric 'his-story'. The Old Man, however, will not recognize this reality and the loss which underlies his sense of completion. He denies this loss, claiming he is 'imaginatively' connected to his wives:

That's right, I was gone! I was gone. You're right. But I wasn't disconnected. There was nothing cut off in me. Everything went on just the same as though I'd never left. (55)

The Old Man's myth of masculine power leads him to believe that he can, in fact, 'speak without words'. In effect, he desires to reproduce the imaginary, pre-symbolic silence of the mirror stage. As the play demonstrates, however, an unmediated communication is impossible, for The Old Man appeals to Eddie to employ words to defend the 'male side a' the thing'. Despite his desire to 'speak without words', to recuperate an unmediated unity of self and world, The Old Man is necessarily in the symbolic realm, a realm of loss where the illusion of such unity can be upheld only by regressive mysticism and male fantasies of frontier heroics and omnipotence.

For a moment, Eddie ignores The Old Man's call and embraces

May. Eddie has been struggling to distance himself from The Old Man, to move away from male fantasies, throughout the play, so May's narrative offers him another opportunity to reject his illusory autonomy. The Countess, the lure of the frontier and further fantasy, however, is too much for Eddie. He must leave. In this way, the play does not posit the exorcism of the imaginary myths; instead, Eddie's departure paradoxically makes it clear that such escape is impossible.

Throughout her narrative, May stands strong, centre stage. She is literally 'off the wall'. But May's subsequent departure indicates that such truth has not brought her stability and completion, only another journey. Further, May no longer clings to the walls of rigid gender codification. She has chosen to speak, to disrupt the frame which Eddie and The Old Man have imposed upon her. And by telling the story from the 'female side', she has also aligned herself with the women of her past, creating the community of women both Eddie and The Old Man so desperately feared.

By leaving May enigmatic, her 'next step' subject to question, the play, moreover, does not put her in 'her place'; it does not cast her into yet another role offered by the imaginary function of the symbolic. Such open-endedness may even indicate Shepard's solution to the problem of female representation. May is neither dutiful daughter-lover nor whorish woman, the two roles most frequently assigned to women; instead she is an anxiety producing question to a system which claims complete control over women. Judith Butler notes, 'perhaps, paradoxically, "representation" will be shown to make sense for feminism only when the subject of "women" is nowhere presumed'.[30] May's mysterious exit, then, creates a gap in the dramatic narrative, thwarting the audience's own desires for certitude, codified meaning and prescriptive gender relations.

In effect, the play concludes by illustrating the anxiety of the symbolic. While May enters the darkness framed by a door, signalling the failure of conventional gender roles, The Old Man on the other side of the stage presents the prescriptive picture: the woman of his dreams, framed, silent, and his 'forever', the extreme position of women in the imaginary, patriarchal structure.

The play, moreover, closes with the Merle Haggard song, '(Remember Me) I'm the One Who Loves You'. Like Eddie and The Old Man, the singer believes he will never be 'subjected' to change:

And through all kinds of weather
My love will never change.
Through the sunshine and the shadows,
Honey, I'll always be the same.[31]

Framed by the two Merle Haggard songs, the play itself becomes another picture, offering us not one vision of fantasy and femininity but two. On one side of the stage is May's absence; on the other, a woman confined by masculine illusion. We are left with the anxiety of two images, two answers: a woman 'framed' by a man's expectations and an empty frame, the opened door, left bare by May who has moved 'out of the picture'. In this way, the play does not solve the problem of gender relations, but instead illustrates the simultaneous but opposing movements of gender and language in the symbolic. The play itself does not succumb to the imaginary's quest for closure, for reconciling these dual functions of the symbolic. Instead, it offers the audience the 'double vision' that imaginary myths persist in eliding, a 'double vision' which, ironically, presents the audience with a clear view of the illusory nature of masculine autonomy and prescribed gender roles.

Notes

1. Don Shewey, *Sam Shepard: The Life, The Loves, Behind the Legend of a True American Original* (New York: Dell, 1985), p. 5.
2. Lynda Hart, 'Sam Shepard's Spectacle of Impossible Heterosexuality: *Fool for Love*',in *Feminist Rereadings of Modern American Drama*, ed. Jane Schlueter (London: Associated University Presses, 1989) pp. 215–17.
3. Florence Falk, 'Men Without Women: The Shepard Landscape', in *American Dreams: The Imagination of Sam Shepard*, ed. Bonnie Marranca (New York: PAJ Publications 1981), pp. 90–103.
4. Bonnie Marranca, 'Alphabetical Shepard', in *American Dreams*, p. 31.
5. Sam Shepard, *Fool for Love and Other Plays* (New York: Bantam 1984), pp. 18–57. All quotations are from this edition; page numbers are given in the text.
6. Sam Shepard, 'Myths, Dreams, Realities – Sam Shepard's America', with Michiko Kukutani, *New York Times*, 29 January 1984, Section 2, p. 26.
7. Bernard Weiner, quoted in Shewey, p. 150.
8. Shewey, pp. 147–48.
9. W. K. Wimsatt, *The Verbal Icon: Studies in the Meaning of Poetry* (Lexington: University of Kentucky Press, 1954).

10. Shepard's work with director Robert Woodruff and the cast of *Buried Child* may also have had an important effect on his female representation. See 'Interview with Robert Woodruff', with Robert Coe, *American Dreams*, p. 156.
11. Falk, p. 95.
12. Jacques Lacan, *Feminine Sexuality*, trans. Jacqueline Rose, ed. Juliet Mitchell and Jacqueline Rose (New York: Norton, 1985), p. 81.
13. Jacques Lacan, *Ecrits: A Selection*, trans. Alan Sheridan (New York: Norton, 1977), p. 4.
14. Jane Gallop, *Reading Lacan* (Ithaca: Cornell University Press, 1985), p. 81.
15. Stephen Heath, "Difference", *Screen* 19, no. 3 (Autumn 1978), 63.
16. Gallop, p. 83.
17. Jacqueline Rose, 'Introduction – II', *Feminine Sexuality*, trans. Jacqueline Rose, ed. Jacqueline Rose and Juliet Mitchell (New York: Norton 1985), p. 47.
18. Lacan, *Ecrits*, pp. 74–85.
19. Rose, p. 43.
20. Both Heath (51–54) and Gallop (pp. 87–92), note Lacan's own lapses into the myth of 'imaginary', the myth his theory tried so desperately to expose.
21. Merle Haggard, *The Way I Am*, MCA, 5929, 1980.
22. Falk, p. 91.
23. Luce Irigaray, *The Sex Which is Not One*, trans. Catherine Porter (Ithaca: Cornell University Press, 1985), p. 170.
24. Annette Kolodny, *The Land Before Her: Fantasy and Experience of the American Frontiers, 1630–1860* (Chapel Hill: University of North Carolina Press, 1984), p. 5.
25. Ibid., p. 9.
26. Heath, 91.
27. Ibid.
28. Lacan, *Ecrits*, p. 84.
29. The history of incest and its prohibition also complicate the problem. See, for example, Claude Lévi-Strauss's *The Elementary Structures of Kinship*, trans. James Harle Bell et al. (Boston: Beacon Press, 1969), and Luce Irigaray's *Speculum of the Other Woman*, trans. Gillian C. Gill (Ithaca: Cornell University Press, 1985). Both concur that the incest prohibition inaugurates society, patriarchy, and the exchange and oppression of women. Women, like material wealth, are exchanged, so it is inevitable that this object must be protected, preserved, and kept intact in order to receive a greater price on the marketplace. Incest, then, signals a violation which ruptures this structure, a triumph over The Old Man; the object of exchange is damaged. Eddie and May bring together the lives The Old Man so desperately tried to separate, and begin a life of their own, without the exchange Lévi-Strauss argues is so necessary for kinship (489). As the play demonstrates, however, this relationship has not escaped the father; it has not revolutionized any relationship. May is still objectified, and Eddie is still ruling the family history.

Further, given the interchangeable nature of women in the sexual marketplace, female roles operate in order to fulfil male desire. A woman's job is to reflect, no matter what her linguistic signifier (mother, daughter, etc.).

The incestuous relationship in the play, then, is far from 'almost irrelevant', as William Kleb concluded in 'Sam Shepard's Free-for-All: *Fool for Love* at the Magic Theatre', *Theatre*, 14 (Summer/Fall 1983), 77–82. It promises an answer, fulfilment, but it is finally enigmatic, a disruptive gap in the text and the gender relations in the play.

30. Judith Butler, *Gender Trouble: Feminism and the Subversion of Identity* (New York: Routledge, 1990), p. 6.
31. MCA Records, 1980.

10

When a Woman Looks: The 'Other' Audience of Shepard's Plays

Susan Bennett

Sam Shepard's now distinguished place in the canon of American drama is without dispute. As William Demastes recently put it: 'Throughout his nearly three decades of playwriting, Sam Shepard has expanded the frontiers of American drama with an energy and inventiveness to rival even Eugene O'Neill'.[1] During at least the last of these three decades, however, Shepard's apparent lack of interest in women as *characters* in his dramas has been often documented. Bonnie Marranca, Joyce Aaron and Florence Falk each in their contributions to Marranca's *American Dreams* (1981) call attention to Shepard's almost exclusive attention to the male figure. Marranca talks of the 'zero gravity of women';[2] Falk of a Shepard landscape where 'the cowboy is the reigning male; consequently, *any* female is, perforce, marginalized'[3] and Aaron of a seemingly radical hope: 'I wish he'd write a play for women!'.[4] Aaron, who performed in the original productions of *Up to Thursday*, *Red Cross* (with its rare solo speech for a female character) and *La Turista*, reminds us that it is not only the critics who have become aware of this remarkable oppression of the female character, but also the performer who is aware of her insignificance in the larger picture of Shepard's myths of America. Their commentary adds up to a rather surprising lapse by a product of the 'cool' and liberated sixties into the restrictive and prescriptive edicts of patriarchy.

Since 1981, of course, Shepard has attempted – perhaps in response to the cumulative effect of these observations – to make some sort of reparation. On *Fool for Love*, first performed in 1983, Shepard commented, 'I was determined to write some kind of confrontation between a man and a woman, as opposed to just men . . . this one is really more about a woman than any play I've ever written, and it's from her point of view pretty much'.[5] And, after *Paris, Texas* (1984) and *A Lie of the Mind* (1985), Felicia Hardison Londré argues, '[t]he masculinization of America, as reflected in the [recent] works of Sam Shepard, is an enlightened recognition of the feminine component at its full value'.[6] But as Shepard and, to some extent, critical opinion has welcomed a reformed gender presentation in his drama, I want here, however, to examine interpretive strategies for the woman who *looks* at Shepard's plays.

While my focus is on an often neglected component in the production/reception relationship – the female spectator – elsewhere Shepard's 'audiences' (seemingly rather homogeneous) have aroused some critical attention. In an interview with Amy Lippman (1983), Shepard offers a rather ambiguous explanation of his attitude to the audiences for his plays:

> [T]he question comes up: what is the audience? Who is the audience? In a way, you write for yourself as a certain kind of audience. In the midst of writing, it always feels as though I'm writing for the thing itself. I'm writing to have the thing itself be true. And then I feel like an audience would be able to relate to it. The theater's about a relationship.[7]

Shepard acknowledges the necessity of relationship(s), but this, as he defines it in this quotation, is clearly problematic. If we look closely at Shepard's response, we see that at first, he apparently denies knowledge of the viewing public and positions himself as audience for his texts. In this way, the author writes in a closed circle; his plays function as personal explorations with the male privileged as creator and recipient of the text. Shepard dismantles this relationship, however, in the promotion of the text itself and its intrinsic 'truth' which marks if not the death, at least the subjugation of the author. Such a claim encases the text in an oppressive New Critical mode which (as Catherine Belsey has described it) relies on 'a naive empiricism-idealism which maintains that words stand either for things or for experiences, and that these inhere timelessly in the phenomenal world or in the continuity of essential human nature'.[8] Finally, of course, Shepard acknowledges the inevitability (although significantly not the centrality) of the audience's relationship to the play in performance. It is nevertheless a relationship which is based primarily on the 'truth' of the text. Notwithstanding these claims for the necessity and/or desirability of textual 'truth', critical discussion of Shepard's audiences has centred upon the dramaturgical strategies employed to engage an apparently homogeneous spectator.[9] We might, I think, consider gender-specific readers/viewers for Shepard's dramas, as well as an 'ideal' audience implied by the strategies of the text, and in this way explore further gender relations in the work of 'our most interesting and exciting American playwright'.[10]

My concern with the female spectator in this re-reading of some of Shepard's work is taken in part from Linda Williams's reading of a conventional refusal of women to 'look' at moments of graphic violence in horror films. She writes:

> When the movie screen holds a particularly effective image of terror, little boys and grown men make it a point of honour to look, while little girls and grown women cover their eyes or hide behind the shoulders of their dates. There are excellent reasons for this refusal of the woman to look, not the least of which is that she is often asked to bear witness to her own powerlessness in the face of rape, mutilation and murder. Another excellent reason for the refusal to look is the fact that women are given so little to identify with on the screen.[11]

Undoubtedly less graphic than the movies to which Williams refers, Shepard's plays nevertheless often represent women in equally disabled roles. Women who read these texts (in performance or otherwise) are positioned in a like frame: they must watch their 'otherness' as signifier of threat and cause of violence and are offered the victim with whom to identify. Powerlessness is the primary characteristic of the female in Shepard's early drama. When, in *Fool for Love*, Shepard becomes self-conscious about his inscription of a female point of view, however, it is particularly interesting that this focus is immediately problematised in his text.

The opening stage direction for this play indicates that '*May sits on edge of bed facing audience, feet on floor, legs apart, elbows on knees, hands hanging limp and crossed between her knees, head hanging forward, face staring at the floor. She is absolutely still and maintains this attitude until she speaks*'.[12] The strategy she offers to the audience is passivity and silence; by contrast, of course, Eddie is revealed through stage business and it is he who initiates the play's action with a speech of some twenty lines. We see him in the opening moments applying resin to the handle of a bucking strap and glove. These stage signs not only denote Eddie's active role in contrast to May's inertia in the microcosmic world of the motel room/stage set, but connote Eddie's participation in a macrocosmic world of social relations where gender determines degrees of power and opportunity. Beyond their immediate signifiers, these actions give Eddie a function outside the onstage male/female relationship and, moreover, offer the audience, at the outset of the drama, the possibility of contextualising him in terms of other male characters in Shepard plays and their cumulative creation of a powerful cowboy myth. These actions, then, not only initiate the narrative, but provide an ideological framework for that narrative. At the same moment in the play, May is viewed as a rag doll, an inactive puppet, whose performance the audience might assume will be triggered, if not controlled, by Eddie's actions and/or words. Yet when this expectation is apparently met, May rejects her inscribed role. She is, it would seem, refusing complicity with Eddie's assumed dominance:

> EDDIE: (*Seated, tossing glove on the table. Short pause.*)
> May, look. May? I'm not goin' anywhere.
> See? I'm right here. I'm not gone.
> (*She won't look.*) I don't know why you won't just look at me.
>
> (21)

Just as Williams describes the role of women in the audience for horror movies, May is positioned here by her 'refusal to look'. Eddie's confusion at May's rejection of her implied role might well be seen as counterpart to Shepard's own realisation of his exclusion hitherto of the female character and/or viewer.

So what of the 'other' audience of Shepard's plays? To what extent does the female spectator refuse to look? Or is it that Shepard's plays are so gender specific as to evict the female spectator or, at the very least, to limit her points of entry into his texts?[13] Again Shepard is apparently conscious of such limitations in point of view: early in *Fool for Love*, May observes,

> You're either gonna' erase me or have me erased.

EDDIE: Why would I want that? Are you kidding?
MAY: Because I'm in the way.
EDDIE: Don't be stupid.
MAY: I'm smarter than you are and you know it. I can smell your thoughts before you even think 'em.
EDDIE: May, I'm tryin' to take care of you. All right?
MAY: No you're not. You're just guilty.

(22)

Here May acknowledges a conventional strategy of erasure, of objectification by her male antagonist or his agents. Her analysis and her retort, however, suggest some possible empowerment as does her strong rejection of Eddie's justification of his behaviour under the role of male protector. Certainly, May's sense of the threat of imminent erasure suggests her awareness of a cultural practice which emphasises her vulnerability as a result of gender differentiation. It is a position which equally applies to May's gender equivalents in the theatre audience as Annette Kuhn reminds us in her description of mainstream cinema practice:

> [S]ocio-biological gender and gendered subjectivity are not necessarily coterminous, so that the specificity of the 'masculine' becomes in some way culturally universalised. If this is indeed the case, it certainly speaks to the hegemony of the masculine in culture that dominant cinema offers an address that, as a condition of being meaningful, must in effect de-feminise the female spectator.[14]

Like May, both Williams and Kuhn suggest a problematised spectatorship for women and such analyses of the effects of spectatorship, as well as possible strategies of resistance, form, I think, a useful approach to Shepard's recent texts. Yet, despite May's awareness at the beginning of *Fool for Love* of the strategies Eddie will most likely use to contain her, it is perhaps a little premature to celebrate the writer's new approach where 'a male perspective does not prevail'.[15] Instead we might look to Shepard's plays, particularly *Fool for Love*, as interrogations which ultimately (and comfortably) confirm, to recall Kuhn's assertion, 'the hegemony of the masculine in culture'.

If *Fool for Love* is the play which Shepard has pointed to as 'about a woman', then we might expect responses to this particular play to demonstrate some flexibility in such a hegemony. Ann Wilson, in her discussion of the spectatorship of Shepard's plays, does not, however, provide a very promising start:

> The interesting aspect of Shepard's exploration of spectatorship in *Fool for Love* is that it is gender-determined. The gaze is male. It is not simply that the figure of the spectator, The Old Man, happens to be a man who constitutes an image of [a] woman, Barbara Mandrell, as the object of desire. The Old Man is also The Father. It is in the figure of The Old Man as The Father that issues of desire and representation intersect. As the desire of the lovers is mediated literally and figuratively by The Old Man in the narrative so the spectators are positioned so that their desire is literally and figuratively mediated by him.[16]

The Old Man, as Wilson suggests, provides a filter through which spectators respond to May. In this way, although Shepard asserts the play is from May's point of view, it is a view which is doubly distanced. It is distanced both by the mediating function of The Old Man and by the hegemonic male gaze. Wilson concludes that May is 'more complex than many of Shepard's earlier female characters, [but] nevertheless is produced within a scene of representation which is over-determined by the masculine'.[17] Such a reading of *Fool for Love* is given weight by responses to the film version of the play in which, of course, Shepard himself played the role of Eddie. A (male-authored) review in the *New York Times* notes:

> As has already been demonstrated . . . the camera likes Mr. Shepard. He has what's usually called 'presence', a psychic weight that has as much to do with emotional gravity as with his lanky Cooperesque frame, his lean face and his crooked, uncapped teeth. Something more important is apparent in his performance as Eddie – a demonic charm that expresses Eddie's sadism as well as his completely guilt-free awareness of what he's doing to May.[18]

While May is undoubtedly more complex – a response indeed to Joyce Aaron's hope for something in Shepard's plays for women – her awareness of the control of the gaze does not ultimately empower her. Shepard closes *Fool for Love* with May destined to repeat her mother's history. May tells The Old Man 'I don't need any of it because I already know the rest of the story. I know the whole rest of the story, see. I know it just exactly the way it happened' (52). When she goes on to tell her mother's 'story' to The Old Man (and to the audience), The Old Man demands another version of the story and then pleads his ignorance of the events May has related. Eddie's rejoinder to The Old Man is simply 'You were gone' (55). May's exit line to Martin only a little later describes Eddie's own exit and echoes The Old Man's desertion of her mother: 'He's gone' (56). If May leaves the play conscious of the prescriptive nature of her role, it is still not an act which suggests an effective resistance, and this is surely emphasised in The Old Man's directions to the audience for their concluding act of reception:

> THE OLD MAN: (*Pointing into space.*) Ya' see that picture over there? Ya' see that? Ya' know who that is? That's the woman of my dreams. That's who that is. And she's mine. She's all mine. Forever.
>
> (57)

The woman is once again reduced to an image, an object of the male gaze, and at this moment even its referent is denied for the audience's own (perhaps different) reading.

Beyond this refusal to facilitate resisting or contending readings either by May or by audience members (female or male), there is an added complication in the reception of Shepard's more recent dramas. This is drawn attention to in the acknowledgement of Shepard's screen presence in the *New York Times* review quoted earlier.[19] Shepard has become a recognised screen actor not only in filmed versions of his works, but in films which have had notable financial and/or critical success in mainstream Hollywood cinema. The attention given to his performances in movies such as *The Right Stuff*, *Crimes of the Heart* and *Baby Boom* has attracted a new demographics in the theatre audiences of his plays. As Steven Putzel has argued, the audience for a later play such as *A Lie of the Mind* is constructed of 'those who know Shepard's previous work [who] have the sense that they have seen it all before and those who come as Shepard groupies . . . armed with pulp-press biographies of their hero'.[20] The new configuration has undoubtedly reshaped the production-reception contract in place at Shepard plays – his works are no longer so obviously avant-garde or even 'new' American drama, but are also supplementary activities to a career privileged by our dominant culture, that of film star. Putzel argues that this has fostered a more naturalistic (and implicitly less challenging) means of production which caters to what he pejoratively labels 'mid-town audience tastes'.[21] Yet such star status for the actor-author might, of course, have the potential for repositioning the gaze with the female spectator, especially when Shepard is seen in a central role in one of his own plays (such as in the film version of *Fool for Love*).[22]

More directly, however, we might examine the female character in *A Lie of the Mind* and the reception strategies this play affords the woman spectator. Rudolf Erben notes the play's more equitable sharing of stage time: 'All the women state their positions as clearly as their husbands do. Lorraine's dialogue with her daughter Sally especially matches those Shepard has written for fathers and sons'.[23] Unlike *Fool for Love*, where the Old Man is used to tilt the balance of an Eddie-May opposition toward a male perspective and male reading, *A Lie of the Mind* indeed offers apparent equity: four female and four male characters. Sheila Rabillard has suggested, however, that such numerical balance is undermined by an imbalance in performance style. She suggests that performance style in this play is sexually differentiated and gives her own gender-specific reading of Shepard's direction (Promenade Theatre, New York City, 1985) of his text:

> [W]omen characters have a stage presence different from the men's. Much of the play's humour comes from the women's lines, because they are self-regarding in a way that the men are not; *they act as their own audiences, and see themselves as they are seen* . . . In this role [Meg], the actress Louise Latham laughed at her character, but without ever breaking out of character; for Meg continually observes herself, and the actress thus earned a great many laughs from self-mocking cues to the audience. At least when the women hold the stage, the spectators at this play are not the victims of a violent commandeering of attention, but sharers of the women's self-regarding gaze.[24] (my emphasis)

I quote Rabillard's reading at some length because it not only reminds us of the gender-specific mediation of (in this instance) the writer-director, but indicates the ability of the performer to point to the on-stage 'reality' as construct. In *A Lie of the Mind* (and not, I think, just in this particular staging), the audience is given an enabling double focus for their reading of the female character. Rabillard observes that:

> Beth dresses in the gaudiest clothes she can find in the final scene, with a tellingly ambivalent effect: she looks equally like a child playing dress-up and like a hooker. This is not, in short, an *Othello* play but almost *Othello* inside-out; the dangerousness of woman's performance is confirmed – the curious alliance between what she appears to others and what she is.[25]

The split between the woman as she is and as she is viewed offers, I believe, a more active role for the female audience of Shepard's play. It affords that oscillation between masculine and feminine identification which Laura Mulvey has suggested can dismantle the hegemony of male spectatorship.[26]

The starting point of *A Lie of the Mind* in many ways matches that of the earlier 'woman' play, *Fool for Love*. In the opening scene we do not see Beth but her passivity is over-determined with Jake twice declaring her dead. The ensuing narrative concerns Beth's coming back from the 'dead' to where, in the denouement, she can reject Jake and pursue her desire for Frankie, a less obviously Shepardian 'hero'. Beth then starts out as a reinvention of May: the passive victim (assumed dead and then revealed to the audience swathed in bandages and inarticulate). Jake's violent dominance of his wife functions as history for the play's action. But, unlike May in *Fool for Love*, Beth, from almost her first on-stage moment, is active and in conflict with male direction:

(BETH *discovers bandage on her head and starts to rip it off. It starts to come apart in long streamers of gauze.* MIKE *tries to stop her but she continues tearing the bandage off.*)[27]

And unlike May she does not anticipate 'erasure', but asserts herself against it: 'You tell them I'm not dead! Go tell them' (5). We see Beth's own oscillation between her prescribed role and her resistance to that role, an oscillation which Mike's ironic commentary in the opening scene of the second act leaves open for an ambivalent audience response: 'Oh, so now you're *not* dead. Today you're not dead. Yesterday you were dead but today you're not. I gotta keep track a' this. Makes a big difference who you're talkin' to – a corpse or a live person' (44). For the woman reader/viewer, it makes an equally big difference who you're asked to identify with – a corpse or a live person. It is possible, of course, to read Beth as victim. She is left brain-damaged by her husband. But here there is also the option to read Beth's acts as resistance, as attempts to reinterpret her possible roles.

In her seduction of Frankie, the boundaries between gender roles are explicitly tested:

> BETH: Pretend to be. Like you. Between us we can make a life. You could be the woman. You be . . . You could pretend to be in love with me . . . You are my beautiful woman. You lie down.
> (BETH *moves in to* FRANKIE *and tries to push him down on the sofa by the shoulders.* FRANKIE *resists.*)
>
> (75–6)

A little later, she marks his otherness from Jake as she labels him 'a woman-man' (76). By contrast, she earlier simply but effectively rejects traditional gender bipartition in her criticism of her father's archetypal macho behaviour:

> This – this is my father. He's given up love. Love is dead for him. My mother is dead for him. Things live for him to be killed. Only death counts for him. Nothing else. This – This – (*She moves slowly toward* FRANKIE.) This is me. This is me now. The way I am. Now. This. All. Different. I – I live inside this. Remember. Remembering. You. You – were one. I know you. I know – love. I know what love is. I can never forget. That. Never. (57)

Beth is left with fragments, but hers is a reality that she actively constructs and the audience's reading is focused toward her act of rebuilding. Beth chooses not to repeat any of the wife/mother roles – her own, her mother's or Lorraine's. Instead she tests possibilities through role play. For the female audience this offers a re-constructed act of viewing. While Beth at first appears as a symptom of the limited receptive strategies of earlier Shepard texts (and, as such, the violence and the damage is a given), her actions finally construct an opportunity for resistance. Hardison Londré suggests that Beth's is a 'new kind of voice in Shepard's work'[28] and indeed it is. It is a voice which refutes the assumption

of a homogeneous audience which holds a male gaze and which
contests the hitherto unchallenged supremacy of the cowboy-hero.
When Amy Lippman asked Shepard whether he thought the media
had certain expectations of his work, the playwright responded:

> Sure. It's hard to know what they're expecting. If they're expect-
> ing me to be myself, I can guarantee that will happen all the way
> down the line. If they're expecting me to be Eugene O'Neill, they
> may be disappointed.[29]

The media and other audiences may be far from disappointed with
work which breaks away from a cultural model which insists on
placing Shepard's writing in the tradition of other white American
males who wrote plays. For the female reader/viewer, at last there
is a Shepard play which does not demand her defeminisation as a
condition of reception.

Notes

1.   William W. Demastes, 'The Future of Avante-Garde Theatre and
     Criticism: The Case of Sam Shepard', *Journal of Dramatic Theory and
     Criticism* 4, no. 2 (Spring 1990), p. 5.
2.   Bonnie Marranca, 'Alphabetic Shepard: The Play of Words' in
     American Dreams: The Imagination of Sam Shepard, ed. B. Marranca
     (New York: PAJ Publications, 1976), p. 30.
3.   Florence Falk, 'Men Without Women: The Shepard Landscape' in
     Marranca, p. 91.
4.   Joyce Aaron, 'Clues in a Memory' in Marranca, p. 174.
5.   Quoted in John Dugdale ed., *File on Shepard* (London: Methuen,
     1989), p. 46.
6.   Felicia Hardison Londré, 'Sam Shepard Works Out: The Masculin-
     ization of America', *Studies in American Drama 1945–Present* 2 (1987),
     21.
7.   Amy Lippman, 'A conversation with Sam Shepard', *Gamut* 5 (Janu-
     ary 1984), 18.
8.   Catherine Belsey, *Critical Practice* (London: Methuen, 1980), p. 19.
9.   See for example Ann Wilson, 'Fool of Desire: The Spectator to the
     Plays of Sam Shepard', *Modern Drama* 30, no. 1 (March 1987), 46–57;
     Steven Putzel, 'Expectation, Confutation, Revelation: Audience
     Complicity in the Plays of Shepard', *Modern Drama* 30, no. 2 (June
     1987), 147–60; Susan Harris Smith, 'Estrangement and Engagement:
     Sam Shepard's Dramaturgical Strategies', *Journal of Dramatic Theory
     and Criticism* 3, no. 1 (Fall 1988), 71-84.
10. Richard Gilman, Introd., *Seven Plays*, by Sam Shepard (London:
     Faber, 1985), p. xi.

11. Linda Williams, 'When the Woman Looks' in *Revision: Essays in Feminist Film Criticism* ed. Mary Ann Doane, Patricia Mellencamp and Linda Williams (Frederick, MD: University Publications of America, 1984), p. 83.
12. Sam Shepard, *Fool for Love and Other Plays* (New York: Bantam, 1984), p. 20. All quotations are from this edition; page numbers are given in the text.
13. For further general discussion of the female spectator, see my *Theatre Audiences: A Theory of Production and Reception* (London: Routledge, 1990), pp. 80–91. A more specific reading of the woman's gaze can be found in Mary Ann Doane's 'Film and the Masquerade: Theorising the Female Spectator', *Screen* 23 (1982), 76–87.
14. Annette Kuhn, *Women's Pictures: Feminism and Cinema* (London: Routledge, 1982), p. 64.
15. Rudolf Erben, 'Women and Other Men in Sam Shepard's Plays', *Studies in American Drama 1945–Present* 2 (1987), 40.
16. Wilson, p. 52.
17. Ibid., p. 56.
18. Vincent Canby, 'Shepard's "Fool for Love"', *New York Times* 6 December 1985, C12, p. 32.
19. Ibid., p. 36.
20. Putzel, 157.
21. Ibid., p. 156.
22. Of interest here are Richard Dyer's 'Don't Look Now – The Male Pin-up', *Screen* 23, vols 3–4 (1982), 61-73; and Steve Neale's 'Masculinity as Spectacle' *Screen* 24, no. 6 (1983), 2–17.
23. Erben, 40.
24. Sheila Rabillard, 'Sam Shepard: Theatrical Power and American Dreams', *Modern Drama* 30, no. 1 (March 1987), 68.
25. Ibid., 68–9.
26. Laura Mulvey, *Visual and Other Pleasures* (Bloomington: Indiana University Press, 1989), p. 37. Jackie Stacey offers a useful comment on this strategy of oscillation; she argues its importance for two reasons: 'it displaces the notions of the fixity of spectator positions produced by the text, and it focuses on the gaps and contradictions within patriarchal signification, thus opening up crucial questions of resistance and diversity'. Stacey, 'Desperately Seeking Difference', *Screen* 28 (1987), 52.
27. Sam Shepard, *A Lie of the Mind* (New York: New American Library, 1987), p. 4. All quotations are from this edition; page numbers are given in the text.
28. Londré, 20.
29. Lippman, 19.

11

Lighting Out for the Territory Within: Field Notes on Shepard's Expressionist Vision

Sherrill Grace

I

I feel like there are territories within us that are totally unknown. Huge, mysterious and dangerous territories.

Sam Shepard*

From the beginning, Sam Shepard's work has provoked debate and elicited strong response. His plays are challenging, intense experiences, usually very violent and always ambiguous, and critics have generally agreed that it is as difficult to say exactly what he means as it is to classify how he writes. One response to this dilemma is to give it up – after all, Shepard's is not a theatre of ideas but of feelings. Another response is merely to celebrate his language, his characters, his stagecraft and to describe what happens on a Shepard stage, thereby adding to the already substantial cult status of the man. But the best response, surely, is to take the plays seriously enough to grapple with them, to try to understand why it is that they move us and what they make us feel – and think. If Shepard is to be called great or major or central, then it behooves us to know why.

In the attempt to clarify and explain, critics have turned again and again to such terms as realist, surrealist, fantastic, gothic, abstract and, always, subjective. More often than not, however, these terms are not well defined and, in their application to a particular play, they tend to confuse the issue.[1] What I want to suggest here is that Shepard's vision is expressionist and that to situate his plays in the context of Expressionism is to see them in an illuminating light. At the very least, Expressionism enables us to account for the realist/non-realist tension and the extreme subjectivity of Shepard's work.

The early modernist movement in the arts known as Expressionism demonstrates clear and well-documented links with Romanticism, *fin-de-siècle* symbolism and the ideas of Nietzsche. Its precursors were Edvard Munch, in painting, August Strindberg, in drama, and Walt Whitman, in poetry, but Expressionism came to be seen as the exclusive preserve of Germany, and it was among the German painters, playwrights, poets, filmmakers, composers and novelists that Expressionism flourished between 1905 and 1933. That Expressionism had an impact beyond German borders and, in fact, reappeared in North America during the forties as abstract expressionism and during the eighties as neo-expressionism is not my immediate concern, any more than I am setting out to argue that Sam Shepard was directly and consciously influenced by Expressionism.[2] It is possible to speak of a writer's expressionist poetics and vision without a reductive search for sources and influences, because the intense subjectivity verging on solipsism that characterises all aspects of expressionist art has played a role in western aesthetics for centuries, and expressivity – the desire to express emotion or thought (as distinct from representing objects) in pigment, music or language – is a human constant.

Nevertheless, before turning to Shepard's plays, it is essential to formulate a working definition of Expressionism that will distinguish it from the far more cerebral process of Surrealism and identify its relationship with extremes of abstract art on the one hand and realist art on the other. Expressionist art is based on the assumption that the individual human being (often the artist herself/himself) has an essential Soul or Self that can be expressed (what I will later describe as the 'expressive fallacy')[3] and that in the expressive act the artist articulates something of more than merely personal, private value or consequence. The pressure towards symbolism, even allegory, is very strong, and gives rise to a common feature of all expressionist literature and drama: the expressionist image, a literalised metaphor that represents an inner felt state in a physical, concrete form. Kafka's Gregor Samsa in *Metamorphosis* is a classic example of this, and the grotesque exaggeration of his condition is typical of expressionist images. In the vocabulary of Expressionism, to depict a man as a bug or vermin (*Ungeziefer*) is to say that he feels like one and to shock an audience or readers into acknowledging similar feelings in themselves.

Characters in expressionist plays may vary from extreme abstractions (such as the Figuren in some of Georg Kaiser's plays or the types in Strindberg's *A Dream Play*) to more realistic creations which invite the possibility of empathy (such as Kaiser's Cashier in *From Morn to Midnight*, the student in Strindberg's *Ghost Sonata*, or Yank in O'Neill's *The Hairy Ape*), but they are never the three-dimensional, psychologically motivated individuals developed in accord with realist conventions. The speech of these characters, especially in the expressionist monologues which mark the high point of their emotional outbursts, is often disjointed, illogical and fragmented; their 'dialogue' is seldom more than words hurled past one another or out into a void. Plot and structure in expressionist works, perhaps especially in plays (where the theatrical experience as distinct from a written text counts for so much), is typically non-linear, fragmented, highly iterative and seldom resolved or concluded; they end abruptly in images of apocalypse or regression. Again, as with the characters, the point is not to develop a logical progression of action and event but to express moments of intense feeling or outbursts of violent conflict, and to juxtapose images or scenes of extreme states of mind (alienation, obsessive passion, despair, hatred), of social collapse, psychological dislocation and ontological uncertainty.

An expressionist poetics enables the writer to articulate a vision that is seldom pretty or comforting. Literary and cultural historians have argued that the rise of Expressionism in Germany in the first quarter of this century was intimately connected with the rise of fascism, and it is impossible to overlook the obsession with murder and power or the pervasive patriarchal violence (sons against fathers, males against females) in expressionist work or to deny the sense of crisis, alienation and collapse that is integral to the movement. At the same time, expressionist art, however muddled in its political message, was an art of protest against the cultural and spiritual bankruptcy of the times, against the horror of war and the capitalist and military agenda of the German state. The artist's nostalgic retreat from such a world into nature or within the territory of his own Soul was not an effective political strategy then and it probably will not be now, but perhaps that is not the point. The expressionist vision brings us face to face with a terrible human cry of terror and warning, a cry that can be heard in O'Neill, Glaspel, Williams and Kennedy, and that echoes through Shepard's work to climax in Beth's shattering scream: 'WHO FELL ME!!!'[4]

II

This play is to be performed relentlessly without a break.
Sam Shepard

Rather than attempt to discuss all of Shepard's plays or submit some of them to an exhaustive analysis in the effort to prove them expressionist, I would instead like to make several general observations about the expressionist qualities of certain plays.[5] There is little to be gained by asserting that all his work is one thing or another or that one play is more expressionist than another. My argument is at once more limited and more focused. I believe there are important expressionist qualities in this playwright's work and that to see his vision as expressionist is both to recognise a central element in his aesthetic tradition and to identify the source of an urgent relevance in his voice.

Beginning with his 'family trilogy' *Curse of the Starving Class* (1978), *Buried Child* (1979) and *True West* (1980), Shepard moves away from the more flamboyant expressive abstraction of much of his earlier work towards a greater realism, but these plays, and the two family plays that follow, *Fool for Love* (1983) and *A Lie of the Mind* (1985), are by no means well-made realist plays. They differ from such predecessors as *Suicide in B♭* (1976) or *The Tooth of Crime* (1972), for example, in that they rely less on obvious stylization (the solos and mock-killings in *Suicide*, the ironic mirroring of the two acts of *La Turista*), exaggerated role-playing and cartoon caricature (*The Tooth of Crime*) or extreme fragmentation of speech (in *Suicide* and *Tooth of Crime*) or dramatic structure (*Turista*). The expressive abstraction of these earlier plays renders them less complex, less powerful emotionally, and paradoxically more cerebral (though possibly no less visually memorable on stage) than the family plays. But it is the move towards realism (and thus towards empathy) that creates an important dramatic tension in the later plays – the tension between abstraction and empathy that is central to all expressionist art and is, to my mind, the key to their haunting power.[6] However straightforward they may seem at first, however careful Shepard may be about realistic details or with characters who seem very familiar, sooner or later an audience is forced to abandon the comfortable realm of logic, clarity, predictability and familiarity for an illogical realm of intense emotion, violent unpredictability and complex symbolic, inner states. And it is at precisely that point, that taut moment, that border between the real and the symbolic, but where both are fully at play, that Expressionism lives.

Expressionist theatre, whether Strindberg's, Kaiser's or O'Neill's, has no monopoly on themes of murder, jealousy, betrayal, violence, madness and obsession, or the ontological crisis of masculine identity (and in the misogynist world of Expressionism the hero or artist figure is usually a male who dominates the stage and every female on it), but these themes recur with depressing predictability and concentrated ferocity in expressionist plays. Why this should be so has something to do with the historical, experiential reality of the individual's belief that he can find his identity in some pre-existent, non-socially constructed essence of Selfhood or Soul, and that he can express (and thereby realise and empower) that essence in language. The expressionist dilemma, it seems to me, can be boiled down to this: faced with an alienating, spiritually bankrupt and repressive society, the individual rebels by turning inward in a desperate belief in and nostalgic longing for some inner, essential truth that can be tapped and that will enable him to reach beyond the immediate, repugnant social reality surrounding him to a transcendent Truth. In Shepard's dramatic lexicon this essence is called 'true west' (even his 'true north' is a true west), and the souls of his heroes are the supposed compasses that will point them in the right transcendent direction. Sickened by their nostalgic longing for origins, and hence for meaning, Shepard's men are all looking for this illusory true west, and they erupt in hatred, violence or destructive, manic obsessions when they fail (as fail they must) to find it. Although Shepard may have put a peculiarly American twist on this dilemma, the quest for origins, and the need to heal some obscure yet crippling wound, has preoccupied western humanity for centuries.

To articulate this vision on the stage, Shepard draws on a rich expressionist poetics. His monologues (sometimes called soliloquies, arias or solos) have a central role to play here. Wesley's outburst in act one of *Curse of the Starving Class* provides a classic

example. He begins, naturalistically enough, filling the wheelbarrow and speaking in short, simple sentences as he recalls the
previous night. But within seconds the relentless repetition of 'I
could hear' and 'I could feel' and of the right-branching sentence
structure establishes a rhythm that will carry him deeper within
himself in the effort to express the emotional truth of his vision.
Eventually his sentences break down into fragments of staccato
phrases which convey, less the story of his father's arrival and
departure, than his feelings about these events.

Buried Child, True West, and Fool for Love all function through non-
linear, dislocated structures. In each there is a clear thread of plot,
of narrative progression from beginning to middle to abrupt end,
but it is not this horizontal movement that controls the dramatic
action or gives rise to the acute tension in each play. Instead,
each develops vertically through a centripetal accumulation of
repeated, but basically similar moments which, in the end, return
the characters to the same position they were in at the beginning
– albeit in states of greater loss (Curse), heightened confusion and
despair (Buried Child), deeper hostility (True West) or a more acute
alienation and withdrawal (Fool for Love and A Lie of the Mind).
Little if anything changes in the sense of improving or significantly
altering the face-offs his characters provoke, little if anything is
learned by these figures. The structure of these plays mirrors their
entrapment within claustrophobic rooms of their own creation to
which their only response can be either a violent gesture of escape
(the final image on the wall in Turista, the exploding car in Curse)
or of a defeated withdrawal (Mom in True West, Tilden mounting
the stairs in Buried Child, Meg's failure in A Lie of the Mind).

Shepard has said that he dislikes resolutions in the theatre because
he finds them false, and in the place of resolution Shepard offers,
time and time again, images of violent (and purposeless) apocalypse, or of exhausted (and profoundly ambiguous) regression.[7]
This opting for apocalyptic destruction or various forms of regressive withdrawal is typical of expressionist art which, by the basic
nature of its enterprise, denies the possibility of alternative com-
promise positions or images of catharsis, let alone harmonious
resolutions. Amongst the earlier plays, Icarus's Mother (1965) ends
with a particularly spectacular image of apocalypse, but Curse of the
Starving Class and Fool for Love also end in similarly useless eruptions
of fire, explosion and destruction.

In Curse the destruction seems utterly negative, pervasive, and so extreme as to verge on parody. The play closes with, outside, a blazing car that has killed Emma, inside, the skinned carcass of the lamb, and the forces of destruction loose on all sides; the only thing the survivors can do is re-tell the father's story of the cat and eagle's fight to the death. *Buried Child*, which concludes with appalling images of regression, offers nothing better. With the young Vince now ensconced on the sofa in Dodge's place and posture and Halie's voice reaching us from 'above the staircase' somewhere, we have simply come full circle back to the beginning – but with what hope for change? Tilden crossing the stage, covered in mud and carrying a small child's corpse that 'mainly consists of bones wrapped in muddy, rotten cloth' gives striking, concrete form to the death and corruption, haunting failure and futility at the core of Shepard's world. This is not an image of resurrection, but of regression to the primordial slime, a grotesque enactment of the desire to return to the womb, and a sign of our destructive illusions that outdoes by far the corpse-in-the-garden warning of Eliot's *The Waste Land*.

In 1918 the German theorist Kurt Pinthus predicted that expressionist writing would have its greatest impact in the theatre because 'there Man explodes in front of Man', and a few years later the critic Albert Soergel claimed that 'Expressionism is lyric outcry [and] dramatic stress'.[8] Shepard's theatre, as created through his sets and stage instructions, demonstrates the continued truth of these remarks. With his careful attention to details of staging, lighting and sound effects he pushes his characters and his audiences well beyond the safe confines of social or domestic realism into the mysterious and dangerous 'territory within'. This territory acquires both claustrophobic tension and destructive violence in *True West* and *Fool for Love* where the sedate interior of a middle-class home is turned into a 'ravaged' cage, or a typical run-down motel room harbours walls and doors that 'boom loud and long'. Outside these private spaces coyotes howl, guns blaze and fires erupt, each activity existing on that line between external plausibility and inner truth.

Equally striking is his use of space and light, particularly spots and blackouts, which contribute to dramatic tension at the same time as they facilitate violent contrasts and incongruous juxtapositions in time and place, and realise – that is provide externalized, literal images of – the spiritual abysses between characters. The staircase leading 'left up into the wings with no landing' in *Buried Child* is a disturbing reminder of this. The empty blackness beyond the playing area further intensifies the sense of alienation, radical loneliness, and dislocation in the souls of the creatures struggling to communicate or define themselves under the lights. All these features can be found in Shepard's theatre, but he spells out what he is trying to achieve with the stage very clearly in the 'Set Description' for *A Lie of the Mind*: 'The impression should be of infinite space, going off to nowhere'.[9]

Among the more recent plays, *Fool for Love* provides the most sustained and effective example of expressionist staging. Even before the 'lights begin to rise slowly on stage in the tempo' of Merle Haggard's song 'Wake Up', the audience has entered the private world of May and Eddie, an impoverished, second-hand world of 'faded' and tired objects where the predominant colour is yellow – yellow table and chairs, a faded yellow exterior door, a yellow bathroom door standing slightly ajar to allow 'a yellow light to bleed onto stage' and a yellow-orange light from a streetlamp outside that shines through the window. Apart from the familiar, conventional association of the colour yellow with jealousy and cowardice, and the obvious relevance of these qualities to the inner lives of the characters, the yellow light establishes a disturbing, unnatural atmosphere right from the start. This atmosphere is further intensified by the 'weird stretching sound' Eddie makes with the bucking strap and by the doors and booming walls which Eddie and May continually slam or strike up against as they circle the room and each other. The Old Man, their father, located in his rocking chair on a small black platform stage left, 'exists only in the minds of Eddie and May', a fine example of expressionist literalised metaphor. Like the entire stage, he is a projection of what most haunts and cripples Eddie and May; he is both within them (in their minds, their genes, their past) and outside them, an expression in physical form of the social and cultural failure of contemporary life. Indeed, I would go further to say that, as the father, he symbolises a wide range of spiritual, psychological and ideological problems in Shepard's world.

The fact that *Fool for Love* must be 'performed relentlessly without a break' is the ultimate reminder that we are, for the duration, exposed to the raw, tormented despair and conflict within two human souls. To the degree that we can connect emotionally with these people, recognising in them not so much a pair of representative, contemporary Americans but our own spiritual anguish and psychological crippling (simultaneously a desire for the object and a rejection of it), it is Shepard's tense balancing between abstraction and empathy, his expressionist staging that makes that recognition possible.

What I call the literalised metaphor in expressionist poetics is a common feature of Shepard's work, and each one of these metaphors deserves the kind of full consideration that is impossible here. The maggot-infested lamb in *Curse of the Starving Class* is a telling example of the blight undermining the early promise of life in the play. The 'curse' itself, of course, is the perfect example of an inner state externalised and, through verbal signification (that is in the constructed world of language), rendered negative. Emma's first menses could (should) just as easily be the literal sign of possibility, but in this patriarchal world of sterility, repression, and violence, the female life force is cursed from the start. The carrots and the child (or whatever it is that Tilden carries up the stairs) in *Buried Child* are equally fascinating and disturbing metaphors, as is the flag in *A Lie of the Mind*. But perhaps the most powerful of the literalised metaphors in Shepard's plays is the Doppelgänger figure in *True West*, for Austin and Lee are distorted mirror images of each other; each is the projection of what the other most loathes and desires, and together they express the destructive division that Shepard sees within the human soul.[10]

III

> I'm taking notes in as much detail as possible on an event that's happening somewhere inside me.
>
> Sam Shepard

In 'Language, Visualisation and the Inner Library', Shepard insists that:

> Language can explode from the tiniest impulse . . . In these lightning-like eruptions words are not thought, they're felt. They cut through space and make perfect sense without having to hesitate for the 'meaning'.[11]

To the degree that he has accurately captured his creative method in these sentences, Shepard has, in fact, articulated the basic expressionist credo. At the same time, he alerts us to what I take to be the central paradox – and challenge – of his art. As human beings we exist in language; we need it to make sense of ourselves and our world, and yet, like all expressionist art, Shepard's statement runs headlong into the 'expressive fallacy'. The implication of Shepard's statement and, I think, of the dilemma in each of his plays, is that there is some essence, some *a priori* reality, some romantic Soul trailing clouds of glory within us that precedes language, and that if we could somehow locate that true inner self we would know ourselves and be able to live emotionally and spiritually better lives. And yet, as one after another of Shepard's characters shows, we must live in a language that can never capture that elusive essence. So Lee and Austin struggle for the 'true story. True to life' until they 'just sorta' echo each other'.[12] Beyond the echo of language, without the identities they construct in words and stories, there is nothing for these two but the violence that reduces human beings to howling animals and finally to the silence of death.

Clearly, Shepard recognises the anguish of this impossible search for the essence that precedes existence or for what Hal Foster calls the 'metaphysics of presence'.[13] What is less clear is whether or not he has recognised the futility of that search and is, therefore, prepared to suggest alternate ways of making sense. This issue, moreover, goes to the very heart of Expressionism for the main charge levelled against it in the past (by Brecht among others)[14] was that in its self-indulgent, morbid championing of the suffering individual Soul and in its romantic belief in personal essence and transcendent Presence, it avoided, to a large degree, a clear articulation of the socio-political basis of human problems, and that this abnegation of responsibility was the sign of incipient fascist tendencies. While it may be pointless to expect political answers from artists, let alone 'ideologically correct' ones, it is nevertheless important to try to understand the underlying assumptions and the significance of their art, especially when they speak as powerfully as Shepard does. A consideration of these questions, however, requires a closer look at both the language and the ending of at least one play, and I will choose *A Lie of the Mind* for this because it seems to me to represent, to date, Shepard's most critically self-aware and important expression of what is 'happening somewhere inside [him]'.

A Lie of the Mind is predicated upon an act of extreme violence. A husband, Jake, has beaten his wife, Beth, so badly that he has almost killed her, and he has certainly caused severe trauma if not irreversible physical damage. Insofar as a reason (motivation, etiology) is given for this act, we are led to believe that he did this, in the first instance, because he was jealous of her acting career. He was at once suspicious of her behaviour with male actors and envious of her ability to play roles, to command language, to lead a separate existence, independent of him. When she developed a complex understanding of reality as a construction ('She tells me this [the play, the role, the theatre] is the real world' (101), he felt threatened because her very existence contradicted his unexamined and inarticulate need to locate the real as a fixed essence within himself, an essence that he could find projected in her, that she in fact would focus and mirror for him. Unable to stand the loss of her comforting mirror-image and threatened by her separate version of reality, he resorted to the physical violence that, in his rage, he believed would re-affirm his authority and dominance.

Given the appalling degree of male violence against women in contemporary Western society, Shepard would appear to have touched an extremely sensitive nerve here and to be tackling an urgent problem. And there can be no doubt, I think, that Beth and what she represents means a great deal to Shepard.[15] However, our understanding of her positive value and of the negative forces that oppose her depends largely upon the roles of the male characters in the play: her brother and father, Frankie and Jake. Here again, there can be little doubt that the men come off badly. Mike is a bully; Baylor is a tyrant with all the weakness and insecurity of a tyrant; Frankie, though comparatively gentle and reasonable, is ineffectual against the patriarchal network of fathers, sons and brothers. And Jake? Well, Jake is a problem. We are invited to feel sorry for him first in act one, scenes two and three, and then in act two, scene four, when his obsessive longing for Beth, whom he sees as part of him, drives him on his journey to Montana; and finally at the end of the play when he is brutalized and defeated himself. What is more, Sally's confession in act three, scene one, shifts a large portion of the blame for Jake's violence from him to his own father who, whether alive or dead, haunts and cripples him.

If it is true, then, that the real curse in Shepard's world is passed on from father to son, then *A Lie of the Mind*, by identifying that curse with such vivid attention to the actual victims of it – the beaten and murdered women, the twisted and destructive men – should be expected by audiences and readers alike to go right to the heart of the problem and demonstrate the costs of continued lying. Whether it does or not, however, is not clear. Beth certainly does articulate, somewhat in the manner of a holy fool, an alternative to the destructive, repressive violence of the patriarchy as embodied in Baylor and Mike (both of whom she rejects) by embracing the gentler Frankie. But Frankie is, at best, luke-warm about accepting Beth and what she represents; he came to this home, after all, as a fraternal ambassador, and he insists that Beth 'belongs' to Jake. No question here of his recognising her separate autonomy as a human being who belongs to herself and makes her own decisions, plays her own roles, and accepts the responsibility for constructing a separate reality. And this ability to play roles, to articulate reality was, if I read Shepard correctly, what Jake tried to destroy and what Shepard is trying to defend.

Still more disconcerting are Jake's final words:

> JAKE: (*To* BETH, *very simple*) These things – in my head – lie to me. Everything lies. Tells me a story. Everything in me lies. But you. You stay. You are true. I know you now. You are true. I love you more than this life. You stay. You stay with him. He's my brother.
>
> (128–29)

Given the context of this play, and of all Shepard's plays, the value of words like 'story' and 'true' is hard to pin down, and as a result Jake's speech raises more questions than it answers. Are stories always lies? Or is it only the patriarchal story that Jake has completely internalised that lies to him? If stories are always lies, then what is the meaning of *A Lie of the Mind*? If, as I suggested above, the need for truth and reality that drove Jake to violence in the first place was shaped by his desire for primordial essence, original, stable 'true west', then what does he now understand by the words 'You stay. You are true'? Has Jake recognised the trap of the 'expressive fallacy'? Has Shepard? What or who exactly is it that Jake now knows as Beth? Surely if he recognises and accepts in her the necessarily constructed nature of reality through language and role-playing, as well as her right to make her own reality, he would not command her to 'stay' with anyone? Is it all right that he give this order because he knows his brother is gentler and, for some inexplicable reason, less contaminated than he is by the curse of the fathers? What does it mean to be Jake's brother? And finally (at least for the present) is Shepard saying that the violent battering of a woman can lead a man (or a woman) to the truth?

My attempted answer to some of these questions brings me back
to the challenge and dilemma of Expressionism. Despite what I
believe to be a sincere attempt on Shepard's part to cut through
the many lies of the mind that deceive us, I am not convinced that
he has yet dismantled the 'expressive fallacy' and shaken off its
strangle-hold on his own thinking. Clearly, the violence of men in a
patriarchal system stands condemned in this play; clearly, Beth tries
to articulate her hope for and the possibility of a gentler, feminised
world. Clearly, she tries to modify the immediate, stultifying and
deceptive reality around her by acting out her vision of a larger
human truth. But just as clearly, Frankie rejects her vision, and
the world at large, represented by her brother, father, mother and
that American flag, remains unaware, unmoved, unassailable and
in charge. I would go further and suggest that in Beth, Shepard
has created his most disturbing literalised metaphor for 'true west'
because, in the final analysis, Beth is offered to us as a projection of
Jake's need (not her own) for that story which is the most deadly of
all illusions: the male dream of pure origin, of essence, of a Reality
that supersedes and erases the reality of a woman beaten, almost to
death, in the desperate effort to preserve and defend that illusion.
Like Gregor Samsa, in *A Lie of the Mind* Beth becomes the outward
and visible sign of that fundamental fallacy, and in the process we
are tempted to forget everything else she represents. What we may
also forget is that, like her, we can, in fact, only and always create a
role within a constructed reality.

Of course, *A Lie of the Mind* does not end with Jake's avowal
and command. In some ways this play reverses the pattern of
earlier ones which move towards a destructive, apocalyptic ending.
Here, the apocalyptic outburst opens the drama which, instead of
revealing a new order of things, runs downhill from that emotional
high into a bizarre serenity at the end. Meg and Baylor, oblivious to
all around them, dominate the stage with their ceremonial folding of
the American flag. In doing so they have withdrawn into the most
traditional of patriarchal/patriotic roles – without any acknowledgement that they are playing roles. Indeed, Meg who keeps this
family going (insofar as it functions at all) retreats even further into a
fog of nostalgic romance at Baylor's kiss. The words with which she
closes the play leave us with a regressive image of life's paradoxes,
antinomies and creative potential reduced to fragments flickering
at the periphery of our vision: 'Looks like a fire in the snow. How
could that be?' The fire burning in the bucket/in the snow is, on

one level, all that remains of Jake's past and, like Meg's question, it throws us back to Lorraine's question: 'Who's comin' back?'. But on another level, the fire in the bucket reminds us of who has been forgotten (Beth) and what has been excluded and repressed in the final moments of the play.

The crucial question this play leaves us with, however, is not who or how, but what: what hope remains for change or understanding in a world where all we can do is beat or be beaten, escape, never to come back, or withdraw inwards and back to a lost past? Like all expressionists, Sam Shepard has taken us on an exploration of the mysterious, dangerous territory within his own soul – and ours. What we find there and what we do with that discovery depends on our willingness to return from that journey with both the experience and the meaning.

Notes

* The quotations that begin each part of this discussion are taken from the following sources: 'Rhythms and Truths', interview with Amy Lippman, *American Theatre* 1, no. 1 (April 1984), 12; *Fool for Love* in *Fool for Love and Other Plays* (Toronto: Bantam, 1984), p. 19; 'Language, Visualisation and the Inner Library' in *American Dreams: The Imagination of Sam Shepard*, ed. Bonnie Marranca (New York: Performing Arts Journal Publications, 1981), p. 215.

1. I will not try to list here all the attempts to classify Shepard's work as 'realist' or 'surrealist', and so on. Some critics, however, run into particular trouble with terminology. In her article 'Alphabetical Shepard', in her book *American Dreams*, Bonnie Marranca calls his work 'realism' (and is obliged to stretch the meaning of the term beyond recognition) and 'melodrama'. She also describes it as 'based on an expressionist view of character' (p. 15), but she does not develop the point. In 'Worse Than Being Homeless', *American Dreams*, pp. 117–25, William Kleb describes Shepard's plays as a mixture of 'the real and the surreal', yet he goes on to mention several features peculiar to Expressionism. Throughout *Inner Landscapes: The Theatre of Sam Shepard* (Columbia: University of Missouri Press, 1984), Ron Mottram notes Shepard's use of characters which are 'projections of his own imagination' (p. 14) and are forced 'to externalize inner states' (p. 153), and comments upon Shepard's predilection for apocalyptic endings and his 'expressive tendencies' (p. 164), but he still insists on thinking of the plays as realistic.

2. I have discussed German Expressionism and its manifestations in North American writing in *Regression and Apocalypse: Studies*

in North American Literary Expressionism (Toronto: University of
Toronto Press, 1989), and in that book I argued that a vital component of American modernism and postmodernism can be traced to
expressionist influences. Sam Shepard stands, I think, in a direct line
with other expressionist writers in the United States such as Thomas
Pynchon, Adrienne Kennedy, Tennessee Williams (in *Camino Real*),
Ralph Ellison, Djuna Barnes, Eugene O'Neill, Susan Glaspell and
others stretching back to Whitman.

3.   I have borrowed the term 'expressive fallacy' from Hal Foster who
also sees this 'metaphysics of presence' as central to Expressionism:
'Such is the pathos of the expressionist self: alienated, it would be
made whole through expression, only to find there another sign of
its alienation . . . for even as expressionism insists on the primary,
originary, interior self, it reveals that this self is never anterior to
its traces, its gestures, its "body"'. See Hal Foster, *Recodings: Art,
Spectacle, Cultural Politics* (Seattle: Bay Press, 1983), p. 62.

4.   Though grammatically a question, Shepard punctuates Beth's cry
as an extreme exclamation; see *A Lie of the Mind* (New York: New
American Library, 1986), p. 5. All quotations are from this edition;
page numbers are given in the text.

5.   I have chosen to concentrate upon *Curse of the Starving Class, Buried
Child, True West, Fool for Love* and *A Lie of the Mind* in part because
I have been able to see one or more production of each and in
part because the particular mix of representation and stylization,
of empathy and abstraction, makes them especially interesting
examples of expressionist poetics. The published editions of these
plays quoted in the text are from *Fool for Love and Other Plays* and
Sam Shepard: Seven Plays (Toronto: Bantam, 1986). All quotations are
from these editions; page numbers are given in the text.

6.   The opposing tendencies of abstraction and empathy were first
described and theorized by Wilhelm Worringer in *Abstraktion und
Einfühlung* (1908); see *Regression and Apocalypse*, pp. 30–34.

7.   In his interview with Amy Lippman, 'Rhythm and Truths', *American
Theatre* 1, no. 1 (1984), Shepard says that he thinks 'it's a cheap trick
to resolve things. It's a complete lie to make resolutions' (10), but
resolution does not necessarily entail contrivance, and violent apocalypse or exhausted regression do not necessarily signify honesty.

8.   Pinthus' remark from his 1918 'Speech addressed to young writers'
is quoted in John Willett, *Expressionism* (New York: McGraw-Hill,
1970), p. 117 and Soergel's is quoted in Armin Arnold, *Prosa des
Expressionismus* (Stuttgart: W. Kohlhammer Verlag, 1972), p. 12 (my
translation).

9.   Sam Shepard, *Fool for Love and Other Plays*, p. xi.

10. The doubling that Shepard creates here is exclusively male, which is
typical of Expressionism, but it could just as easily involve a female,
and Shepard suggests as much with characters like May and Beth.

11. Marranca, *American Dreams*, p. 217.

12. *Seven Plays*, pp. 42, 55.

13. See note #3. In her important study, 'Great Expectations: Language

and the Problem of Presence in Sam Shepard's Writing', in *Sam Shepard: A Casebook*, ed. Kimball King (New York: Garland, 1988), pp. 135–53, Ann Wilson examines Shepard's work from a Derridean perspective and comes to some interesting conclusions about both the problematics of his language and his American literary tradition. When she notes, for example, that the 'failure of language to reveal fully what it signifies' (p. 138) is central to Shepard and that the 'nostalgic yearning for an authentic self is perhaps the most striking feature common both to Shepard's writing and Whitman's' (p. 140), she has identified what I am describing here as his struggle with the 'expressive fallacy' of Expressionism.

14. The original debate over the ideology of German Expressionism is set forth in Ernst Bloch's 'Diskussionen über Expressionismus', *Erbschaft dieser Zeit* (Frankfurt: Suhrkamp Verlag, 1962), translated as 'Discussing Expressionism' by Rodney Livingstone in *Aesthetics and Politics*, ed. Ronald Taylor (London: NLB, 1977). See also Stephen Eric Bronner's thorough reconsideration of the debate in 'Expressionism and Marxism: Towards an Aesthetic of Emancipation', *Passion and Rebellion: The Expressionist Heritage*, ed. Stephen Eric Bronner and Douglas Kellner (London: Croom Helm, 1983), pp. 411–53; Siegfried Kracauer, *From Caligari to Hitler* (Princeton: Princeton University Press, 1947), and Benjamin Buchloh, 'Figures of Authority, Ciphers of Regression: Notes on the Return of Representation in European Painting', *October* 16 (1981), 39–68.

15. It could be argued that Beth is Shepard's artist surrogate in this play, or perhaps his muse. Either way, her tragic fate holds little hope for the artist's message which, like Cassandra's, is misunderstood and dismissed.

12

'I Smash the Tools of my Captivity': The Feminine in Sam Shepard's *A Lie of the Mind*

Jane Ann Crum

I

The critical discourse surrounding Shepard and the feminine is probably best represented by Bonnie Marranca's summation:

> . . . he has not radicalized the way women interact in dramatic form, neither has he given them a new language . . . . The voice – of consciousness, of the emotions, of reason, of triumph, and of failure, too – and finally, of America – is a man's voice.[1]

Marranca calls for 'a female language' to be added to the other languages Shepard has mastered, at which time the 'silent voices' (the female characters) will tell their stories.

According to Marranca, the women in Shepard's plays (with the exception of Cavale in *Cowboy Mouth*)[2] exist only in the background, playing subservient roles that lack the imaginative range present in the male characters. But behind Marranca's critique lies an unspoken value system which ascribes merit to female characters who would attain such attributes as dominance and autonomy. Marranca does not want 'the feminine' as a presence in Shepard's work so much as she wants female characters who speak and act with the authority of men. In other words, the women portrayed should be empowered *as men are empowered* in order to participate more fully in the unarguably patriarchal world Shepard creates.

While Marranca's suggestions may be plausible in their context, certain feminist theorists provide an alternative view. Hélène Cixous' concept of *écriture féminine*[3] (feminine writing) includes, even embraces, such writers as Antonin Artaud and Jean Genet, and warns against confusing the sex of the author with the sex of the writing. To write a feminine text, the author need not be a woman, but must implement Derrida's notion of *différance*, or more specifically, 'split open the closure of the binary opposition and revel in the pleasures of open-ended textuality'.[4] On a political level, this notion of feminine writing is integrally related to the idea of power. Rather than complying with the patriarchal binary thought which has dominated Western philosophical systems (i.e. activity/passivity; culture/nature; head/emotions; rational/sensitive; the first term of each sequence being inevitably perceived as male or superior while the second term is continually linked to the feminine or inferior side),[5] the very act of feminine writing rejects binary opposition and challenges the power structures which result from phallogocentrism.

If, as Marranca has stated, one of the most problematic aspects of Shepard's writing is his 'consistent refusal or inability'[6] to create viable female characters, *A Lie of the Mind* would seem to negate the no-woman's land of the earlier plays, not simply because brain-damaged Beth is one of the most extraordinary characters in his canon, nor because its subject is the relations between man and woman. Character and thematic content aside, *A Lie of the Mind* offers two diverse models of feminine revolution, two methods by which the female characters liberate themselves from submissive roles and activities and achieve 'the landscape of the female body'.[7] Set into motion with the confession of a brutal act of patriarchal violence, the parallel dramaturgy of *A Lie of the Mind* underscores dual models of feminine reaction to male oppression, the first characterised by a ritualised burning of the father's house, the second a gradual transformation of the sexual and economic exchanges between men and women.

At first glance, one of these models appears to be the most active in the sense that Lorraine and Sally vacate and destroy the father's house. A radically aggressive move, their action supports a feminist viewpoint which considers power a peculiarly male obsession and vigorously attacks what it perceives to be an all-pervasive and universal misogyny.[8] This model also upholds the ideal of autonomy, a synonym for everything denied women living under patriarchy –

economic, social, creative, and physical freedom, and in this case, freedom from history. As Lorraine sees it, only one course of action guarantees self-preservation. Her son Jake, to whom she has offered sanctuary and sustenance, has abandoned her as his father did before him: 'He's run off to the wild world when he could've stayed here under my protection. He could've stayed here forever and no one could've touched him'.[9] Bereft, yet angered, Lorraine admits defeat, but only in the context of the men's failure: 'You can't save the doomed! You make a stab at it. You make the slightest little try and you're doomed yourself' (89). If she and her daughter are to be 'saved', another road must be taken, and that road leads toward revolution.

II

. . . I smash the tools of my captivity, the chair the table the bed. I destroy the battlefield that was my home. I fling open the doors so the wind gets in and the scream of the world. I smash the window. With my bleeding hands I tear the photos of the men I loved and who used me on the bed on the table on the chair on the ground. I set fire to my prison . . .
                    Ophelia, from Heiner Müller's *Hamletmachine*[10]

Lorraine and Sally engage in leave-taking. Their men, husband and father, sons and brothers, are gone; only the house, a place of indeterminate walls without ceilings containing only a bed and a chair, remains. Into a metal bucket are tossed 'odd papers and paraphernalia from the men' (115), three items described in exact detail: a letter describing a baseball scholarship, a blue rosette ribbon from a livestock show, and plastic model airplanes of World War Two fighters and bombers. No hint of sentimentality is evidenced for the things discarded. The silence of their individual activities (the mother reading travel brochures, the daughter haphazardly examining the *bricolage*[11] of the past), is broken by phrases such as: 'Naw, toss it' (116), and 'Naw, burn it' (117). Into the bucket goes 'all the junk in this house that they left behind for me to save' (94), junk Lorraine believes was left 'to keep me on the hook' (96). Each item is associated with male identity and male pursuits: the baseball field, one of the few sites of approved male bonding, the first place ribbon, suggesting the love of competition; and miniature airplanes, commercialised icons of the wars of men. A single item is saved, a photograph from the 1940s of the mother and her sorel mare taken during a Frontier Days parade, to be secreted in Sally's purse with the simple explanation 'I just like the picture' (117).

A peculiar quietness exists between mother and daughter; prolonged, intimate silences that result from persons grown accustomed to each other's presence, an affability they have never evidenced before. Then, casually and without fanfare, they rise from their positions, the mother from the bed, the daughter from the chair, and Lorraine strikes a blue-tipped wooden match whose flame lights the papers in the bucket. The lights around them fade, the fire in the bucket continues to glow, and we imagine them outside the house on the parched yellow grass that characterizes the winter months of the southwestern states. Perhaps we remember a previous scene, when Lorraine wishes for a wind which will let in Ophelia's 'scream of the world': 'One a' them fierce, hot, dry winds that come from deep out in the desert and rip the trees apart' (97). Even as the lights dim around the blaze they have ignited, we envision their celebration as they watch the conflagration of the father's house.

> LORRAINE: Nah – maybe we won't run. Maybe we'll just stand out there on the front lawn, the two of us, and watch it burn for a while. Sing a song maybe. Do a little jig. Then we'll just turn and walk away. Just walk.
> SALLY: Well, we're not gonna have any place to come back to, Mom.
> LORRAINE: Who's comin' back?
>
> (120)

Their calm deceives, their quietude beguiles, for this is not a simple departure, but a conscious, verbalized, act of destruction. Like doctors working without benefit of antibiotics, they cut out the infected flesh, the 'disease' (92) the father left behind him which still inhabits his deserted wife, and cauterize the wound. Like Müller's Ophelia, they set fire to their prison of chairs, beds, and photos of men they loved, and escape male parameters. Ophelia takes her revolution into the streets. Lorraine and Sally journey to another continent, to Sligo county near Connaught, a place remembered fondly by a maternal grandmother, a place where the mere mention

of Lorraine's maiden name will provide them with safe harbour on
a green isle surrounded by the waters of the Atlantic. From desert to
ocean, from dry winds to moist breezes, their action catapults them
out of the narrative, out of recent history and into the legendary
past. Lorraine and Sally's rejection of the phallus returns them to
the motherland.

But the fire in the bucket still burns and its flames serve as the
visual transition to the opposite side of the stage. There, in another
state, in another father's house, a young woman helps support an
injured man and, with a soft embrace, lays her head on his chest.
Her mode of dress is described as 'bizarre' (111) an odd assortment
of green tights, short woollen bobby socks, a tight pink skirt, a fuzzy
turquoise-blue sweater, and black high heels. Yet this strange, even
perverse, attire is accompanied by a *bricolage* of another sort, one
which has not been discarded, but which bedecks the owner. Here
is an assemblage of symbols of faith and hope both secular and
sacred: 'charm bracelets and a silver chain around her neck with
a St. Christopher medal, a gold cross and a rabbit's foot' (111).
The young couple stands silent and unmoving, a silhouette of
two bodies entwined, Frankie stiff and distraught as he watches
his older brother disappear into the winter night, Beth's slight form
a living crutch as she holds him upright. Again we hear words from
a previous scene when she insists 'once we're together, the whole
world will change. We'll be in a whole new world' (114).

Taking no notice of their daughter's presence in the room or the
activities in which she is involved, Meg and Baylor fold a large
American flag. Baylor instructs his helpmate in the task; Meg,
attired in nightclothes, works obediently, 'staying put' (129) as her
husband shuffles slowly towards her. The stripes disappear into the
gradually thickening folds of the triangle and, at last, the white stars
on the field of blue are uppermost. With a triumphant cry 'There!
Look at that! We did it, Meg!' (130) Baylor picks up his wife and
*'twirls her around, then sets her down and kisses her on the cheek, holding
flag up'* (130).

We are party to a domestic miracle of sorts, as is evidenced by
Meg's reaction to a husband who has not kissed her in twenty years,
for she 'holds her hand to her cheek' (130) and steps away from
him, staring around the room as if 'bewildered', yet another and
more substantial miracle is in the making. Never taking her hand
from her cheek, Meg turns and stares out toward the porch, still
unaware of Frankie and Beth, and after a long pause, she speaks the

words that comprise the transformation of which she is a part, for her vision changes, and as a newly-born Sybil, a prophetess, a literal 'see-er' and figurative 'seer', she looks across time and space and explodes the careful conventions of stage reality which have been observed throughout the theatrical event, an unspoken agreement between spectator and performer that the theatre space, visually separated by a chasm of darkness, suggests two states as disparate as Oklahoma and Montana, and two houses, the interior landscapes of women, frequented by mothers as dissimilar as acerbic Lorraine and enigmatic Meg. In this moment, a violent tear in the fabric of reality, Meg announces/questions her counterpart's revolutionary act: 'Looks like a fire in the snow. How could that be?' (131).

Here, in the closing moments of *A Lie of the Mind*, the duality of Shepard's dramaturgy is bridged by *la mystérique*, a term used by Luce Irigaray to describe mystic language or discourse, the only place in the history of the West in which women spoke eloquently in a public forum. This place is one 'where consciousness is no longer master . . . where "she" . . . speaks about the dazzling glare which comes from the source of light that has been logically repressed'.[12] As read through Irigaray's definition of *la mystérique*, Meg experiences the loss of subjecthood through the disappearance of the subject/object opposition, something Toril Moi believes to hold 'a particular appeal for women, whose very subjectivity is . . . denied and repressed by patriarchal discourse'.[13] In this manner, Meg, who has been described as 'dozing through life',[14] and seems an initially comic figure when she cannot distinguish her existence from that of her mother (a woman who is described by Baylor as 'crazy' and by Meg as 'pure female'), achieves dignity by her ability to venture across the abyss which separates 'that place' from 'this place' and dissolves the difference between 'I' and 'not I'. Her mystical experience eludes logic, rejecting rational thought processes in favour of ecstatic revelation. Baylor insists on the separation of categories: 'A deer is a deer and a person is a person. They got nothin' to do with each other' (104). Meg intuits that such separations are meaningless, that while her mother hadn't 'any trace of male', her daughter's 'got male in her' (104), and that Baylor's logic aside, 'Some people are like deer. They have that look – that distant thing in their eyes' (104).

In addition to its aura of mysticism, Meg's utterance assumes the importance Roland Barthes ascribes to speaking last, a position whereby the speaker 'assign[s] a destiny to everything that has been said, to master, to possess, to absolve, to bludgeon meaning'.[15] Her final words, then, confer upon Meg the power of assigning meaning, of putting into perspective the entire event of the play. Lorraine and Sally have departed, their fire burns after them, and in tones of wonderment, Meg recognizes and questions the effectiveness of their act. It is Meg who confirms that 'the female one needs – the other . . . the male' (105), and despite her observation that 'the male one – doesn't really need the other' (105) or, at least his need is not 'the same' as the female, she also predicts that because the male doesn't know what he needs, he 'ends up dead. By himself' (105).

In accordance with Meg's prophecy, Mike and Jake depart the world of the play of their own volition; Mike assigning his role as son to Jake, and Jake relinquishing his role as husband to Frankie, who by extension will become son to Meg and husband to Beth. Lorraine's husband abandons his family, but like Laius at the crossroads 'ends up dead' as the result of an Oedipal confrontation with his son (which takes the form of a maniacal bar-hopping race between the curiously unnamed father and Jake). A chronic alcoholic, he is dubbed 'doomed' (89) by his wife, 'one a' them hopeless men' (94) who 'doesn't know what he needs' (105). He 'goes off by himself' (105), a rejection of his role as husband and father, only to tape pictures of his family to the wall of his trailer (a habitat best suited to a wanderer) amongst such public personalities as Bing Crosby, Ginger Rogers, Ida Lupino, Gene Autry, and Louis Armstrong, an act which leads his daughter to believe that 'he must've spent a lot of time talking to these faces . . . Trying to make a family out of us all. So we'd know each other' (90). This pitiable act of fictionalising a family is contrasted with Sally's description of him as he turns on her when he lies drunk and battered on the street, a 'deep, deep hate that came from somewhere far away' (93) in his eyes as he snarls at her 'like a crazy dog' (94). The dichotomy that destroys men is this inability to align manhood (the father's attempted besting of his son in a self-destructive drinking contest, Jake's repeated fits of violence in the face of his uncertainty of his wife's affections) with husband/parenthood (the father's picture-worship of his family, Jake's avowal that he loves Beth 'more than this earth' (124)). Father and son, who abandon and batter, are abandoned in turn by Lorraine and Sally; yet this first model of revolution – one which rejects male power to hinder or harm the female – ends in sterility as the women vacate the patriarchal landscape of the American continent. If the continuation of the species is to be assured, it is for Meg, the seer, and Beth, the truth-sayer, to re-socialize the invalid men who find themselves in the company of women who exist in altered states.

Admittedly, the two men on whom continuance lies do not come into the female preserve by choice. Ron Mottram[16] applies the Freudian term 'castration' to Frankie's thigh wound, yet fails to point out that Baylor, too, with his cracked and bleeding feet, is equally immobilized. Inability to move freely may be a unique interpretation of castration, but seems fitting since they are sequestered in a place not of their choosing. Baylor's injury is self-inflicted, the result of days spent in his primitive hunting shack. His remedy, mink oil (used to waterproof leather), seems a stubborn, even martyred rejection of antiseptic ointments that could heal his open wounds. Baylor, the 'hunter/wanderer' (as described by Rosemarie Bank)[17] who has been forced to occupy a new space, the women's interior landscape, as a result of his injury and the blizzard which rages outside the house, is responsible for Frankie's entry into this world of women. Frankie comes 'crashing through that stand of aspen like a freight train' (50) and is shot like an antlered buck. Frankie's entrance into the house results in Mike's self-banishment, since he refuses to frequent his parents' house if it shelters any kin of the enemy: 'I'm not stayin' in the same house with the brother of the man who tried to kill my sister! I'm not doin' that' (52).

Mike's rage throughout the play emulates that of the vengeful Furies, but reverses their gender, since Chthonic female deities traditionally punished those who broke the bonds of oikos, the ties of blood. Because Beth demonstrates no intention of punishing Jake, Mike assumes the role of revenger:

> You wormed your way in, didn't you? Pretty cute. I'm not forgettin' anything. Everybody else might forget but I'm not. Far as I'm concerned you and your brother are the same person. (52)

Jake's insistence on his inability to 'forget' implies his separation from the forgetfulness that exists in his mother (her seeming inability to disassociate herself from her mother's identity) and his sister (whom he accuses of daily vacillations: 'Oh, so now you're *not* dead. Today you're not dead. Yesterday you were dead but today you're not. I gotta keep track a' this' (44). Mike's revenge comes to fruition in the taming of Jake (a third incident of a male immobilised by another male), but by this time his act is meaningless, not the least because Jake has passed out of the realm of Beth's memory. Lacking the capacity for forgetfulness towards wrongs committed in the past, his brutal traumatisation of Jake should be judged in the context of Meg, who when informed that Jake will be made to apologise to her, replies: 'Nobody has to apologize to me. Nobody has ever offended me in any way' (113). It is this rigidity, this inability to forget, and by extension, to forgive, that forces Mike outside the enclave of the family.

In a macabre sequence in Act II, scene 3, Mike dumps the hindquarters of the buck he has shot on the living room floor, announcing his intention to mount the 'rack', the unarguably phallic antlers of the 'trophy buck' (79), and restating in a symbolic sense Frankie's position as 'prize', a trophy shot by Baylor who will eventually be claimed by Beth. This transformation of men into animals is a constant and irrefutable construction on Shepard's part. Mike's taming of Jake, driving him like a 'draft horse' (120) with the flag as reins; Sally's description of her father as a mad dog or a rooster pecking at hens and chicks, likening his dead body to something 'splattered all over the road like some lost piece of livestock' (95); all of these images suggest the 'other-ness' of the male, the animal and by extension, the inhuman qualities of these doomed and hopeless men.

III

Let us imagine . . . a real liberation of sensuality, that is, a transformation of our relationship to our body (– and to another body), an approximation of the immense material organic sensual universe that we are. Then 'femininity', 'masculinity', would inscribe their effects of difference, their economy, their relationships to expenditure, to deficit, to giving, quite differently.

Hélène Cixous, 'Sorties', *La jeune née*[18]

To begin a consideration of the second model of revolution, the one which redeems even as it rebels and redetermines how power might be transformed/shared between genders, we must first locate its origins. The most incisive question would seem to be the one on which all events hinge, namely, why does Jake 'kill' Beth? This particular emphasis, although it may not be factual, has special import as it relates to the beating as the instigating action of the play as well as the locus of the second model of revolution. There is evidence that he has beaten her before (FRANKIE: 'So you beat her up again' (11). SALLY: 'There was other times when you said you'd killed her – when you thought you'd killed her – remember?' (60)), yet never to this degree.

> JAKE: I killed her.
> (*Pause*)
> FRANKIE: You killed her.
> JAKE: That's right.
> FRANKIE: She stopped breathing?
> JAKE: Everything stopped.
>
> (11)

'Everything stopped', and in that moment, in Jake's mind, Beth dies. Her crime is one of property, for although she 'denied it flat' (8), he believes she gave what is rightfully his (the pleasures of her body) to another man. Probably the most telling passage in this diatribe against her comes at the very beginning of the third scene as he remembers her applying sweet-smelling oils ('Coconut or Butterscotch') to her body.

> I'd watch her oiling herself while I pretended to be asleep. She was in a dream, the way she did it. Like she was imagining someone else touching her. Not me. Never me. Someone else. (8)

Even a cursory reading of what follows clarifies that Jake's theory of Beth's sexual involvement with another man (the so-called 'actor-jerk') is pure fantasy, a fiction devised to divert his attention from a notion so disturbing that he must invent a masculine adversary rather than face the fact of his wife's burgeoning sexual autonomy. The 'someone else' is Beth herself, since her session with the oils is autoerotic, an act which defies duplication by the male. In *This Sex Which Is Not One*, Irigaray posits female eroticism as plural rather than the 'one', the phallus-dominated sexuality of the male of the species:

> But *woman has sex organs more or less everywhere*. She finds pleasure almost anywhere. [The] geography of her pleasure is far more diversified, more multiple in its differences, more complex, more

subtle, than is commonly imagined – in an imaginary rather too narrowly focused on sameness.[19]

Alone with her oils, her scents, the textures of her skin, Beth becomes both object and subject, lover and loved one, sexually aroused without necessity of touching her genitalia, a sexuality so foreign to Jake, that all logic aside, there must be 'another'. 'Everything changed', he explains, but those changes do not seem to be Beth's affections/desire for Jake, but a liberation of her being to the point that she becomes 'unrecognisable', and threatening to the degree that he must divest himself of her. His masculine prejudice toward sexuality, that pleasure cannot exist without possession, that satisfaction can be reached only through manipulation or penetration, is negated by Beth's unique brand of eroticism. What he cannot possess or understand he must degrade or kill, and love becomes war.

As the victim of Jake's vicious attack, Beth is most often seen as the leading tragic character by those who read the play as a document of failure.[20] At the same time, although we may react sympathetically to her as an abused woman, it is undeniable that her injury successfully transports her to another realm, an avenue of self-hood where her use of language supersedes patriarchal logic. While most critics concede that Beth's altered voice reveals truths of a sort not usually spoken aloud between adults (i.e. about Meg: 'You – you a love. You – you are only this. Only. You don' know. Only love' (46). About Baylor: 'He's given up love. Love is dead for him. My mother is dead for him' (57)), they complain that she is 'confused and dramatically limited'.[21] Yet in the first scene of Act II, having left the hospital and entered her father's house, she becomes an undeniably active force, refusing to support Mike's ill-conceived notion of vengeance ('You make – you make a war. You make a war. You make an enemy. In me. In me! . . . You – you have a feeling. You have a feeling I'm you. I'm not you!' (45)), even as she accepts her role as one who has been transformed:

This – This – (*She moves slowly toward* FRANKIE.) This is me. This is me now. The way I am. Now. This. All. Different. I – I live inside this. (57)

It is no wonder that Beth is continually described as damaged goods, a pathetic victim, a speaker lacking coherence, for '[h]ers are contradictory words, somewhat mad from the standpoint of reason, inaudible for whoever listens to them with ready-made grids, with fully elaborated code in hand'.[22] To understand Beth one must listen differently, or as Irigaray recommends, with another ear: 'as if hearing an "other meaning" always in the process of weaving itself, of embracing itself with words, but also of getting rid of words in order not to become fixed, congealed in them'.[23]

This longing to subvert logos, to undermine exact meanings, to admit that words, in and of themselves, are unfit to translate certain concepts that oppose patriarchal thinking, requires another language. In her discussion of *la mystérique*, Irigaray proposes two alternatives: 'to keep quiet, or else utter only a sound so inarticulate that it barely forms a *song*'.[24] Such a song, inarticulate as it may be to those who listen only for exact definitions, is sung by Beth during her conversion of Frankie. Here is the 'liberation of sensuality' envisioned by Cixous, where divisions of the feminine and the masculine are supplanted, where Frankie could become 'a woman-man', a 'better man' who is 'without hate'; a 'sweet man' not afraid of softness or gentleness, a man who can accept the male in Beth as freely as she welcomes the female residing in Frankie (76).

Beth sings of what Cixous has called 'the other bisexuality',[25] one which rids us of the old oppositions between masculine and feminine without ending in a neutered void which denies the pleasure of sexual difference. According to Cixous, this new order does not do away with differences, but 'stirs them up, pursues them, increases their number',[26] thus celebrating the multiplicities of desire. The paradigm for Cixous' new sensuality is Beth's shirt-play as she kneels by Frankie's side, revealing the signs of her femininity as she removes the shirt she has borrowed from her father and attempts to wrap it around Frankie's injured leg, then buttoning up the shirt, clenching her fists, sticking out her chin and strutting, proclaiming 'Now, I'm like the man'. Pretending, she says, 'fills' her, while 'Ordinary is empty'. Her rejection of traditional sexuality (signified by the shirt-play) forces us to witness the difference of the female body. Her breasts, either bare or slightly concealed by lingerie,[27] serve as a reminder of her femininity even as the shirt 'brings me a man', that is, allows her to feel like a man (75).

Having used the phrase 'Frankie's conversion', it seems necessary to point out that this scene has also been described as 'Frankie's feminisation',[28] and that more than one critic agrees with Ron

Mottram's assessment that Beth's attempt to make 'Frankie be a
woman'[29] (a misleading statement since she repeatedly uses the
word 'man' in her descriptions of his re-socialisation) is unsuccessful. The evidence for this reading seems connected to a regrettable
cult of Shepard criticism which would read every play as a variation
on one theme – the failure of American family life. The mereness,
not to mention the monotony, of this approach, both in theatrical
and textual terms, threatens to reduce *A Lie of the Mind*. Are we
to believe, as Mottram apparently does, that Frankie wants to (or
will) leave Beth because of his parting words to his brother's back,
'You gotta take her with you! I never betrayed you! I was true to
you! (129)'. Or are we to put our faith in the unbroken embrace
which ends the Frankie/Beth scene and the weightiness of Meg's
vision, made under the influence of a kiss, occupying as it does
the sovereign position of the one who speaks last? *A Lie of the Mind*
resembles no other Shepard play, either in terms of its parallel
structure or its final image of redemption. And in no other play
does the affirmative ring so truly. As Cixous reminds us, citing
Molly Bloom in James Joyce's *Ulysses*, 'The feminine affirms'.[30]

Both Cixous and Irigaray consider generosity the most unique
and superlative quality of the feminine. The root of this generosity
resides in biological reproduction, since it is the mother who gives
all to the child without thought of return. The blood which courses
through the fetus, the milk which springs from the breast, all of these
fluids, the waters of life, are given long before the child achieves the
means by which to reciprocate maternal affection. Cixous describes
the *puissance féminine* (the strength of the feminine) as: 'The more
you have, the more you give the more you are, the more you give
the more you have'.[31] She sets this contiguous notion of power in
opposition to that of the man, who gives in order that the circuit
of exchange may be broken, to the end that he may owe nothing to
anyone. The Realm of the Gift, Cixous' system of feminine economy,
derives its power not from the fear of separation (The Realm of the
Proper [or property] attributed to the male's fear of castration), but
from an open-ended notion of exchange. Toril Moi credits Cixous'
Realm of the Gift as one of the few means by which the feminine
can subvert patriarchal order.

> . . . the gift is perceived as establishing an inequality – a dif-
> ference – that is threatening in that it seems to open up an
> imbalance of *power*. Thus the act of giving becomes a subtle

means of aggression, of exposing the other to the threat of one's own superiority.[32]

Generosity, then, would seem to be the basis of Meg and Beth's revolution in *A Lie of the Mind*, a solution entirely opposite to Lorraine and Sally's choice to flee the fatherland, and as mysterious and subtle as theirs is conscious and verbalized. Meg kneeling to remove Baylor's boots; Beth placing the stool under Frankie's leg; Beth offering the shirt as a bandage, not just once but again as Frankie falls to the floor; Meg opening the tin of mink oil and applying it to Baylor's feet; in each case the woman gives and slowly, gradually, that giving begins to upset former models of patriarchal exchange.

The clearest example of feminine aggression achieved by means of altering the method of exchange occurs in the third act sequence between Meg and Baylor when she ministers to his feet. Their physical position for this activity suggests a master and slave relationship, or in a Christian context, Christ washing the feet of the disciples. Christ, with his marked proclivity for giving (and who is described by Irigaray as 'That most female of men, the Son'),[33] would seem an apt example of generosity as a redemptive force. Meg may kneel submissively at Baylor's feet, yet note that she instigates the giving rather than obeying his command.

> BAYLOR: (*Slamming tin into the arm of the chair*) Goddamn these tins! They make everything nowadays so they won't come open! Nothin' comes open anymore.
> MEG: Here, let me do it.
> BAYLOR: (*Hands tin to* MEG) You do it.
> MEG: (*Taking tin*) I am doing it.
>
> (101)

Once the tin is easily opened by Meg, Baylor requests that she apply the oil, using the excuse of a sore back as currency – he has injured himself providing food for the table (carving the venison Meg declares she hates) and thus she owes him her efforts on his behalf. When Meg hesitates, thereby rejecting an unsatisfactory bargain, Baylor restates his position more forcefully:

> (BAYLOR *hands the Mink Oil back to* MEG. MEG *takes it. She hesitates.*)
> MEG: I should get back upstairs and check on BETH.

BAYLOR: Just do my feet, would ya please!
(MEG *kneels and starts to rub Mink Oil into* BAYLOR'S *feet.*
BAYLOR *lays his head back on the chair and closes his eyes*).

(102)

Acquiescing to his demand might appear passive, but even as she assumes her role as healer (causing Baylor to declare 'that is as close to heaven as I been in a long time' (102)), Meg begins her critique. Her action, to give him surcease from pain, puts him in her debt, and the resulting imbalance of power allows her the opportunity to question his activities. The first salvo fired concerns his self-destructive tendencies: 'you sit out there in that shack for hours on end letting your feet freeze. That doesn't make any sense, Baylor' (102). To his defense of hunting as 'a way of life', she counters: 'We don't need to kill animals anymore to stay alive. We're not pioneers' (103). Having been defeated in his argument with Meg, Baylor has no choice but to retreat. This he does by issuing another order based on the earlier transaction, that is, his exhaustion stems from his activities on her behalf. Having previously established that these activities are unwarranted by anything other than his refusal to join 'the modern world', Meg effectively wins the encounter, only to be overpowered by his refusal to communicate: 'Just rub that stuff into my feet and stop tryin' to pick a bone with me. I'm too tired to argue' (103).

Another sequence follows in which Meg draws closer to the matter which most concerns her, namely, what she believes to be his fast-approaching retreat from husband/parenthood into isolation and death. That she touches on the truth is indicated by his burst of activity as he 'sits up fast', pulling his feet away from her (thus refusing her gift), and shouts: 'All right. All right! Stop rubbing my feet now. Go on upstairs! Go on. I've heard enough a' this' (105).

Her generosity may be rebuffed, but Meg stands fast, watching him as he tries to reach his socks. The most violent confrontation follows, Baylor 'tremb[ling] with rage' (106), understanding that he is in her debt, hating his need for her even if that necessity is as simple as handing him the socks he cannot reach. At this point, Meg gives him permission to leave, probably the most generous action she can perform. Her intuitive reading of his resentments, 'If only your life was free of females, then you'd be free yourself' (106) is affirmed by Baylor as 'truth'; and, again, she rejects the false values of his Realm of the Proper:

Nobody's crazy, Baylor. Except you. Why don't you just go. Why
don't you just go off and live the way you want to live. We'll take
care of ourselves. We always have. (106)

Baylor's notion of caretaking is to 'waste my days away makin' sure
they [the women] eat and have a roof over their heads and a nice
warm place to go crazy in' (106), a male exchange of goods given
to free the giver of indebtedness and ungraciously given at that.
Meg's offer, 'freely given, exempt from masculine transactions:
enjoyment without a fee, well-being without pain',[34] releases him
without thought of return.

That Baylor sulks after her departure, indulging in a fit of impotent rage, would seem evidence of her success: his economic strategies have been rendered powerless in the face of her generosity.
Yet this encounter does not redeem Baylor, nor does it prove his
re-socialisation. The proof of his conversion will come only in the
last minutes of the play, when Meg gives him the gift of her
cooperation as she helps him fold the flag, and Baylor, without
forethought or hope of return, gives her the gift of his affections
in the form of a kiss, a gift he has withheld from her for twenty
years.

Given the bitterness of their former scene, this kiss becomes a
transaction of enormous scope, resonating richly with Irigaray's
vision of an 'economy of abundance',[35] and merging subtly with
the image of Beth supporting Frankie, the two seemingly locked
forever in a close embrace. Here, in the visual text, is to be found the
masculine and the feminine involved in commerce of another kind,
'exchanges without identifiable terms, without accounts, without
end . . . Without additions and accumulations'.[36]

Assigning authorial intent remains the trickiest of propositions,
yet in *A Lie of the Mind*, whether consciously or unconsciously,
Shepard embraces the feminine. Here is to be found what Marranca
longs for, women with imaginative range, women endowed with a
new language, and a substantial 'landscape of the female body'.[37]
Two revolutions offer two solutions to patriarchy, to take flight
from the 'fatherland' or to redeem those men made invalids by its
systems through the generosity of the female spirit. Neither solution
is without substantial cost. Shall Sally, who never 'had' a man, take
flight with the result that the joys of difference are never celebrated,
or shall Beth, battered by male hands, continue her labour on their
behalf, trusting that 'a transformation of our relationship to our

body (– and to another body)'[38] will evolve? A single kiss and a grudging embrace hold no promise of Utopia, yet the miraculous image of 'fire in the snow' remains – binary opposites existing side by side, neither consuming the other, abiding in an unforeseen and unimaginable state of grace.

Notes

1. Bonnie Marranca, "Alphabetical Shepard: The Play of Words", in *American Dreams, The Imagination of Sam Shepard*, ed. Bonnie Marranca (New York: Performing Arts Journal Publications, 1981), p. 31.
2. In her discussion of Cavale, Marranca gives Patti Smith credit for writing this part for herself, thus denying Shepard's part in the creation of 'the only truly dominant, autonomous female character in the plays'. Marranca, p. 31.
3. Cixous's term is related to Derrida's notion of writing as *différance*. Since writing lacks the *presence* of the speaker, the field of signification becomes widespread; 'writing – textuality – acknowledges the free play of the signifier and breaks open what Cixous perceives as the prison-house of patriarchal language'. Toril Moi, *Sexual/Textual Politics: Feminist Literary Theory* (New York: Routledge, Chapman and Hall, 1988) p. 107.
4. Ibid., p. 108.
5. 'Whenever an ordering intervenes, a law organizes the thinkable by (dual, irreconcilably; or mitigable, dialectical) oppositions. And all the couples of opposition are *couples*'. Hélène Cixous [In collaboration with Catherine Clément], *La Jeune née* [*The newly born woman*] (Union Générale d'Editions, 10/18, 1975). This excerpt from 'Sorties' is translated by Ann Liddle in *New French Feminisms*, ed. Elaine Marks and Isabelle de Courtivron (New York: Schocken Books, 1981) pp. 91–92.
6. Marranca, p. 30.
7. Ibid., p. 31.
8. Consult Françoise Parturier's 'An Open Letter to Men' or Françoise D'Eaubonne's 'Feminism or Death' for an example of a more radical and less theoretical feminism than either Hélène Cixous or Luce Irigaray. Both essays can be found in Marks and Courtivron's *New French Feminisms* (see note 5).
9. Sam Shepard, *A Lie of the Mind* (New York: New American Library, 1986), p. 87. All quotations are from this edition; page numbers are given in the text.
10. Heiner Müller, *Hamletmachine and Other Texts for the Stage*, ed. and trans. Carl Weber (New York: Performing Arts Journal Publications, 1984), pp. 54–55.
11. Lévi-Strauss' term refers to the construction of a system (be it personal, philosophical, literary, etc.) based not on immaculate creation

but on an assemblage, a collage of pre-existent fragments and pieces. For a discussion of *bricolage*, see Jacques Derrida, 'Structure, Sign and Play in the Discourse of the Human Sciences' in *Twentieth Century Literary Theory*, ed. Vassilis Lambropoulos and David Neal Miller (Albany: State University of New York Press, 1987), pp. 35–60. I am indebted to Shawn Levy for introducing me to this term and providing the reference cited.

12. Luce Irigaray, *Speculum of the Other Woman*, trans. Gillian C. Gill (Ithaca: Cornell University Press, 1985), p. 191.
13. Moi, p. 136.
14. Rosemary Bank, 'Self as Other: Sam Shepard's *Fool for Love* and *A Lie of the Mind*'. *Feminist Re-Readings of Modern American Drama*, ed. June Schlueter (Rutherford, N.J.: Fairleigh Dickinson University Press, 1989), pp. 234–35.
15. Roland Barthes, *A Barthes Reader*, ed. Susan Sontag (New York: Hill and Wang, 1982), p. 450. The citation is from *A Lover's Discourse*, trans. Richard Howard (New York: Hill and Wang, 1978).
16. Ron Mottram, 'Exhaustion of the American Soul: Sam Shepard's *A Lie of the Mind*', in *Sam Shepard: A Casebook*, ed. Kimball King (New York: Garland, 1988) p. 98.
17. Bank, p. 235.
18. Cixous, p. 97.
19. Luce Irigaray, *This Sex Which Is Not One*, trans. Catherine Porter and Carolyn Burke (Ithaca, New York: Cornell University Press, 1985), p. 28.
20. 'Beth is the central character of the play. She is not only the victim of Jake's aggression, and so is at the heart of the play's principal event, but, like Cassandra, the one with the clearest vision and the one with the most to lose. If the characters can be seen as tragic, hers is the greatest tragedy'. Mottram, p. 99. 'Of all of Shepard's characters, Beth and Jake in *A Lie of the Mind* are the most profoundly shattered victims of gender conflict and nuclear family psychology'. Lynda Hart, *Sam Shepard's Metaphorical Stages* (New York: Greenwood Press, 1987), p. 105.
21. Hart, p. 106.
22. Luce Irigaray, *This Sex Which Is Not One*, p. 29.
23. Ibid., p. 29.
24. Luce Irigaray, *Speculum of the Other Woman*, p. 193.
25. Cixous differentiates 'the other bisexuality' from the classic conception of bisexuality, which,'squashed under the emblem of castration fear and along with the fantasy of a "total" being (though composed of two halves), would do away with the difference experienced as an operation incurring loss, as the mark of dreaded sectility'. Hélène Cixous, 'The Laugh of the Medusa', trans. Keith Cohen and Paula Cohen, in *Women's Voices: Visions and Perspectives*, ed. Pat C. Hoy II, Esther H. Schor, and Robert DiYanni (New York: McGraw-Hill, 1990), p. 487.
26. Ibid., p. 488.
27. Shepard leaves the question of Beth's nudity open. He stipulates

that she wears jeans and is barefoot, but makes no mention of any undergarments. Frankie's anxiety on this point (his continual requests that she put the shirt back on), would seem to suggest nudity. When I attended the premiere production of *A Lie of the Mind* (Promenade Theatre in New York City, 1985) Beth (Amanda Plummer) wore a brassiere made of a sheer, almost transparent fabric with the result that her breasts were covered, yet visible. Since Shepard directed this production, one might assume this costume to be his choice, although it is just as possibly the result of the actor's preference.

28. Mottram, p. 98.
29. Ibid., p. 98.
30. '"And yes", says Molly, carrying *Ulysses* off beyond any book and toward the new writing; "I said yes, I will Yes".' Hélène Cixous, 'The Laugh of the Medusa', p. 488.
31. The translation is by Toril Moi in *Sexual/Textual Politics*, p. 115. The citation, from Hélène Cixous' *La Jeune née*, is unfortunately excluded from the English translation contained in *New French Feminisms*. Moi's reference is as follows: *La Jeune née* (en collaboration avec Catherine Clément), Paris: UGE, 10/18, p. 230.
32. Moi, p. 112.
33. Luce Irigaray, *The Speculum of the Other Woman*, p. 199.
34. Luce Irigaray, *This Sex Which Is Not One*, p. 197.
35. Ibid.
36. Ibid.
37. Marranca, p. 31.
38. Bank, p. 235.

13

A Motel of the Mind: *Fool for Love* and *A Lie of the Mind*

Felicia Hardison Londré

> is it a motel room
> or someone's house
> is it the body of me alive
> or dead[1]

These lines from a poem beginning with the words '3:30 a.m.' in Sam Shepard's *Motel Chronicles*, evoke the mental dislocation of waking up at night in an unfamiliar room. The motel room and the disoriented effect are also integral to *Fool for Love* and *A Lie of the Mind*. Although Shepard has always made effective use of scenic metaphors, these two plays offer particularly intriguing examples of a correlation between the *fait théâtral* – that is, any physical object that is visible to the audience – and the mental states of the characters as they relate to the meaning of the play as a whole.

In the course of the action of many of Shepard's plays, a character brings in some unusual artifact from outside: a live lamb in *Curse of the Starving Class*, an enormous quantity of freshly-dug carrots in *Buried Child*, dozens of stolen toasters in *True West*, a steer rope used for lassoing the bedpost in *Fool for Love*, and in *A Lie of the Mind* 'the severed hindquarters of a large buck with the hide still on it'.[2] Although the dramatic device may seem reminiscent of Eugene Ionesco's proliferation of objects in his Absurdist plays of the 1950s, there is a subtle difference. Whereas Ionesco was concerned with the overwhelmingness of inanimate objects, Shepard uses these *faits théâtrals* to create a sense of dislocation. When such objects are brought into the kitchen or living room of an ordinary home, the home is denatured. The motel room of *Fool for Love* is in effect a

denatured home in that May lives there but keeps her belongings
in the bathroom for security. Both the motel and the denatured home
are products and reflections of the unstable world inhabited by
Shepard's characters. His characters try to bind themselves together
in family units, but they succeed only briefly. In *A Lie of the Mind*,
for example, Beth remembers, 'This room was – where we all were
– together' (48); but her father Baylor has long since been spending
most of his time out in his hunting shack. And Sally – representing
the play's other family – says, 'I started thinkin' about this whole
thing. This family. How everything's kinda – shattered now' (61). In
Fool for Love, May recounts a detached vision of family life, recalling
how she and her mother went 'peering in every window, looking
at every dumb family' until they found her father sitting down to
supper with another wife and child.[3]

Shepard's denaturing of the family living room is a process that
finds its ultimate expression in the motel room. His use of the
motel-room setting for *Fool for Love* and in several scenes in Act 1 of
A Lie of the Mind culminates a long historical evolution of theatrical
loci, each underscoring a dramatic focus specific to the era. The
setting for neoclassical tragedy was always an antechamber, a tragic
site that Roland Barthes describes as

> the eternal space of all subjections, since it is here that one *waits*.
> The Antechamber (the stage proper) is a medium of transmission;
> it partakes of both interior and exterior, of Power and Event, of
> the concealed and the exposed. Fixed between the world, a place
> of action, and the Chamber, a place of silence, the Antechamber
> is the site of language: it is here that tragic man, lost between the
> letter and the meaning of things, utters his reasons.[4]

With the gradual demise of tragedy and elevated language, the antechamber gave way to the nineteenth-century drawing room, which
evolved in turn into the living room of modern family drama – or
its variant, the kitchen. In certain respects, Shepard's motel room
is closer to the neoclassical antechamber than to the middle-class
living room. The living room suggests a stable environment as a
context within which, according to traditional dramaturgy, a disturbance upsets the balance and a conflict ensues, but a dénouement
signals a return to stability. This pattern prevailed for most of
twentieth-century drama, even in plays that used the rented room
as a setting, plays ranging from *fin-de-siècle* bedroom farces like

Feydeau's *L'Hôtel du Libre-Echange* to George Abbott's *Room Service* or Neil Simon's *Plaza Suite*. Those plays, furthermore, imply an upscale urban context, as do even such variants as the Mexican resort hotel of Tennessee Williams's *The Night of the Iguana* or the motel room of Preston Jones's last play *Remember*. Not only are the middle class aesthetic and the urban context absent from Shepard's plays, but instability and impermanence are the givens of their dramaturgy. Like the neoclassical antechamber, Shepard's motel room is, in Barthe's words, 'a medium of transmission'; it is a way station between the larger world (often equated with the road or highway as a place of action) and what Barthes calls 'the Chamber, a place of silence'.

In Shepard's dramaturgy, the 'place of silence' is not a royal *inner sanctum*, but the surrounding blackness that represents the outer edge of consciousness. The motel rooms of *Fool for Love* and *A Lie of the Mind* are minimally concretised milieux that seem to float in a void. They reify a transitory state between dream and waking, a state in which incongruous or anachronistic elements can appear, as if dredged up from another place and time to reinforce a current perception. Certainly, the introduction of objects like an armload of carrots or the hindquarters of a deer can serve to evoke a larger world – the rural outdoors – outside the confines of the stage setting. More importantly, however, the unconventional quality of such objects in their settings reinforces a dreamlike sense of the surreal. This interpolation of isolated elements carrying old associations into a new context is one of the most striking features of Shepard's postmodernism.

Shepard's motel rooms are occupied by a character or characters whose perceptions – like those of a Strindbergian artist-dreamer – shape, and perhaps distort, the reality offered to the audience. However, Shepard's postmodernist sensibility enables him to shift the identity of the dreamer, the central consciousness that conjures up the *fait théâtral*, from one character to another. In *Fool for Love*, the dream mode is aurally indicated when the play opens with a song entitled 'Wake Up'. There is a surrealistic quality about the recurrent slamming of doors throughout the action, as the stage directions call for a microphone and bass drum hidden in the frames, causing the doors to boom *'loud and long'* (26). The intensity of colour in the cheap and sparsely furnished motel room contrasts with the empty blackness outside. A separate level of reality is established for a small extended platform with black floor, black curtains, and a grey and black blanket on a rocking chair, where The Old Man sits observing the action in the motel room. Shepard states that The Old Man *'exists only in the minds of* MAY *and* EDDIE, *even though they might talk to him directly and acknowledge his physical presence.* THE OLD MAN *treats them as though they all existed in the same time and place'* (15).

If The Old Man exists in the minds of both May and Eddie, the play necessarily reifies a split consciousness. At the same time it may be that May and Eddie, The Old Man's progeny, exist as the projections of his mind. There is some evidence to suggest that he might be the dreamer, especially since he remains largely in a position of passive repose, only occasionally intruding into the action. Not only does The Old Man get the last word in the play, but the explosion that jolts the play to an end arises most probably from his need to end a nightmare in which the story is not coming out as he would have it. Still, it is possible to see The Old Man and May and Eddie as the products of one another's memories and imaginative fancies. One is reminded of Guildenstern's line in Tom Stoppard's *Rosencrantz and Guildenstern Are Dead*: 'A Chinaman of the T'ang dynasty – and, by which definition, a philosopher – dreamed he was a butterfly, and from that moment he was never quite sure that he was not a butterfly dreaming it was a Chinese philosopher'.[5]

A Lie of the Mind is even more complex in its apparent shifting of the central consciousness from one character to another. According to Shepard's set description, 'in the First Act there are no walls to define locations – only furniture and props and light in the bare space. In the Second and Third Acts walls are brought in to delineate the rooms on either side of the stage' (xi). It might well be assumed that a dream mode is represented in Act 1, while Acts 2 and 3 represent the dreamers' return to a more objective reality. Throughout Act 1, both Beth and Jake are mentally and physically in transit. After an opening scene which occurs in a 'huge dark space' relieved only by a highway pay phone and a pale yellow full moon, Scenes 2 through 6 of Act 1 alternate between Beth's hospital room and Jake's motel room. Beth, having been beaten and left for dead by her husband Jake, has been diagnosed as brain damaged. Although her speech is largely incoherent to her brother Mike as well as to the audience, she – like the dreamer whose dream carries its own coherence – clearly embodies a very self-contained consciousness, as exemplified by her insistence in Scene 4: 'You gan' stop my head. Nobody! Nobody stop my head. My head is me' (19). She does not participate at all in the dialogue between Mike and her parents in Scene 6, but her presence in bed 'upstage in very dim light' offers the visual suggestion that she is the dreamer of the scene. In Jake's parallel scenes, he becomes increasingly incoherent. When Scene 5 begins, he sleeps covered with a blanket on the couch in his motel room 'in very dim light', while his brother Frankie discusses his condition with their mother and sister. Jake awakes to interact with them, but loses consciousness again by the end of the scene. The last scene of Act 1 (Scene 7), also positions Jake as the dreamer. He has been brought back to his own former bedroom in his mother's house to be nursed back to health, but he seems not to recognize the room. The scene builds to Jake's vision of Beth, uninjured and very beautiful. But with dreamlike discontinuity, *eros* gives way to *thanatos*: Jake makes a move toward her and the apparition disappears. Jake is left staring at his empty bed, its erotic associations giving way to its evocation of sleep or death. Jake's attention is then redirected to the box containing his father's ashes.

Acts 2 and 3 of *A Lie of the Mind* are composed of scenes with sequences alternating between Jake's bedroom and the living room of Beth's parents' ranch house in Montana. Both Beth and Jake, now well on the way to recovery, are no longer merely passive observers, but are able to interact with others. However, all except one of these scenes incorporate a reclining figure, one who might be described as the dominant or most objective consciousness of the scene, and who does not succumb to a dream state. In Jake's bedroom his sister Sally lies in his bed under the blanket; she is to fool their mother Lorraine into thinking that Jake is still there, while he makes his way to Montana to see Beth. In another scene, it is Lorraine who lies bundled up in Jake's bed, shaking with cold chills and nursed by Sally. The last scene in Jake's room has Lorraine again lying on his bed, but this time fully dressed, as she reminisces about the past and plans a future. In the Montana scenes, Jake's brother Frankie is largely confined to the sofa where he is deposited after being shot in the leg by Beth's father Baylor, who mistook Frankie for a deer. Despite the pain of his wound and the uneasiness he feels about Beth's attentions to him while he remains trapped in the snowbound house, he retains a superior consciousness. That is, he takes the role of the dreamer without entering a dream state. He functions as an objective observer of the war between men and women in that household. Indeed, he occupies a kind of middle ground between the sexes in that Beth is drawn to his gentle masculinity and calls him a 'woman-man' (76). Baylor's having mistaken Frankie for a deer reinforces that ambiguity, if we can apply the view expressed in 'The Sex of Fishes', a short piece in Shepard's *Hawk Moon*: 'The gun looked male through and through. The deer were female, even the bucks'.[6]

In most of these instances in *A Lie of the Mind*, the reclining figure – that is, the one who functions most nearly to a central consciousness in each scene – is covered by a blanket. The stage directions specify several times that the blanket is wrapped tightly around the body so that only the head sticks out – like a mummy. The mummy-like appearance indicates a transitory state of being; it identifies a state, like sleep, in which the person appears dead while the mind continues to function in some capacity. In the first hospital scene, Beth unwinds long streamers of gauze bandages from her head and asks: 'Am I a mummy now?' Yet in the next breath she insists, 'I'm not dead' (5). In the Montana scenes, Frankie appears to be emotionally dead, as – out of loyalty to his brother – he resists Beth's advances; and yet Beth can sense the life in him. Whatever else may be wrong with Beth, she displays a barometric sensitivity to others' capacity for love. She comments that her father has 'given up love', and she knows that Frankie – despite his protests – could love her. When she and Jake are finally going to see each other in the last scene of the play, Beth remarks: 'He's dead' (122). Certainly, Jake is dead from her emotional perspective, as she has transferred her love to Frankie. Jake declares his love to Beth, but realizes that he has forfeited her love and tells her to stay with Frankie. Jake becomes the play's last mummy, objectively conscious enough to remove himself as an obstacle to Beth's happiness. This is visually reinforced when he picks up the blanket, wraps himself in it up to his shoulders, and exits into darkness.

As a potential carrier of meaning, the blanket takes additional focus in the Montana sequences of Act 3 with the development of a running rivalry over it between Frankie and Baylor. In Scene 2, Baylor pulls it from Frankie, and the two have a tug of war with it. Both are semi-incapacitated, Frankie with his leg-wound and Baylor with frozen feet, but possession of the blanket seems to confer authority, first when Baylor wraps it around his feet, then when Frankie jerks it back and encases himself in it 'like a mummy' in preparation for Beth's entrance. At the end of that scene, Baylor rips the blanket off Frankie and 'slowly wraps himself in the blanket all the way up to his neck' (114), leaving Frankie vulnerable to Beth.

Later, Baylor sleeps in his chair with the blanket wrapped tightly
around him while Beth tucks a throw rug around the shivering
Frankie. When Baylor is startled awake, he lets the blanket fall
to the floor. Beth unobtrusively takes it and covers Frankie 'like
a mummy' with it. When Mike picks Beth up and carries her to
the porch to force her to look at Jake, she pulls the blanket along
with her. Baylor grabs the blanket from Beth before she can return
it to Frankie, but Baylor's attention is instantly diverted to the
American flag that Jake had draped around himself for the journey
to Montana. It is while Baylor and Meg are occupied with folding
the flag that Jake wraps himself in the blanket and departs.

If the blanket serves as a kind of talisman, whether allowing its
wearer to attain the mummy's superior consciousness or simply
affording protection from cold and aggression, the American flag
seems to serve as a still more powerful, and perhaps ironic, version of it. The flag first appears when Lorraine pulls it out from
under Jake's bed and reminds him that it was given to him at
his father's funeral. When Jake makes his amazing journey from
southern California to Montana, he wraps the flag around himself
for warmth; otherwise he wears only his underwear and his father's
leather flying jacket, since Lorraine has hidden Jake's pants. At the
ranch, he is captured by Mike who takes the flag and forces Jake to
walk on his knees to the main house. Mike enters the house with
the flag wrapped around his rifle, but Baylor takes it from him to
show respect for it. Baylor and his wife Meg together fold the flag
properly, and their success in this joint endeavour prompts him to
kiss her for the first time in twenty years. Baylor's last line, the
penultimate in the play, suggests that – having now shown his first
hint of sensitivity toward a woman – he will be the next dreamer: 'I
don't wanna' get woke up in the middle of a good dream' (130).

As his meticulous stage directions indicate, Shepard has a clear
sense of what he wants the audience to see on the stage. Even in *True
West* – a rare instance in which he specifies a 'realistically constructed' setting – he states: *'No objects should be introduced which might
draw special attention to themselves other than the props demanded by the
script'.*[7] His scenic *dépouillement* invests his chosen visual signifiers
with added weight or multivalent associations. The blanket/flag,
for example, carries many cultural referents ranging from the security blanket of the *Peanuts* comic strip to the patriotic symbolism of
the flag. When the blanket is used to wrap a person like a mummy,
that person retains a clear awareness of his surroundings despite

the physical constriction that deters action. Possession of the flag, as it passes from Lorraine to Jake to Mike to Baylor, seems to endow those characters with a sense of moral complacency. In addition, significations accumulate within Shepard's own canon as the same objects reappear in different guises from one play to another: leg wounds, blankets, rifles, fire, etc. The absent father of Jake, Frankie, and Sally in *A Lie of the Mind* is described in terms very much like The Old Man we see in *Fool for Love* (who is clearly an incarnation of Shepard's own father as described in *Motel Chronicles*).

Shepard's motels – and even his hotels, as in *Geography of a Horse Dreamer* and *La Turista* – strongly evoke a sense of spatial and temporal mobility. The best examples of a comparable use of scenic metaphor would be Tennessee Williams's *Camino Real* and William Hauptman's *Domino Courts* and *Gillette*. Yet even Kilroy of *Camino Real* and the men in Hauptman's plays are to a certain extent defined by their stage milieu. Shepard's characters are not. The motel room of *Fool for Love* is no more descriptive of May and Eddie than are Austin and Lee characterized by their Mom's suburban kitchen in *True West*. Shepard's characters, in general, belong to the highway; the motel room setting expresses only their restlessness. It is a pit stop in lives that are characterised by impermanence. Shepard's male characters are literally and figuratively on the road to becoming their fathers. Eddie repeats the pattern of The Old Man's life by loving two women, May and the unseen 'Countess'. Mike achieves identification with Baylor by shooting his father's deer on the last day of the season and taking over the hunting shack. Jake relives his father's story when he walks on bloodied knees to his showdown. Only Frankie breaks the pattern, it is suggested, by bonding with a woman. The plays abound with dialogue references to identity that recall Strindberg's dream mode. In *Fool for Love*, for example, Eddie says: 'You know we're connected, May. We'll always be connected' (31). In Act 1 of *A Lie of the Mind*, Beth says of Jake: 'Heez in me'. Later she creates a role reversal with Frankie: 'Now, I'm like the man . . . You could be the woman. You be' (74). In this essay on the play, Ron Mottram has demonstrated 'an intricate web of interlocking actions' that 'identifies the characters with each other even while they remain separated in their own spaces'.[8]

Within the settings of *A Fool for Love* and *A Lie of the Mind*, the single most important *fait théâtral* is the bed. The 'cast iron four poster single bed' in *Fool for Love* is placed almost at the centre of a room whose only other furnishings are a metal table and two matching metal chairs. *A Lie of the Mind* features four 'beds': the hospital bed, the couch in Jake's motel room, Jake's bed at home, and the sofa in the Montana living room. Like the blanket, the flag, and other objects, the bed is an archetypal object that carries overlapping connotations. It certainly reinforces the undercurrent of sexual tension in *Fool for Love*. It is a place for healing in *A Lie of the Mind*. In both plays it is also the locus for a different level of consciousness, a place where the mind can create new realities. If the motel room represents a kind of isolation from the realities of ordinary life, then the bed is a stage within that stage metaphor. It is the launching pad for so many crowded thoughts – truths, lies, fictions – that the dreamer may long to take refuge in action. The characters are bent on leaving the stage, either to be swallowed up in the blackness of the unconscious or to encounter a real world as emblematised by the road. Or perhaps they will achieve both – a hope that Shepard expresses in his '3:30 a.m.' poem:

> what thoughts
> can I call allies
> I pray for a break
> from all thought
> a clean break
> in blank space
> let me hit the road
> empty-headed
> just once.[9]

Notes

1. Sam Shepard, *Motel Chronicles* (San Francisco: City Light Books, 1982), pp. 20–21.
2. Sam Shepard, *A Lie of the Mind* (New York: First Plume Printing, 1987), p. 79. All quotations are from this edition; page numbers are given in the text.
3. Sam Shepard, *Fool for Love and Other Plays* (New York: Bantam, 1984), p. 53. All quotations are from this edition; page numbers are given in the text.
4. Roland Barthes, *On Racine* (New York: Hill and Wang, 1964), p. 4.
5. Tom Stoppard, *Rosencrantz and Guildenstern Are Dead* (London: Faber and Faber, 1974), p. 43.
6. Sam Shepard, 'The Sex of Fishes' in *Hawk Moon* (New York: PAJ Publications, 1981), p. 77.

7. Sam Shepard, *True West* in Sam Shepard, *Seven Plays* (New York: Bantam, 1981), p. 3.
8. Ron Mottram, 'Exhaustion of the American Soul: Sam Shepard's *A Lie of the Mind*' in *Sam Shepard: A Casebook*, ed. Kimball King (New York: Garland, 1988), pp. 101–5.
9. *Motel Chronicles*, pp. 20–21.

Index

Aaron, Joyce, 10, 16, 168, 173
Action, 9, 16; the body in, 62;
   memory and, 60–62;
   minimalist stage setting and,
   137; performance and, 61–62
Albee, Edward, 15
All My Sons (Miller), 116, 123, 126
Allen, Jennifer, 99
American Place Theatre, 9, 100
Anaphoric language, 25
Andrew, Dudley, 23
Angel City, 3, 13, 43, 134; cliché
   in, 84–85; as collage, 84;
   deconstruction of authorial
   originality in, 79–80, 83, 86,
   87, 88–89; minimalist stage
   setting in, 137; modernist
   search for presence and, 93;
   representation of performance
   and, 94
Anti-Intellectualism in American Life
   (Hofstadter), 79
Artaud, Antonin, 142, 197
Avant-garde theatre in 1960s, 117

Baby Boom, 174
Baez, Joan, 103
Barthes, Roland, 110, 201–2, 216
Beckett, Samuel, 81
Belsey, Catherine, 169
Bigsby, Christopher, 131
Bishop's Company Reperatory
   Players, 10
Back Bog Beast Bait, 8
Blau, Herbert, 81
Blue Bitch, 135
Bowie, David, 87
Brecht, Bertold, 152
Brook, Peter, 142
'Brownsville Girl' (Dylan,
   Shepard), 104
Buried Child, 6, 12, 15, 35, 79,
   107–9, 111–12, 183, 186,

188; conventions of modern
   realism and, 118–21; legacy
   of avant-garde and, 133–34;
   Oedipal usurpation in, 123,
   124; superrealism and, 145;
   stage setting of, 142–43
Butler, Judith, 164

Caffe Cino, 9
Camino Real (Williams), 222
Chaikin, Joseph, 8, 10, 13, 59, 150
Chase, Mary, 2, 11
Chelsea Hotel, 100
Cherry Orchard, The (Chekhov),
   119, 126
Chicago, 10, 12, 16
Cixous, Hélène, 7, 197, 207, 208,
   212n, 213n
Collage, 84, 94
Corrigan, Robert, 134
Cowboy Mouth, 100, 106, 112;
   pastiche and, 103; role-playing
   in, 104; 'The Second Coming'
   (Yeats) and, 101–3; theme of
   outlaw in, 100–1
Cowboys, 12, 13, 14, 135
Cowboys #2, 12; planes of reality
   juxtaposed in, 139
Crimes of the Heart, 174
Curse of the Starving Class, 12, 15,
   16, 35, 79; compared with
   texts of Ibsen and Chekhov,
   126–27; convention of the
   problematic father and,
   125–26; conventions of modern
   realism and, 118; critical
   reception of, 136–37; expressionist staging in, 184–86,
   188; legacy of avant-garde
   and, 133–34; minimalist stage
   setting of, 137; planes of reality
   juxtaposed in, 139; postmodern
   'schizophrenia' and, 140–42;

225

and, 118; deconstruction of authorial originality in, 79–80; 83, 86, 87–88, 89–90; legacy of 1960s avant-garde and, 134; performance and, 94; planes of reality juxtaposed in, 139; supperrealism and, 143–44

Unseen Hand, The: postmodern condition and, 133
Up to Thursday, 10, 12, 13, 15, 168

Waste Land, The (Eliot), 93
Weales, Gerald, 136–37, 138
Weiner, Bernard, 151

Wenders, Wim, 42; *see also*: *Paris, Texas*
Wetzsteon, Ross, 144
Whitman, Walt, 181
Who's Afraid of Virginia Wolfe (Albee), 116, 126
Wild Duck, The (Ibsen), 119
Wilder, Thornton, 2
Williams, Linda, 170
Wilson, Ann, 173, 194–95n
Winnicott, D. W., 73

Zinman, Toby Silverman, 147n
Zola, Emile, 81
Zoo Story, The (Albee), 117